Women in Power in Post-Communist Parliaments

Women in Power in Post-Communist Parliaments

Edited by Marilyn Rueschemeyer

and Sharon L. Wolchik

Woodrow Wilson Center Press
Washington, D.C.

Indiana University Press
Bloomington and Indianapolis

EDITORIAL OFFICES

Woodrow Wilson Center Press
Woodrow Wilson International Center for Scholars
One Woodrow Wilson Plaza
1300 Pennsylvania Avenue, N.W.
Washington, D.C. 20004-3027
Telephone: 202-691-4029
www.wilsoncenter.org

ORDER FROM

Indiana University Press
601 North Morton Street
Bloomington, IN 47404-3797
Telephone: 800-842-6796
Facsimile: 812-855-7931
iuorder@indiana.edu
http://iupress.indiana.edu

2 4 6 8 9 7 5 3 1

Library of Congress Cataloging-in-Publication Data

Women in power in post-communist parliaments / edited by Marilyn Rueschemeyer and Sharon L. Wolchik.
    p.   cm.
    Includes bibliographical references and index.
    ISBN 978-0-253-35433-4 (hardcover : alk. paper) — ISBN 978-0-253-22169-8 (pbk. : alk. paper)
    1. Women in politics—Europe, Eastern. 2. Women in politics—Europe, Central. 3. Women legislators—Europe, Eastern. 4. Women legislators—Europe, Central. 5. Post-communism—Europe, Eastern. 6. Post-communism—Europe, Central. 7. Europe, Eastern—Politics and government—1989– 8. Europe, Central—Politics and government—1989– I. Rueschemeyer, Marilyn, 1938– II. Wolchik, Sharon L.
    HQ1236.5.E852W657   2009
    328.082′0943—dc22

                                                                                    2009008791

**Woodrow Wilson
International
Center
for Scholars**

The Woodrow Wilson International Center for Scholars, established by Congress in 1968 and headquartered in Washington, D.C., is the living, national memorial to President Wilson.

The Center is a nonpartisan institution of advanced research, supported by public and private funds, engaged in the study of national and world affairs. The Center establishes and maintains a neutral forum for free, open, and informed dialogue.

The Center's mission is to commemorate the ideals and concerns of Woodrow Wilson by providing a link between the world of ideas and the world of policy, by bringing a broad spectrum of individuals together to discuss important public policy issues, by serving to bridge cultures and viewpoints, and by seeking to find common ground.

Conclusions or opinions expressed in Center publications and programs are those of the authors and speakers and do not necessarily reflect the views of the Center staff, fellows, trustees, advisory groups, or any individuals or organizations that provide financial support to the Center.

The Center is the publisher of The Wilson Quarterly and home of Woodrow Wilson Center Press, dialogue radio and television, and the monthly newsletter "Centerpoint." For more information about the Center's activities and publications, please visit us on the web at www.wilsoncenter.org.

Lee H. Hamilton, President and Director

Contents

List of Tables and Figures   ix

Acknowledgments   xiii

1 Women in Power: The Issues   1
Marilyn Rueschemeyer and Sharon L. Wolchik

Part I. Women in Six National Parliaments

2 Women in the Russian State Duma   25
Linda J. Cook and Carol Nechemias

3 Women's Representation in the Polish Parliament and the
Determinants of Their Effectiveness   61
Renata Siemieńska

4 What Difference Do Female Deputies Make in the
Slovene Parliament?   93
Milica G. Antić

5 Women in Parliament in the Czech Republic   111
   Sharon L. Wolchik

6 East German Women in the Parliament of Unified Germany   131
   Marilyn Rueschemeyer

7 The Return of the King: Women in the Bulgarian Parliament   161
   Kristen Ghodsee

Part II. Perspectives of Women Parliamentarians

8 Russian Women Parliamentarians: In Their Own Voices   193
   Compiled and Translated by Carol Nechemias

9 The Perspective of the Head of the Parliamentary Women's
   Group in Poland   205
   Senator Dorota Kempka Speaks with Agnieszka Majcher

10 A Specialist in Culture in the Slovene Parliament   223
    Majda Širca

11 Negotiating the Czech Parliament   231
    *An Interview with Anna Čurdová, House of Deputies,
    Czech Parliament*

12 My Entry into Politics during the Time of German
    Reunification: Where Do East German Female Politicians
    Stand in Europe Today?   235
    Constanze Krehl

13 Women in Politics in Bulgaria   243
    Kina Andreeva

14 Women in Power: Concluding Thoughts   251
    Marilyn Rueschemeyer and Sharon L. Wolchik

    Selected Bibliography   267

    Contributors   277

    Index   281

Tables and Figures

Tables

1.1 Members of national parliaments by country and gender,
1990–2005   4

2.1 Women in the Russian State Dumas, 1993–1995 to 2007–2011   30

2.2 Political recruitment and women's pathways to the
Russian State Duma   37

2.3 Women deputies and representation of women's interests
in the Russian State Dumas   49

3.1 Women deputies in the Polish Sejm during the first, second,
and third terms   64

3.2 Women among candidates for and deputies elected to the
Polish Sejm in 2001   66

3.3 Composition of election committees in the 2001 Polish
Parliamentary election   71

3.4 Share of women among parliamentarians in the Polish
     Sejm, 2005   73

3.5 Numbers of women and men deputies elected to the Polish
     Sejm in 2007   73

3.6 Membership of women in the committees of the Polish
     Sejm elected in 2005   78

3.7 Participation of women in the Polish Senat committees
     elected in 2005   79

3.8 Number of terms in the Polish Parliament of deputies
     elected in 2007   79

3.9 Chairs of the committees in the Polish Parliament elected
     in 2007   80

4.1 Women deputies in the Slovene Parliament, 1990–2004   97

4.2 Women deputies in the Slovene Parliament by party, 1992,
     1996, 2000, and 2004   98

4.3 Female members of the Slovene Parliament by party and by
     occupation, 2000–2004   101

4.4 Members of the Slovene National Assembly by party and
     gender, 2000–2004   104

5.1 Women deputies in the lower house of Parliament, Czech
     Republic, various election years   113

5.2 Women deputies in the Czech Republic by party, 1996–2006 116

5.3 Women in government in the Czech Republic, 2009   118

6.1 Election results in the eastern German and western German
     federal elections, 1990–1998   137

6.2 Members of the German Bundestag elected in 2002, by party
     and gender   140

6.3 The occupations of eastern German women members of
     Parliament, 2002–2006   143

6.4 Members of the 2005 German Bundestag, by party
     and gender   149

6.5 Election results for the 2005 Bundestag in western and
eastern Germany 150

7.1 Women in the Bulgarian Parliament, 1976–2005 164

7.2 Women in the Bulgarian National Assembly by party, group,
or coalition, 1997–2001 and 2001–2005 166

7.3 Personal background of the members of the Bulgarian
Parliament interviewed for this study, 2001–2005 171

7.4 Gender composition of the Bulgarian Parliamentary
committees, 2004 175

7.5 Women in the fortieth Bulgarian National Assembly by
party, group, or coalition, 2005 186

7.6 Women candidates in the top five places on their parties'
lists in the 2005 Bulgarian Parliamentary elections 187

Figures

3.1 Percentage of women and men in a Polish survey who
did not agree with the statement "Men are better suited to
politics than women," 1992–2005 68

3.2 Responses in a Polish survey to the statement "Some believe
that women should play the same role in business, industry,
and politics as men; others believe the woman's place is at
home," 1992–2005 69

3.3 Desirable traits of politicians attributed to women and men
in a Polish survey, May 2005 70

12.1 The growth in the number of female parliamentarians in
the German Bundestag, 1949–2002 238

12.2 Number of women in the German Bundestag by party, 2005 238

12.3 Quotas for the numbers of women and men in the Parliament
of the German state of Saxony, 2006 239

12.4 Number of women in the European Parliament by party, 2005 239

12.5 Women members of Parliament in the nations admitted to
the European Union in 2004 240

Acknowledgments

It is difficult to know how to begin to express our gratitude to all the people who made this volume possible. A workshop at the Woodrow Wilson International Center for Scholars brought together not only the researchers on post-Communist parliaments but also a number of visiting parliamentarians who worked intensely with us. At our meetings, it was wonderful to be with these visitors, who contributed so much with their questions and comments. All this would not have been possible without the support of the Woodrow Wilson Center as well as the contributions of Brown University's Watson Institute for International Studies and the Institute for European, Russian, and Eurasian Studies at George Washington University. At the Woodrow Wilson Center, Martin Sletzinger, director of the East European Studies program, and Nida Gelazis, program associate and editor, did the complicated organizational work for the conference and were patient and supportive. We also want to thank Thomas Biersteker, director of the Watson Institute, and Abbott Gleason and Dietrich Rueschemeyer, both at Brown, as well as Blair Ruble, director of the Kennan Institute at the Woodrow Wilson Center, for their help and advice.

Melissa Aten's help in editing chapters, tracking down references, and keeping us organized during the period of our research was invaluable. We also want to thank Nancy Meyers and David Szakonyi for their work at critical junctures. And we thank Joe Brinley and Janet Rabinowitch for their guidance and efforts in moving our book toward publication. The final preparation of the manuscript, which calls for enormous concentration and patience, was greatly aided by Yamile Kahn, managing editor of the Woodrow Wilson Center Press, and Alfred Imhoff, who copyedited the book.

Finally, for all of us who have spent hours researching in the parliaments, our respect for the work and difficulties that parliamentarians must negotiate will likely remain with us for the rest of our lives, and so will our appreciation for the support and help given us by so many of them and their assistants. A number of them are directly thanked in our chapters.

We dedicate this book to the women parliamentarians and the women who are now heads of state in post-Communist Europe and Eurasia. May they have a positive impact on the lives of their citizens, and may they contribute to a world where ambition and competition are modified by compassion and commitment to the common good.

Marilyn Rueschemeyer
Sharon L. Wolchik

Women in Power in Post-Communist Parliaments

Chapter 1

Women in Power: The Issues

Marilyn Rueschemeyer and Sharon L. Wolchik

It has frequently been observed that women are underrepresented in positions of political leadership throughout the world. But there are signs that this pattern is changing. Recently, women have been elected to top posts in Chile (president), Latvia (president), Germany (chancellor), and the United States (speaker of the House of Representatives); Hillary Clinton ran a high-profile U.S. presidential campaign and was then appointed secretary of state; and increasing numbers of women are being elected to national legislators in many countries. For most of the 1970s and 1980s, the proportion of national legislative offices held by women was highest in Sweden, where it averaged 14 percent.[1] By 2008, women accounted for 47.3 percent of legislators in Sweden and 45.3 percent in Rwanda.[2]

Although these trends represent great progress compared with earlier periods, women are still underrepresented in positions of power throughout the world. Early studies of women and politics also documented a pattern that holds today: The more important the position, the lower women's representation in that body. This law of increasing disproportion, which has

1

also been found to characterize the representation of minorities in political positions,[3] appears to hold in countries with different overall levels of women's representation. These trends, which were first studied in the United States (where only 16.3 percent of the members of the House of Representatives are women)[4] and other advanced Western countries,[5] were also documented in Communist and other nondemocratic polities. Thus, women were well represented among the symbolic governmental elites, but their exercise of power within the realm of the effective political elites—the Communist Party—was limited and followed a similar pattern.[6]

Similar trends have been evident in the post-Communist world since the end of Communism in the period 1989–91. Although women played important roles in ousting Communist systems in Central and Eastern Europe and in the former Soviet Union, they continued to be marginalized politically as political leaders and citizens worked to construct democratic political orders, establish market economies, and reassert their countries' independence on the world stage.[7] From research conducted by scholars both inside and outside the region, we have learned a great deal about women's participation in politics as voters and citizens, as well as about their voting preferences and party affiliations. Numerous public opinion polls and survey research projects have documented women's political attitudes and values, as well as their policy preferences and how these differ from those of men. Scholars have investigated the routes that women commonly take to reach positions of political power and the impact of different systems of political recruitment on women's chances of being successful candidates.[8] Similarly, we now know much more than we did about women's organizations and movements in the post-Communist world.[9] The harsh impact of war on women, as in the former Yugoslavia, has also received attention.[10]

We also know that the patterns that held in the post-Communist world soon after the fall of the old system are changing somewhat, as women's proportion of legislators, if not of members of the government, has increased over the last several elections in many post-Communist countries (table 1.1). Thus, as in other areas of the world, women are more frequently achieving positions of political power than they did a decade or so ago. However, though we now know a great deal about women's participation at the mass level and the extent of their representation in national parliaments, the particular women who have arrived in positions of political power in post-Communist Europe have received relatively little attention. This book focuses on these women. Still fewer in number than their male colleagues, they are nonetheless important political actors whose roles merit investigation.

The chapters that follow focus on the roles of women in power in six post-Communist European and Eurasian countries. They are based on extended interviews with women, and in some cases men, who are members of the national legislatures of Bulgaria, the Czech Republic, Poland, Russia, and Slovenia. We also included members of the German Bundestag who represent constituencies in eastern Germany, the former German Democratic Republic. We chose these countries as a sample of post-Communist countries that share certain characteristics and at the same time differ in ways that highlight certain aspects of politics that could be expected to have an impact on women's participation in political leadership. Thus, all these countries have elections, and in contrast to the situation in some post-Communist countries, all have a political space that is open enough for women and other nongovernmental groups to function. Similarly, with the exception of Russia, which is both European and Eurasian, all are European countries that share a common heritage and history as well as a Communist experience that, although different in many respects, had a number of common features. Finally, all the countries studied, again with the exception of Russia, are members of the European Union, which has a commitment to promoting women's equality in all areas, including politics.

At the same time, each country examined in this volume has specificities that reflect its geographic location, history, and traditions. Poland is the most Catholic of the countries we have included and illustrates the impact of the Church on politics. The inclusion of eastern Germany both allows comparison of patterns in the two parts of Germany and permits us to see what impact, if any, a different pattern of transition from Communism, one that involved the reincorporation of a formerly Communist area into a larger state, has had on women's political roles. The Czech Republic, although nominally Catholic, has been a largely secular country for at least the last century and a half and was one of the most developed countries to become Communist; it also had a longer experience with democracy in the interwar period than the other countries analyzed in this volume. Slovenia, one of the most developed areas of the former Yugoslavia, adds a country where Communism was far less intrusive and repressive than in most of the other countries covered in this volume and where levels of contact with the West were much greater, as they were in Poland. The Bulgarian case brings in a country at a somewhat lower level of development, whose religious tradi-

Table 1.1. Members of national parliaments by country and gender, 1990–2005

Country and Membership	1990	1995	2000	2001	2002	2003	2004	2005
Bosnia and Herzegovina								
Female								
Members of national parliament	..	..	12	3	3	7	7	7
Percentage of total for both sexes	..	..	28.6	7.1	7.1	16.7	16.7	16.7
Male								
Members of national parliament	..	..	30	39	39	35	35	35
Percentage of total for both sexes	..	..	71.4	92.9	92.9	83.3	83.3	83.3
Bulgaria								
Female								
Members of national parliament	..	26	26	63	63	63	63	50
Percentage of total for both sexes	..	10.8	10.8	26.2	26.2	26.2	26.2	20.8
Male								
Members of national parliament	..	214	214	177	177	177	177	190
Percentage of total for both sexes	..	89.2	89.2	73.8	73.8	73.8	73.8	79.2
Czech Republic								
Female								
Members of national parliament	29	21	30	30	34	34	34	34
Percentage of total for both sexes	14.1	10.3	15.0	15.0	17.0	17.0	17.0	17.0
Male								
Members of national parliament	177	183	170	170	166	166	166	166
Percentage of total for both sexes	85.9	89.7	85.0	85.0	83.0	83.0	83.0	83.0
Estonia								
Female								
Members of national parliament	12	11	18	18	18	19	19	19
Percentage of total for both sexes	11.9	10.9	17.8	17.8	17.8	18.8	18.8	18.8
Male								
Members of national parliament	89	90	83	83	83	82	82	82
Percentage of total for both sexes	88.1	89.1	82.2	82.2	82.2	81.2	81.2	81.2
Hungary								
Female								
Members of national parliament	28	43	32	32	35	38	38	35
Percentage of total for both sexes	7.3	11.1	8.3	8.3	9.1	9.8	9.8	9.1
Male								
Members of national parliament	358	343	354	354	351	348	348	350
Percentage of total for both sexes	92.7	88.9	91.7	91.7	90.9	90.2	90.2	90.9

	1	2	3	4	5	6	7	8
Latvia								
Female								
Members of national parliament	21	21	21	17	17	17	9	..
Percentage of total for both sexes	21.0	21.0	21.0	17.0	17.0	17.0	9.0	..
Male								
Members of national parliament	79	79	79	83	83	83	91	..
Percentage of total for both sexes	79.0	79.0	79.0	83.0	83.0	83.0	91.0	..
Lithuania								
Female								
Members of national parliament	31	31	15	15	15	24	25	10
Percentage of total for both sexes	22.0	22.0	10.6	10.6	10.6	17.5	18.0	7.1
Male								
Members of national parliament	110	110	126	126	126	113	114	131
Percentage of total for both sexes	78.0	78.0	89.4	89.4	89.4	82.5	82.0	92.9
Poland								
Female								
Members of national parliament	93	93	93	93	60	60	60	62
Percentage of total for both sexes	20.2	20.2	20.2	20.2	13.0	13.0	13.0	13.5
Male								
Members of national parliament	367	367	367	367	400	400	400	398
Percentage of total for both sexes	79.8	79.8	79.8	79.8	87.0	87.0	87.0	86.5
Romania								
Female								
Members of national parliament	37	37	37	37	37	25	25	..
Percentage of total for both sexes	11.2	10.7	10.7	10.7	10.7	7.3	7.3	..
Male								
Members of national parliament	294	308	308	308	308	318	318	..
Percentage of total for both sexes	88.8	89.3	89.3	89.3	89.3	92.7	92.7	..
Russian Federation								
Female								
Members of national parliament	44	44	34	34	34	34	46	..
Percentage of total for both sexes	9.8	9.8	7.6	7.6	7.6	7.7	10.2	..
Male								
Members of national parliament	403	406	415	415	415	407	404	..
Percentage of total for both sexes	90.2	90.2	92.4	92.4	92.4	92.3	89.8	..

(continued)

Table 1.1. Continued

Country and Membership	1990	1995	2000	2001	2002	2003	2004	2005
Serbia and Montenegro								
Female								
Members of national parliament	4	9	9	..	..	10	10	10
Percentage of total for both sexes	2.9	6.5	6.5	..	..	7.9	7.9	7.9
Male								
Members of national parliament	134	129	129	..	..	116	116	116
Percentage of total for both sexes	97.1	93.5	93.5	..	..	92.1	92.1	92.1
Slovakia								
Female								
Members of national parliament	22	22	21	21	21	29	29	25
Percentage of total for both sexes	14.7	14.7	14.0	14.0	14.0	19.3	19.3	16.7
Male								
Members of national parliament	128	128	129	129	129	121	121	125
Percentage of total for both sexes	85.3	85.3	86.0	86.0	86.0	80.7	80.7	83.3
Slovenia								
Female								
Members of national parliament	12	12	9	11	11	11	11	11
Percentage of total for both sexes	15.0	13.3	10.0	12.2	12.2	12.2	12.2	12.2
Male								
Members of national parliament	68	78	81	79	79	79	79	79
Percentage of total for both sexes	85.0	86.7	90.0	87.8	87.8	87.8	87.8	87.8
Ukraine								
Female								
Members of national parliament	..	17	35	35	24	24	24	24
Percentage of total for both sexes	..	3.8	7.8	7.8	5.3	5.3	5.3	5.3
Male								
Members of national parliament	..	433	415	415	426	426	426	426
Percentage of total for both sexes	..	96.2	92.2	92.2	94.7	94.7	94.7	94.7

Note: .. = not applicable.
Source: Data from the United Nations Economic Commission for Europe
(http://w3.unece.org/pxweb/dialog/varval.asp?ma=001_gepdnatparliament_r&ti=members+of+national+parliament+by+sex%2c+measurement%2c+country+and+year&path=../database/stat/30-ge/05-publicanddecision/&lang=1).

tions are both Orthodox and, among its Turkish citizens, Muslim. It has experienced a less direct transition to democracy and a slower transition to a market economy.

Russia provides an even sharper contrast to most of the other countries on a number of dimensions. Most relevant for our purposes is the fact that the Communist period was significantly longer and the post-Communist political transition has been less complete. After a promising, though hardly trouble-free, start on the road to democracy under Boris Yeltsin, Russia has become a hybrid political system variously described as an "illiberal" democracy, a semiauthoritarian polity, or a semiconsolidated authoritarian system in which Vladimir Putin and his associates dominate politics and the legislature has limited independence.

The Setting: Communist and Post-Communist Politics

Women's political roles in the countries included in this volume have been influenced by a number of factors. Three of the most important that merit attention before we turn to the questions that animated our research are their experiences with Communism, the transitions they have undergone since the end of Communism, and the growing influence of outside actors.

It is the first of these factors that distinguishes these countries from other European countries. Although all the countries examined in this volume except Russia are now members of the European Union, they share a particular history that continues to have an impact on their politics and economies. In the political arena, the Communist period was characterized by a one-party system in which the Communist Party monopolized political power and dominated the government and economy; attempted to control and shape education, the media, and the arts; and oversaw the associational life of the society through its control of the few other small political parties permitted and the mass organizations that were the only associations allowed for most of the period. The party also oversaw efforts, which were only partially successful at best, to politicize all areas of life to secure its own power and prevent independent challenges to the system.

This effort to remake society according to the strictures of Marxist-Leninist ideology also included attempts to wean the population away from religion as an organizing principle and create allegiance to the values approved by the Communist Party. These systems, which were imposed from above and from outside in all the countries except Yugoslavia—where Tito and the Partisans came to power largely through their own efforts to expel the occupiers at the end of World War II—came to rely increasingly on coercion to control their populations and secure their rule. The reliance on force, evident in purge trials, labor camps, and the imprisonment of perceived as well as real opponents, declined after the death of Stalin and the resulting campaign of de-Stalinization that began in 1956. But coercion remained a fallback tool for Communist elites to use even as they shifted their emphasis, in most cases, to a mixture of material incentives and the selective use of coercion against dissident intellectuals as their formula for ruling in the latter part of the Communist period.

This brief overview of some of the central elements of the Communist system is not meant to imply that Communism worked the same way everywhere in the region. There were clearly important differences in the way the system worked and in the leeway for individual expression and nonconformity in Poland, as well as Hungary, and in countries with more hard-line leaderships, such as Bulgaria, Czechoslovakia, and East Germany. But the organizational structures and principles of rule were similar.

Among the countries included in this book, the organization of politics and the nature of Communism—and hence, its legacy—differed most in Slovenia. As a member of the Yugoslav federation until Slovene leaders declared independence in 1991, Slovenia was part of what Dennison Rusinow termed "the Yugoslav experiment."[11] Thus, after Yugoslavia was expelled from the Communist community in 1947, Tito and his colleagues developed a form of political organization that allowed more autonomy for republic-level governments and, in theory, required the Communist Party to lead by example rather than force. Economic decisionmaking was also decentralized, though most property continued to be "social" rather than private. Although the party leadership retained a great deal of control, other groups in society had more room to operate, and intellectual life was less controlled than in other Communist countries. The citizens of Yugoslavia—including those in Slovenia, the most developed part of Yugoslavia, which became the republic most integrated into the West before the end of Communism—had much greater opportunity to travel and much greater exposure to intellectual, political, and other developments in the rest of Europe. Although the Communist Party remained the only official party, the citizens and leaders of Slovenia thus had very different experiences than those in most of the other countries under consideration.

One feature that all the Communist countries, including the former Yugoslavia, shared was an official, explicit commitment to women's equality.

On the basis of the writings of Marx, Engels, and Lenin, the Soviet and Central and Eastern European leaders enshrined a commitment to the full equality of women in their constitutions and included measures forbidding discrimination against women in their laws. Although these laws were often ignored in practice, they (together with other higher-priority elite commitments) led to a pattern of change in women's roles that was both common across the Communist countries and distinctive compared with changes that occurred more spontaneously in women's roles in other societies. Briefly put, women's roles changed significantly in terms of their educational access and employment outside the home, although important inequalities remained in both areas. There was far less change in women's actual exercise of political power or their role in the effective Communist Party elite as opposed to the more symbolic, governmental elites, and even in the division of labor within the family.[12]

This uneven pattern of change in women's roles created burdens for women and their families, including the often-discussed "double burden" of work and housework, as well as benefits in the provision of important services, such as child care and paid maternity and child care leave with guaranteed return to one's job—thus enabling women to use their skills and become part of a work collective, which, if successful, provided important practical and emotional supports. In the post-Communist period, particularly immediately after the end of Communism, there were women as well as men who reacted to these burdens by rejecting the ideal goal of gender equality. Although they clearly knew that the "equality" celebrated by party leaders on official occasions such as International Women's Day was not true equality, many nonetheless either saw the emphasis placed on women's economic roles under Communism as excessive and called for a greater focus on women's maternal roles or, linking the goal of gender equality to the old system, rejected it as well. Public opinion polls indicate that these attitudes changed somewhat in the recent past, but they had an impact on popular perceptions of women's roles in politics as well as other spheres and, we would argue, continue to have an influence in post-Communist societies.

The activities of women leaders have also been influenced by several aspects of the politics of transition. In the early post-Communist period, largely inexperienced political leaders faced a number of complex and difficult tasks as they sought to change constitutions, adopt or change laws to allow the development of a private economy, reorient political institutions to function democratically, recruit and train new political leaders and bureaucrats, facilitate the repopulation of their countries' associational space, and foster political cultures supportive of democracy. They also had to deal with the persistent political and economic roles of the Communist Party and its officials and oversee all the tasks involved in creating a market economy. In this complex, demanding context, issues related to women's status, and particularly women's equality, were often judged as secondary and shunted aside.[13]

Although many of the early tasks of the post-Communist transition have been accomplished in both the political and economic realms, numerous elections have been held, and we have seen the emergence of people who define themselves as "professional" rather than "amateur" politicians, political life continues to bear some of the hallmarks of the early transition. Thus, even today, political parties continue to be fleeting organizations in many cases, as political leaders leave established parties and form new ones. Levels of party identification remain low, and parties frequently disappear, to be replaced by new ones, between elections. Nongovernmental organizations abound, but many have few members and only weak links to the groups whose interests they seek to articulate. Although many citizens continue to support democracy and few wish to return to Communism, nostalgia for the services and security of the old days does surface, particularly among those who have not gained much from the shift to the market. Trust in political leaders and in political institutions remains low, in part as a reflection of the Communist era, but undoubtedly also in part in reaction to the many missteps made by inexperienced or personally ambitious, shortsighted leaders. The citizens of the post-Communist countries also continue to have lower levels of political efficacy and are less likely to engage in political acts beyond voting than their counterparts in more established European democracies.

In Russia, we have seen what many analysts consider to be de-democratization—a retreat from efforts to consolidate democracy and a return to semiauthoritarian rule. During the mid-1990s, the development of new political parties remained weak, and an unreformed, hard-left Communist successor party dominated the political scene. Nonetheless, parties did have some links with electoral constituents, and they had some representative role. Under the Putin presidency, a single "party of power," United Russia, dominated the legislature. United Russia was generally subordinate to the president, had very shallow roots in society, and made little effort to represent societal interests. This situation persists under the presidency of Dmitri Medvedev, as Putin has assumed the post of prime minister.

We also want to draw the reader's attention to recent economic trends in the region. After declines in production that, at least formally, equaled or surpassed those occurring in the United States during the Great Depression, the economies of the Central and Eastern European countries under consideration have recovered. Until mid-2008, many of them were experiencing growth rates higher than those of most other European countries. Clearly, the shift to the market produced positive results at the macroeconomic level. However, it is important to note that these benefits have not reached all parts of the populations of these states equally. The economic transition has created winners and losers in all these societies. Inequality soared in what had been very egalitarian societies—even the Communist Party elite enjoyed fewer material privileges than many of today's winners—and poverty and unemployment became urgent public policy issues. The recent worldwide crisis has been felt throughout the region, and some countries have been very badly affected.

In general, the young, urban, better-educated, and male segments of the population have benefited the most from the shift to the market, as well as those members of the Communist elites who were able to translate their political advantages into economic resources as Communism was ending. Young, urban, well-educated women have also gained new opportunities. And though it is too simple to paint all other women as victims of the transition, many women—including those who were older, less educated or skilled, and rural—did in fact face a good deal of hardship, particularly in the early years of the transition. Single-parent families, most of which are headed by women, also suffered disproportionately from the decline in social services and state subsidies. Thus, statistics about growth rates, improvements in productivity, and the overall standard of living must be tempered by the realization that the benefits of the shift to a market economy have not reached all groups equally. In Russia, where the shift to the market, like the political transition, has not progressed as far as in Central and Eastern Europe, poverty and inequality remain well above pretransition levels, though economic growth since 1999 has improved the living standards and well-being of many.

A final element that must be kept in mind when examining the women in power in the six countries considered here is the fact that all these nations are now far more susceptible to and interact with a much greater variety of outside actors than under Communism. This trend is especially noticeable in the Central and Eastern European countries. With the possible exception of Slovenia—where, as discussed above, the Communist system operated very differently than elsewhere in the region and where, as a result, there was much greater contact with the rest of Europe before the end of Communism—the opening of borders and the end of tight political control have exposed both political leaders and ordinary citizens to many more outside influences and actors of all types. Those most relevant for our purposes are the European Union and the transnational women's networks, groups, and individuals based in the United States and the rest of Europe. In eastern Germany, the creation of a unified Germany and the impact of western German institutions and policies is of course of paramount importance.

Although the Central and Eastern European countries regained their ability to act independently on the world stage with the end of Communism, the European Union has had an enormous influence not only on the policies but also on aspects of the institutional structures of the post-Communist countries that have sought and gained EU membership. U.S. and European feminists were early supporters of efforts to establish gender studies centers and women's studies programs at universities, and contact between women activists within and outside the region continues in the framework of the EU and other institutions. Russia, of course, has not applied to join the EU and so has not been subject to the same pressures and requirements as the Central and Eastern European countries. However, even in Russia, many kinds of outside actors, including international financial institutions, multinational corporations, and nongovernmental organizations such as women's groups, have also been active.[14]

The Research Questions

The results of the research presented in this volume, which was designed to focus on several common sets of questions and important issues specific to each country, were first made public in April 2005 at a conference in Washington organized by the editors of this volume and sponsored by the East European Studies Program and the Kennan Institute of the Woodrow Wilson International Center for Scholars and cosponsored by the Watson Institute at Brown University and the Institute for European, Russian, and Eurasian Studies at George Washington University.[15] Each researcher, guided by a common set of questions elaborated during several preparatory meetings, interviewed or arranged interviews with a sample of women, and in some cases men, who were deputies in their national parliaments in 2004. In addition to the common questions, the researchers also focused to some degree on issues of importance in individual countries. More detail on these interviews is included in each country chapter that follows (part I, chapters 2 through 7). Each chapter also discusses changes in women's representation in parliament and other relevant developments that have occurred since the initial research was completed.

As part of the project, we were eager to allow women leaders to speak for themselves. Thus, in addition to our interviews, we invited a woman deputy from each country discussed in this volume to reflect on her experiences as a political leader. Several of these women attended the conference in Washington. The women leaders whose voices are reflected in this book were asked to address a number of common questions. As their contributions illustrate, each has spoken in her own voice and has chosen to address issues of particular concern in her country and to her (part II, chapters 8 through 13).[16]

Our research into women's roles in exercising power in post-Communist states focused on six sets of issues. First, how did women decide to run for political office, and what factors helped or hindered them in their quest to be elected? How did they become interested in political careers, and what kinds of support have they received during their campaigns and as legislators? Second, what roles do women play in post-Communist legislative elites? What committees do they serve on, and what activities do they see as most important? Third, how do women in power see their roles? Do they see themselves as advocates for women in any sense, or do they define themselves primarily in terms of their party affiliations or the interests of their constituencies as a whole?

Fourth, to what extent have women been able to achieve their goals, and what areas have been the focus of their activities? What barriers or obstacles have they faced, and what issues do they see as most important for their countries and for women?

Fifth, we were interested in women's relationships with other political actors, such as their parties, and members of interest groups and nongovernmental organizations, including women's groups. We wanted to know how women deputies interacted, if at all, with women from other parties to articulate women's interests and how effective they were in getting issues of particular interest to women and issues related to women's equality onto the political agenda. We were particularly interested in "the difference women make"[17]—that is, the impact of differing levels of women's representation on policies toward women, the range of issues considered, and other aspects of the way legislatures function. Sixth and finally, we were interested in learning what influence outside actors, including Western feminists and international organizations, such as the European Union, have had on how issues of particular concern to women and issues related to women's equality fare in the political arena in the eyes of women legislators.

The literature on women in political leadership in other contexts provided insights into what we anticipated we might find. Almost all the legislatures examined were elected by proportional representation. The exception is Russia, because the Duma at this time relied on a system of half proportional representation and half single-member districts. In proportional representation systems, which are generally thought to be more favorable for women's representation than single-member districts,[18] candidates' positions on party lists are critical determinants of who actually gets seats in parliament. Thus, we hypothesized that women would identify party leaders and work in their party organizations as critical factors in their decisions to become active in politics and their success in getting into parliament. At the same time, we know from studies of women in other contexts that some women enter national political life after lengthy work as volunteers or activists. We expected that party loyalties and a party's role as a reference group would be less in the case of women leaders who entered politics by this route, even though they also were dependent on party lists for election.[19]

In the second area, we anticipated, based on studies of women leaders elsewhere, that women deputies would play a secondary role in leadership positions in the legislatures and that they would choose and/or be channeled into serving on committees that deal with issues traditionally thought to be women's issues—such as social affairs, family and children, and health and education—and would less often be members of the higher-prestige committees generally thought to be more important, such as defense, foreign affairs, and the budget. We did not know how women deputies would view their own success in achieving their goals. Given evidence of various forms of discrimination against women in these studies and women's clear recognition of the persistence of certain prejudices and stereotypes, as evident in mass public opinion polls, we anticipated that women deputies, who are almost uniformly highly educated, would perceive or be aware of traditional or discriminatory attitudes and behaviors within parliament. Conversely, given the high educational levels and professional accomplishments of women legislators as a group and the influences on mass elite political culture in other areas, we also thought it possible that women deputies would not encounter or perceive great difficulties due to their gender.

Studies of women in powerful positions in other countries outside the post-Communist world indicate that they are divided in how they view their roles. Many clearly see themselves primarily, if not exclusively, as representatives of their voters or constituencies. However, some women legislators in other contexts also see themselves as having a special responsibility to articulate and defend the interests of women. Others, although seeing themselves largely as general representatives, in fact through their committee assignments, effectively focus their activities on areas of special significance to women.[20]

Women leaders in other countries also tend to see social issues as somewhat more important than do their male counterparts. Similarly, legislatures in which there are higher levels of women's representation have different kinds of policy outcomes. We anticipated that women deputies in post-Communist states might be particularly likely to see these issues as important, given the impact of the shift to the market on the situation of less advantaged groups in these societies and the disproportionate share of the burdens of this shift borne by women—especially older, rural, less-educated women, and single mothers.

The patterns of cooperation of women deputies in other countries' legislatures vary. In all, party affiliations and membership in parliamentary clubs, or ideological orientations, are primary identities for women as well as for men. The influence of these factors is particularly strong in parliamentary systems, especially those whose electoral systems rely on closed party lists to select candidates. At the same time, women leaders have overcome these obstacles to cooperate. Some have founded ongoing women's groups or caucuses, as in the United States and Poland. Others have set up ad hoc coalitions to advocate cooperatively certain laws or measures that have a particular impact on women or address issues of particular concern to women. In some cases, contact with and pressure from women's organizations or groups outside the legislature have facilitated this cooperation.

We anticipated that the barriers to this kind of cooperation would be substantial in most of the countries we investigated. Because these nations' political parties are generally weaker and more often appear and disappear than those in many more established democracies, these parties may have less influence on women deputies. Conversely, given the absence of a strong women's movement and the small number of feminist organizations in most of the post-Communist world, there is likely to be less pressure on women deputies to focus on issues of special interest to women.[21]

We also expected a number of factors to hinder the effectiveness of women deputies in getting issues of special concern to women onto the political agenda, particularly those directed at advancing or promoting gender equality. As is illustrated by the ongoing debate about "critical mass"—the proportion that a group of legislators needs to reach to be effective, once thought to be 30 percent for women—there is no necessary link between the numerical representation of women and substantive representation. As many scholars have argued in other contexts, a host of other factors—ranging from electoral systems to the orientation of party members toward issues of particular concern to women and feminism, the length of time women have served in office, and the strength of links between women leaders and women's groups outside legislatures[22]—influence how women see their roles and their possibilities of getting issues onto the political agenda. Women's political values and attitudes, as well as their own definitions of their roles, also have an impact. There is evidence from other cases that it does make a difference if there are "women in the house" or legislature.[23] Numbers do seem to matter, although the threshold is unclear. Scholars have also suggested that it is necessary to differentiate between the impact of differing levels of women's representation in legislative bodies on politics as a workplace (attitudes toward women legislators, levels of hostility toward or agreement with feminist objectives, etc.) and policy outcomes.[24] As Sarah Childs and Mona Lena Krook have argued, and as the chapters that follow reflect, it is thus necessary to shift our focus from the question of "what women do" when they hold political office to "what specific women do."[25] At the same time, it is important to note that in our cases, as in most other legislatures worldwide, women still constitute a relatively small minority of legislators. Therefore, we anticipated that it would be unlikely for them to already have had a marked impact, independent of their male colleagues, on the kinds of legislation adopted.

Finally, we wanted to investigate the role of outside actors in influencing the perspectives of women parliamentarians in post-Communist Europe and Eurasia. Here, our expectations derived less from the experiences of women in other countries than from the role of outside actors in the region in general after the end of Communism. As numerous scholars have documented, outside governments, international organizations such as the European Union, NATO, and the International Monetary Fund, and transnational networks of nongovernmental organizations and activists have had an enormous impact on institutions, policies, and life in these societies. In contrast to the interwar era, when outside actors were either uninvolved or saw these newly independent or re-created states as fair game for economic and political penetration, in the post-Communist era, international actors have been far more supportive.[26]

Two of these outside actors were of particular interest to us: the European Union and Western women's organizations and feminist activists. Given the EU's commitment to the principle of gender equality and the inclusion, made explicit at the Copenhagen Summit in 2002, of antidiscrimination legislation as part of the package of laws that states wishing to join the EU must adopt, as well as periodic monitoring of progress on gender issues as part of the accession process,[27] we anticipated that women leaders would be aware of and would positively evaluate the EU's role in this area. We also anticipated that women deputies might be aware of the activities of Western women's and feminist groups, because numerous groups and individuals from other European countries and the United States have been active in the region, particularly in the early years after the end of Communism. We were not, however, sure whether the role of such groups and individuals would be evaluated positively. "Feminism" was a dirty word among many groups in the population, including, until recently, many intellectuals. Although negative attitudes toward feminism appear to be changing, many Central and Eastern European women appear to share the view of some intellectuals (who consider themselves feminists and are certainly advocates for women) that the experiences of Western feminists have little to tell them given the peculiarities of their experiences under Communism.[28]

As the chapters that follow illustrate, our research supported some of our hypotheses and called others into question. Our results also varied according to the nature of the transition and recent political and economic developments in individual countries. Although all the post-Communist nations discussed in this volume faced similar tasks at the outset of the transition period, the speed with which these tasks have been undertaken, as well as the methods used and degree of success, have differed considerably among the six countries. As a result, although all have experienced large-scale political, economic, social, and psychological changes since the end of Communism, the nature of these simultaneous transitions has been different in each case. As the chapters by researchers and activists alike illustrate, both these commonalities and differences have shaped the experiences and perspectives of women leaders in the region.

In conducting our research, we had to consider one issue faced by all those who focus on post-Communist European states: whether it still makes sense to view these countries as post-Communist or whether, particularly now that most Central and Eastern European countries are part of the European Union, we should simply see them as European. As the conception of this volume indicates, we believe that it still makes sense to view the countries studied as post-Communist—given, in this case, the impact of the common pattern of gender role change under Communism and the reaction to that pattern after Communism.

However, it is also important to view our conclusions within the framework of the ongoing integration of these post-Communist countries into Europe. For all the countries we consider, except Russia, in this respect our work is a snapshot of how women exercise power in countries that, now that they have joined the European Union, are beginning a long and presumably deepening process of integration. It will be for later observers and activists to determine whether the trends we discuss still reflect the post-Communist era or more properly belong to the start of a new one in which politics in these countries, and the women who play roles in political leadership, are influenced far less by their past than by their status as an integral part of Europe.

Notes

1. See Julie Ballington and Azza Karam, *Women in Parliament: Beyond the Numbers* (Stockholm: International Idea, 2005).

2. United Nations Development Program, *United Nations Human Development Report 2007/2008: Fighting Climate Change—Human Solidarity in a Divided World* (New York: United Nations Development Program, 2007), http://hdr.undp.org/en/media/hdr_20072008_en_complete.pdf, table 29, "Gender Empowerment Measure."

3. See Robert Putnam, *The Comparative Study of Political Elites* (Englewood Cliffs, N.J.: Prentice Hall, 1976).

4. Inter-Parliamentary Union, "Women in National Parliaments," http://www.ipu.org/wmn-e/classif.htm. Also see "Women Officeholders Fact Sheets and Summaries," provided by the Center for American Women in Politics, Eagleton Institute of Politics, Rutgers University, http://www.cawp.rutgers.edu/Facts.html#congress.

5. See Walter S. G. Kohn, *Women in National Legislatures: A Comparative Study of Six Countries* (New York: Praeger, 1980); Joni Lovenduski, *Women and European Politics: Contemporary Feminism and Public Policy* (Amherst: University of Massachusetts Press, 1986); Barbara J. Nelson and Najma Chowdhury, eds., *Women and Politics Worldwide* (New Haven, Conn.: Yale University Press, 1994); and Virginia Sapiro, *Political Integration of Women: Roles, Socialization and Politics* (Urbana: University of Illinois Press, 1983).

6. See Gail W. Lapidus, *Women in Soviet Society: Equality, Development and Social Change* (Berkeley: University of California Press, 1980); Dorothy Atkinson, Alexander Dallin, and Gail Warshofsky Lapidus, eds., *Women in Russia* (Stanford, Calif.: Stanford University Press, 1977); and Sharon L. Wolchik and Alfred G. Meyer, eds., *Women, State, and Party in Eastern Europe* (Durham, N.C.: Duke University Press, 1985).

7. See Marilyn Rueschemeyer, ed., *Women in the Politics of Post-Communist Eastern Europe,* rev. and expanded ed. (Armonk, N.Y.: M. E. Sharpe, 1998); Valentine M. Moghadam, ed., *Democratic Reform and the Position of Women in Transitional Economies* (Oxford: Clarendon Press, 1994); Mary Buckley, ed., *Perestroika and Soviet Women* (Cambridge: Cambridge University Press, 1992); Susan Gal and Gail Kligman, *Politics of Gender after Socialism* (Princeton, N.J.: Princeton University Press, 2000); and Jane S. Jaquette and Sharon L. Wolchik, eds., *Women and Democracy: Latin American and Central and Eastern Europe* (Baltimore: Johns Hopkins University Press, 1998). Also see the bibliography for additional sources.

8. See Richard E. Matland and Kathleen A. Montgomery, eds., *Women's Access to Political Power in Post-Communist Europe* (Oxford: Oxford University Press, 2003); and Alena Heitlinger, "Women in Eastern Europe: Survey of Literature," *Women's Studies International Forum* 8, no. 2 (1985): 147–52.

9. See Valerie Sperling, *Organizing Women in Contemporary Russia: Engendering Transition* (Cambridge: Cambridge University Press, 1999); Alena Heitlinger, ed., *Émigré Feminism: Transnational Perspectives* (Toronto: University of Toronto Press, 1999); and Barbara Einhorn, *Cinderella Goes to Market: Citizenship, Gender, and Women's Movements in East Central Europe* (London: Verso Books, 1993).

10. See Sabrina Ramet, ed., *Gender Politics in the Western Balkans: Women and Society in Yugoslavia and the Yugoslav Successor States* (University Park: Pennsylvania State University Press, 1999).

11. Dennison Rusinow, *The Yugoslav Experiment 1948–1974* (Berkeley: University of California Press, 1977).

12. After the fall of Communism, scholars and Western feminists flocked to many of the formerly Communist countries, and the literature on women's roles in politics and their status burgeoned. See the bibliography for some of this literature. Early works in English on the status of women under Communism include Barbara Jancar, *Women under Communism* (Baltimore: The Johns Hopkins University Press, 1978); Hilda Scott, *Does Socialism Liberate Women? Experiences from·Eastern Europe* (Boston: Beacon Press, 1974); Marilyn Rueschemeyer and Christiane Lemke, eds., *The Quality of Life in the German Democratic Republic: Changes and Developments in a State Socialist Society* (Armonk, N.Y.: M. E. Sharpe, 1989); Lapidus, *Women in Soviet Society;* Dorothy Atkinson, Alexander Dallin, and Gail Warshofsky Lapidus, eds., *Women in Russia* (Stanford, Calif.: Stanford University Press, 1977); and Wolchik and Meyer, *Women, State, and Party in Eastern Europe.* See the chapters that follow on individual countries for references to some of the literature on women's issues by scholars in the countries studied, much of which, with the exception of Poland and Yugoslavia, developed largely after the end of Communism.

13. Along with other scholars, we have dealt at some length with the nature of the transition and women's roles in the transition, as well as in bringing down Communism, and the impact of the transition on women's situation. See, e.g., Jaquette and Wolchik, *Women and Democracy;* Rueschemeyer, *Women in the Politics of Post-Communist Eastern Europe;* Barbara Einhorn, *Citizenship in an Enlarging Europe: From Dream to Awakening* (London: Palgrave Macmillan, 2006); Nanette·Funk and Magda Mueller, eds., *Gender Politics and Post-Communism: Reflections from Eastern Europe and the Former Soviet Union* (London: Routledge, 1993); and Tanya Renne, ed., *Ana's Land: Sisterhood in Eastern Europe* (Boulder, Colo.: Westview Press, 1997). Also see the sources listed in the bibliography at the end of the present volume. Materials dealing specifically with women leaders in the post-Communist world are much less numerous. See the bibliography and the individual chapters for references to these works.

14. See Leah Seppanen Anderson, "European Union Gender Regulations in the East: The Czech and Polish Accession Process," *East European Politics and Societies* 20, no.1 (2006): 101–25; Einhorn, *Citizenship in an Enlarging Europe;* Katya M. Guenther, "Understanding Policy Diffusion across Feminist Movements: The Case of Gender Mainstreaming in Eastern Germany," *Politics & Gender* 4, no. 4 (2008): 587–613; Vlasta Jalušić and Milica Antić, *Prospects for Gender Equality Policies in Central and Eastern Europe,* Social Consequences of Economic Transformation in East Central Europe Pro-

ject Paper 79 (Vienna: Institute for Human Sciences, 2000), http://www.iwm.at/publ-spp/soco79pp.pdf; and Joanna Regulska and Magda Grabowska, "Will It Make a Difference? EU Enlargement and Women's Public Discourse in Poland," in *Gender Politics in the Expanding European Union,* ed. Silke Roth (Oxford: Berghahn Books, 2008), 137–54.

15. For brief summaries of the conference proceedings, see Nida Gelazis, ed., *Women in East European Politics,* East European Studies Special Report (Washington, D.C.: Woodrow Wilson International Center for Scholars, 2005).

16. Given the very difficult situation of the few women deputies in the Duma, in the Russian case, we decided to use their responses to a number of questions raised in the interviews.

17. Michele L. Swers, *The Difference Women Make: The Policy Impact of Women in Congress* (Chicago: University of Chicago Press, 2002).

18. Matland and Montgomery, *Women's Access to Political Power.*

19. Manon Tremblay, "The Substantive Representation of Women and PR: Some Reflections on the Role of Surrogate Representation and Critical Mass," *Politics & Gender* 2, no. 4 (2006): 502–11.

20. For studies of the impact of these factors in other political contexts, see Michael B. Berkman and Robert E. O'Connor, "Do Women Legislators Matter? Female Legislators and State Abortion Policy," in *Understanding the New Politics of Abortion,* ed. M. Goggin (Newbury Park, Calif.: Sage, 1994); Kathleen A. Bratton and Leonard P. Ray, "Descriptive Representation, Policy Outcomes, and Municipal Day-Care Coverage in Norway," *American Journal of Political Science* 46, no. 2 (April 2002): 428–37; Rebecca Howard Davis, *Women and Power in Parliamentary Democracies* (Lincoln: University of Nebraska Press, 1997); Lyn Kathlene, "In a Different Voice: Women and the Policy Process," in *Women and Elective Office: Past Present and Future,* ed. Sue Thomas and Clyde Wilcox (New York: Oxford University Press, 1998), 188–202; Sue Thomas, "Voting Patterns in the California Assembly: The Role of Gender," *Women and Politics* 9, no. 4 (1989): 43–53; and Sue Thomas, "The Impact of Women on State Legislative Policies," *Journal of Politics* 53, no. 4 (November 1991): 958–76.

21. For information on the development of political parties and party systems in post-Communist Europe and Russia, see Herbert Kitschelt, Zdenka Mansfeldova, Radoslaw Markowski, and Gabor Toka, *Post-Communist Party Systems: Competition, Representation, and Inter-Party Cooperation* (Cambridge: Cambridge University Press, 1999); Tomáš Kostelecký, *Political Parties after Communism: Developments in East-Central Europe* (Washington, D.C., and Baltimore: Woodrow Wilson Center Press and The Johns Hopkins University Press, 2002); Paul G. Lewis, *Political Parties in Post-Communist Eastern Europe* (London: Routledge, 2000); Anna M. Grzymala-Busse, *Redeeming the Communist Past: The Regeneration of Communist Parties in East-Central Europe* (Cambridge: Cambridge University Press, 2002); and Robert Moser, *Unexpected Outcomes Electoral Systems, Political Parties, and Representation in Russia* (Pittsburgh: Pittsburgh University Press, 2001).

22. See, especially, Sandra Grey, "Numbers and Beyond: The Relevance of Critical Mass in Gender Research," *Politics & Gender* 2, no. 4 (2006): 492–502. For analyses that emphasize strong links to women's organizations as key, see Irene Tinker, "Quotas for Women in Elected Legislatures: Do They Really Empower Women?" *Women's Studies International Forum* 27, nos. 5–6 (2004): 531–46; and Irene Tinker, "Assumptions

and Realities: Electoral Quotas for Women," *Georgetown Journal of International Affairs,* Winter–Spring 2009, 7–14.

23. See Swers, *Difference Women Make.*

24. See Drude Dahlerup, "The Story of the Theory of Critical Mass," *Politics & Gender* 2, no. 4 (2006): 511–22.

25. Sarah Childs and Mona Lena Krook, "Should Feminists Give Up on Critical Mass? A Contingent Yes," *Politics & Gender* 2, no. 4 (2006): 522–30.

26. See Ronald Linden, *Norms and Nannies: The Impact of International Organizations on the Central and East European States* (Lanham, Md.: Rowman and Littlefield, 2003); Milada Anna Vachudova, *Europe Undivided: Democracy, Leverage, and Integration after Communism* (Oxford: Oxford University Press, 2005); and Jan Zielonka, ed., *Democratic Consolidation in Eastern Europe, Volume 1: Institutional Engineering* (Oxford: Oxford University Press, 2001).

27. Open Society Institute, *Monitoring the EU Accession Process: Equal Opportunities for Women and Men* (Budapest: Open Society Institute, 2002).

28. See Jiřina Šiklová, "Feminism and the Roots of Apathy in the Czech Republic," *Social Research,* Summer 1997; and Hana Havelkova, "Abstract Citizenship? Women and Power in the Czech Republic," in *Gender and Citizenship in Transition,* ed. Barbara Hobson (New York: Routledge, 2000). See also Susanne Kraatz, Dorothee de Neve, and Silvia von Steinsdorff, "Osteuropaforschung ohne Frauen?" *Osteuropa* 5 (2003): 635–46.

Part I

Women in Six National Parliaments

Chapter 2

Women in the Russian State Duma

Linda J. Cook and Carol Nechemias

This chapter focuses on women deputies in Russia's State Duma—their pathways to power and experiences as professional legislators. Among the cases included in this volume, the Russian Federation has elected the lowest percentage of women deputies during the post-Communist period.[1] With the introduction of competitive elections during perestroika, the percentage of women in the national legislature fell dramatically, and in the newly independent Russian Federation, the share of seats held by women dropped over the course of three elections from 13.5 percent in 1993 to 10.2 percent in 1995 and then to 7.5 percent in 1999. The December 2003 parliamentary contest reversed that trend, as women increased their share of seats to 9.8 percent, and in the December 2007 election they increased it further, to 14 percent.

The authors thank Marilyn Rueschemeyer, Nadezhda Shvedova, Sharon Wolchik, and the participants in the Conference on Women in East European Politics at the Woodrow Wilson International Center for Scholars, April 2004, for comments on earlier versions of this chapter.

The downward spiral that marked the 1990s ran counter to developments in Western Europe and in several other former Communist states, where women registered gains in national parliaments. Overall, Russia continues to lag behind the worldwide average figure for women, holding 16.3 percent of seats in the lower houses of national legislatures as of the end of 2005.[2] More significantly, the increase in women's representation from 2003 has coincided with growing executive dominance and authoritarianism in Russia's political system and with the collapse of the legislature's independent role.

The dearth of women in the State Duma during the 1990s served as a telling reminder that women remained sealed off from "big politics" during Russia's relatively democratic period. What, then, have been the obstacles to women's access to the State Duma? What are the characteristics of those women who have secured election as deputies? Did these women follow particular recruitment patterns? And does women's presence make a difference? Have women deputies sought to define, advocate, and defend women's interests? Have they worked within their parties or across party lines to advance policy goals related to those interests? Here, we explore these issues through the unique prism of Russian women parliamentarians' personal accounts of their experiences in the hallways of power.[3]

The Interviews: Setting the Stage

This research draws on in-depth interviews with women deputies, who recount their own stories concerning their backgrounds, candidacies, political commitments, priorities, and work in the State Duma.[4] Interwoven throughout the interviews are comments on whether gender matters, and if so, how. The interviews were conducted during February and March 2004, following the December 2003 parliamentary elections and thus early in the fourth session of the Russian State Duma. (For more discussion of Russian women deputies' views based on these interviews, see chapter 8.)

There were twenty-five interviews with former women deputies, including nineteen of the forty-four women elected in the December 2003 parliamentary election; five Women of Russia (WR) deputies who served from 1993–95; and one woman deputy elected to the State Duma in 1993, 1995, and 1999. The nineteen interviews with women deputies elected in December 2003 reflect the spectrum of political forces in the fourth State Duma; they include twelve of the twenty-six women aligned with United Russia

(UR), two of the six women from the Communist Party of the Russian Federation (CPRF), both of the women deputies from the Liberal Democratic Party (LDP), one of the four women from Rodina (Motherland), and two of the four independent or unaligned women deputies. Overall, 43 percent of the women deputies elected to the fourth State Duma session were interviewed, a firm foundation for identifying commonalities and patterns. The inclusion of a small group of former women deputies, mainly from WR, strengthens our capacity to track change over time in the lives and roles of women deputies.

The political setting in which these women forged their legislative careers has undergone dramatic transformation since 1993, when the first State Duma was elected. First, initial parliamentary elections showed great volatility: Parties formed, dissolved, and reformed; public support for individual parties shifted sharply from election to election; and most parties were too weakly rooted in Russian society to effectively mediate between society and the state.[5]

Second, there is a widespread perception that electoral politics has become more biased as well as dirtier, that "parties of power" have used state-controlled media and other administrative measures to tilt the playing field in their favor, including the Kremlin sponsorship of "official" opposition parties.[6] Third, the 2003 and 2007 parliamentary elections and the 2004 and 2008 presidential elections mark the emerging dominance of a state-controlled party of power—UR—that represents the ruling group rather than elements of civil society.[7]

Fourth, the surge in political activism that occurred during perestroika and the early 1990s has receded along with Russia's enthusiasm for democracy.[8] Research suggests that Russia is among the least advanced—outside Central Asia—of the post-Communist countries in democratization and the rule of law, while ranking among the lowest in the world with respect to trust in public institutions, in political parties, and in election procedures.[9] The impact of these factors on women's prospects for holding public office and for advancing a "women's agenda" will be discussed in greater detail in the following sections of this chapter.

Women in the Duma

Table 2.1 provides an overview of women's participation in the Dumas of the Russian Federation, including overall numbers of deputies and representation in leadership positions. Each Duma is made up of 450 deputies. In the first four elections, held in December 1993, 1995, 1999, and 2003, half the deputies were elected in single-member districts (SMD) and half on the basis of party lists, with a 5 percent threshold in the national vote required for a party to gain representation. For the December 2007 election, the system was changed to exclusively party list elections with a 7 percent threshold, a measure that enhanced the Kremlin's dominance of the electoral process by eliminating independents as well as governor-sponsored candidates. In each Duma, the stronger parties formed factions and deputy groups that provided access to leadership positions and legislative resources.[10] The main party affiliations of women deputies, as well as their programmatic commitments, shifted over the five Dumas.

The outcome for women in 1993 was shaped overwhelmingly by the success of WR, which nominated only women, gained 8 percent of the vote, and elected twenty-three deputies, more than one-third of the total number of women. WR formed a faction that was committed to the defense of women's interests; its deputy, Alevtina Fedulova, gained a position as a Duma deputy chair; and it worked through the Committee on Women, Family, and Youth, an important source of legislative policy initiative. Its success "helped substantially to legitimize a place for women in the new nation's politics" and made their inclusion part of the electoral strategies of other, especially left and centrist, parties.[11] In 1995 the CPRF, the liberal Yabloko, and the propresidential Our Home Is Russia substantially increased their nominations of women candidates, contributing to WR's demise as an electoral force (though conflicts within WR also played a role). The party narrowly missed passing the 5 percent barrier in the 1995 election, seating only three SMD deputies. In 1999, WR gained only 2 percent of the national vote and no seats, ending the near-term prospects for a significant women's party in Russia. The overall number of women deputies fell to forty-six in 1995 and thirty-four in 1999, and they were spread across parties of various orientations and ideologies.

In the 1995 Duma, the largest group of women was affiliated with the CPRF, the only party that allocated seats to women nearly in proportion to the original list (9 percent elected vs. 11 percent nominated on party lists, a policy that was apparently followed for this election only). The CPRF and its political allies dominated the second Duma, and women from these left-wing parties and factions constituted a majority of women deputies overall.[12] The CPRF deputy Svetlana Goryacheva became a Duma deputy chair, Alevtina Aparina headed the Committee on Women and Families, and women chaired two additional "social" committees. However, few held leadership roles in the parties and there were no women heads of Duma factions or deputy groups. By the 1999 election, the CPRF had begun to weaken, and its contingent of women shrank. In 2003 the CPRF nominated the largest number of women in both proportional representation and SMD races (a total of forty-eight) but seated only six, and the party's influence generally was eclipsed.

From the 1999 Duma election, the largest contingent of women was affiliated with UR, a propresidential party of power that was formed by a merger of Unity and Fatherland–All Russia shortly after the election. UR included almost half the women deputies in 1999 and a majority in both 2003 and 2007. In the last two elections, both the total number of women and the number elected on party lists rose substantially, showing that UR promoted women more than most of Russia's previous legislative parties. UR's heightened interest in promoting women may have been foreshadowed before the December 2007 parliamentary election, when a September reshuffling of President Vladimir Putin's cabinet led to the appointment of two women as government ministers, lending a female touch to the then all-male Russian government. The two women—the health and social development minister, Tatyana Golikova, and the economic development minister, Elvira Nabiullina—not only continue to hold their positions under President Dmitri Medvedev but also form part of a new executive body called the Presidium, a group of key government officials that meets weekly with now–Prime Minister Putin.

Two cabinet positions, however, is rather paltry, as is the modest record of women's legislative leadership positions in the third, fourth, and fifth Dumas, all dominated by UR, which held a two-thirds majority of seats after the 2003 and 2007 elections. In the third Duma, UR's Lyubov Sliska and Irina Khakamada of the small Union of Right Forces served as Duma deputy chairs, and the CPRF's Alevtina Aparina headed the Committee on Women, Family, and Youth. In the fourth Duma, all five women who held leadership positions represented UR, and in the fifth the three Duma deputy chairs and three committee chairs assigned to women went to deputies from UR and its allied party, Just Russia.

Of other parties that have crossed the party list threshold, the liberal Yabloko enjoyed success in the 1993, 1995, and 1999 elections, and it has exhibited a consistently strong record on the nomination of women deputies and a progressive stance on gender issues. The nationalist LDP has a comparatively poor nomination record and is sometimes overtly sexist on issues

Table 2.1. Women in the Russian State Dumas, 1993–95 to 2007–11

Measure	First Duma, 1993–95	Second Duma, 1995–99	Third Duma, 1999–2003	Fourth Duma, 2003–7	Fifth Duma, 2007–11
Women in the Duma					
Number	60	46	34	44	63
Percent	13.5	10.2	7.5	9.8	14
Elected					
Single-member districts	26	31	20	21	
Party lists	34	15	14	23	62
Party or bloc affiliation, number of women members	WR, 23; LDP, 5; CPRF, 3; Yabloko, 2; Russia's Choice, 2; DPR, 1; Independent/SMD,[a] 24	CPRF, 17; Yabloko, 6; OHR, 5; LDP, 1; WR, 3; Other, 4; Independent, 10	CPRF, 11; Unity, 7; FAR, 7; URF, 4; Yabloko, 2; Independent, 3	UR, 26; CPRF, 6; LDPR, 2; Rodina, 4; Yabloko, 1; Independent, 5	UR, 44; Just Russia, 11; Communists, 4; LDP, 4
Leadership positions in the Duma	Deputy chair (Fedulova, WR)	Deputy chair (Goryachev, CPRF)	First deputy chair (Sliska, UR); deputy chair (Khakamada, URF)	First deputy chair (Sliska, UR)	Deputy chairs (Gerasimova, UR; Zhurova, UR; Sliska, UR)
Committee chairs	Women, Family, and Youth; Health Protection; Education, Culture, and Science	Women, Family, and Youth; Ecological Protection	Women, Family, and Youth; Problems of the North and Far East; Ethics	Women, Family, and Youth; Health Protection; Problems of the North and Far East; Natural Resources	Women, Family, and Youth; Health Protection; Problems of the North and Far East; Natural Resources, Conservation and Environmentalism

Committees with strong representation of women, number of women members	Women, Family, and Youth, 8; Education, Culture, and Science, 6; Health Protection, 6; Budget, Taxes, Banks, and Finance, 6	Women, Family, and Youth, 5; Budget, Taxes, Banks, and Finance, 6	Women, Family, and Youth, 6; Budget, Taxes, Banks, and Finance, 4	Budget and Taxes, 6; Culture, 5; Labor and Social Policy, 4	Budget and Taxes, 10; Women, Family, and Youth, 7; Labor and Social Policy, 7; Health Protection, 5; Affairs of the Federation and Regional Politics, 4

Note: CPRF = Communist Party of the Russian Federation; DPR = Democratic Party of Russia; FAR = Fatherland–All Russia; LDP = Liberal-Democratic Party; OHR = Our Home Is Russia; URF = Union of Right Forces; UR = United Russia; WR = Women of Russia.

[a]In the 1993 election, party affiliation was not listed on the single-member ballot; women elected through that route are listed as independents, though some of them were nominated supported by various parties or blocs. The SMD entry refers to the number of women elected via that route.

Sources: Andrei Maximov, *Maximov's Companion to the 1995 Russian Duma Elections* (Moscow: Maximov Publications, 1996); *Maximov's Companion to Who Governs Russia* 1, no. 1 (1995): 96–127; *Maximov's Companion to Who Governs Russia* 3, no. 2 (1998): 189–244; *Maximov's Companion to Who Governs Russia* 4, no. 2 (1999–2000): 183–240; *Rossiia v Tsifrakh 2000* (Moscow: Goskomstat, 2001), 48; Iulia Shevchenko, "Who Cares About Women's Problems? Female Legislators in the 1995 and 1999 Russian State Dumas," *Europe-Asia Studies* 54, no. 8 (2002): 1201–22 (the citation is on 1219); Nadezhda Shvedova, "Short Description," unpublished; Valerie Sperling, *Organizing Women in Contemporary Russia* (Cambridge: Cambridge University Press, 1999), 117; N. A. Shvedova, *Prosto slozhnom: Gendernoie prosveshchenie* (Moscow: Antikva, 2002), 123; "The Russian Federation Votes: 2003–04, Single-Mandate-District Winners by Party," Radio Free Liberty / Radio Europe, http://www.rferl.org/specials/russianelection/archives/single.asp; "The Russian Federation Votes: 2003–04, Party-List Winners by Party," Radio Free Liberty / Radio Europe, http://www.rferl.org/specials/russianelection/archives/partywinners.asp; Radio Free Liberty / Radio Europe, *RFE/RL* 11, no. 238, part 1, December 28, 2007; http://www.duma.gov.ru.

of civic equality. These and other small parties have elected small numbers of women deputies. However, the parties that have mattered by far the most—in terms of seating the largest contingent of women deputies and representing women's interests in legislative agenda setting and policy-making—have been WR in the first Duma, the CPRF in the second Duma, and UR in the third, fourth, and fifth Dumas. The bulk of our interviews thus focused on deputies from these three parties, and the remaining discussion concentrates on them.

Why So Few Women Deputies? Obstacles and Challenges

Researchers have identified a number of barriers to women's access to high-level legislative seats. There is a substantial literature documenting obstacles to women's election to national legislatures, and this chapter directs attention in a selective fashion toward those factors highlighted either by women parliamentarians themselves or by scholars particularly concerned with women's political opportunities in post-Communist countries. These factors include the Soviet Communist legacy, gender ideologies, women's socialization, women's presence in recruitment or "eligibility" pools, and aspects of the political system such as the type of electoral system, incumbency rates, and political parties' role as gatekeepers in the nomination process.

The Soviet Communist Legacy

The Soviet Communist gender system advanced three principles: (1) a commitment to a concept of gender equality that emphasized women's participation in the labor force as the key to their liberation and independence, (2) a commitment to state policies directed toward making it possible for "mother-workers" to combine motherhood with full-time work, and (3) a commitment to a version of equality that stressed natural or biological differences between men and women. The Soviet approach to women's issues led to significant achievements for women in terms of their integration into the workforce and their educational levels, including inroads into traditional male occupations and the professions. By the mid-1970s, virtually all women of working age worked full time or were students, women constituted more than half the Soviet labor force, and 50 percent of students in higher education were women. Substantial proportions of professional women were employed as academics, agronomists, engineers, scientists, economists, and physicians. Yet a glass ceiling kept women out of leading positions in the Soviet Union; at the close of the Soviet era, just 6.5 percent of managers in the Russian Republic were female and the proportion of women in the political elite, as measured by membership in the Central Committee of the Communist Party of the Soviet Union, hovered consistently around the 3 percent level.[13]

According to A. A. Temkina, a prominent gender studies scholar at the European University in Saint Petersburg, "the peculiarities of the [Soviet] gender system and the social construction of gender influenced and continue to influence women's political behavior in the transition period."[14] She draws attention to the ways in which Soviet women's political opportunities were constricted, to gender ideologies, and to the heritage of declarative or formal equality rather than real equality. Although the antidemocratic character of Soviet Communism constrained political participation in general, there were peculiar features associated with women's political roles.[15] A key pattern involved women's absence from leading party and state positions coupled with a quota system that ensured substantial female representation in institutions lacking political power. Those institutions especially involved the USSR Supreme Soviet and lower-level legislatures, which, while providing a facade of democracy, frequently utilized women deputies for symbolic or decorative purposes. These practices advanced stereotypes of women as powerless political figures chosen by powerful male politicians—the proverbial textile worker or milkmaid. Moreover, the strong association between gender quotas and the Communist past has complicated efforts in the post-Soviet era to present numerical goals and/or quotas as progressive measures designed to enhance democratic representation.[16]

Another legacy of the past involves the concentration of women political activists in a "ghetto" of second-tier political positions. This pattern included government departments and party officials specializing in policy areas like education, social benefits, youth, children, culture, propaganda, and light industry. Even here, women were more likely to be found at the local and regional levels than the federal or all–Soviet Union level. These positions carried less status and meshed with widespread gender stereotyping of women as defenders of children, the elderly, and the family.

Soviet-era gender consciousness reinforced these patterns of women's political participation. The Soviet explanation for differences in "feminine" and "masculine" personality traits, interests, and careers stresses biology rather than socialization. Lynne Attwood's work on Soviet sex-role social-

ization suggests that beginning in the 1970s an upswing in traditional thinking occurred, as an unfavorable demographic situation spurred a desire to
promote traditional gender roles.[17] Equality did not mean identity; women
were described as different from men in character, as soft, emotional, sin-
cere, gentle, delicate, thoughtful, kind, sensitive, and understanding. Mary
Buckley points out that Soviet ideology rejected as bourgeois feminism the
idea that "casting woman as the main child rearer, cook, shopper, washer,
and cleaner might result in gender inequalities."[18] Thus, the Soviet era accounted for women's absence from political office as stemming from nature, from immutable and eternal causes, with no injustice—unfair societal
discrimination—to redress. It was assumed that women, destined for motherhood as well as the workforce, opted for a lesser (though not inconse-
quential) role in the workplace and the polity, one that allowed them to de-
vote their energies to fulfilling their duties as mothers and wives.

At the end of the Soviet period, women were political outsiders, lacking
access to high-level decisionmaking. On paper, the Soviet Union had performed admirably, with equal rights for women embedded in a series of
Soviet constitutions (1918, 1936, 1977), a tradition continued in the 1993
Russian Federation Constitution.[19] But in reality, considerable inequalities
existed in many areas of life, particularly with respect to high-level politics.

Gender Consciousness in Post-Soviet Russia

In contrast to the Soviet era, we can now draw on survey research to delve
into contemporary public attitudes toward women's rights. Public opinion
polls show considerable opposition to women holding high-level political
office. According to a 2003 survey, 35 percent of the population (41 percent
of men and 30 percent of women) endorsed the view that "politics is not
women's business."[20] Sixty-three percent of the population declares itself
ready to vote for a woman as president, but 31 percent strongly oppose the
idea.[21] A survey conducted only among women and with somewhat different wording found a strong preference for males in high-level politics;
63 percent of women would vote for a man when asked how they would
vote if the presidential contest was between a man and a woman.[22]

Popular attitudes militate against women building support among women
as a means of launching political careers. When asked what should be the
main direction of women's organizations, overwhelming majorities of Russian women reject the view that women's groups should struggle for women's
rights or fight against gender discrimination. Instead, they believe women's

organizations should provide psychological and material support, help women secure work, and defend children. In any case, very few women—less than 2 percent—participate in women's groups; the bulk of women have no interest in participating, have never turned to women's groups for assistance, or knew nothing about such groups. Despite their recognition that women do not enjoy equal access to the political arena or to high-paying jobs, a majority of women (59 percent) believe that there are no so-ciopolitical differences between the interests of men and women and that it is therefore unimportant whether men or women defend those interests. When queried as to whether they would turn to a male or female local po-litical figure, both competent to solve an important personal problem, women narrowly favored the woman officeholder (by 53 to 47 percent).[23] Opposition to women in politics, the weakness of women's organizations, and the lack of women's solidarity do not bode well for women's prospects for rallying citizens to the cause of increasing women's political clout.

Women's Political Ambition

Turning to our interviews, we began by asking whether these women as-pired to run for the State Duma. A lack of political ambition, as an aspect of women's socialization, often is cited as a reason for the paucity of women in public office, in particular higher-level political offices. Did these women plan to enter the national political fray? Are they politically ambitious? Though most of the women deputies had years of social and political ac-tivity behind them on the local or regional level, few dreamed about pursu-ing a political career on the national stage. In general, the women deputies regard their foray into "big politics" as unplanned, as a matter of chance or fate rather than as the culmination of lifelong personal goals. One deputy responded that she had never before thought about running for the State Duma, while another considered the proposal to run the result of chance, as she happened to be attending a program for women leaders that brought her into close contact with the WR leader Ekaterina Lakhova. UR women deputies make comments to the effect that "the republic governor made the suggestion—it was not my initiative" and "I did not consciously want to run, but my leadership role with professional unions thrust me into a close connection with [them]." A CPRF deputy stressed that "I didn't make the decision; the party organization made the decision."

In a few cases, women actively sought national office. These women cite convictions and patriotism, outrage over Boris Yeltsin's policies and the collapse of the USSR, or work at the local level in building up their parties' organization as factors that led them to step forward as their parties' candidate. These motivations were more typical for Rodina and LDP women deputies; the handful of UR deputies who pointed to their own personal decision to run typically came from a business background or had experience with nongovernmental organizations (NGOs). The bulk of the women deputies, however, entered the national political arena because they were recruited, selected, or urged to run by others. We will explore this topic in greater detail when we turn our attention to the role of gender in the recruitment process.

Recruitment Pools

Are women present in recruitment pools, and do they have the proper credentials or background for a career in "big politics"? Two streams of recruitment predominate in Russian politics: the old *nomenklatura,* who adapted to new circumstances and fill various high-status positions, and the smaller but growing infusion of personnel drawn from the world of big business. Fifteen of our twenty-five women deputies followed the first pathway, having honed their leadership and organizational skills within the Komsomol, trade unions, and/or the CPRF (table 2.2). Overwhelmingly, they worked at the local or regional level in the traditional sphere of women's political activism: as Komsomol secretaries, as heads of departments like education or social welfare, or as trade union or women's council activists. Some had electoral experience at lower levels of the political hierarchy before running for the State Duma. Overall, these women characterized their work in terms of helping others through *obshchestvennaia rabota* (public or social work), and they clearly relished that work as a central value in their lives.

This route to political office plays to women's strengths—ties to regional elites, local name recognition, and professional visibility. Our women deputies often pointed to their reputations for service within their communities, as well as support from political parties or local political machines, as key factors that permitted them to compensate for a resource they lacked—money. One deputy noted that as a deputy head at the regional level, she was a well-known person who regularly conducted radio and television programs on "Your Social Guarantees"; another remarked that she had worked for eighteen years in the same city district, the last five as the top administrator, so that she was well known; still another considered that

Table 2.2. Political recruitment and women's pathways to the Russian State Duma (number of women members)

Background	United Russia, 12	WR, 5; Independent, 2; Various, 1	LPD, 2; CPRF, 2; Rodina, 1
Nomenklatura	9	WR, 4	CPRF, 2
Business	1	Various, 1	
Civil society	2	Independent, 1	LPD, 2
Academia	2	WR, 1; independent, 1; Rodina, 1	
Report contact with women's organizations	8	WR, 5; various, 1	CPRF, 1

Note: CPRF = Communist Party of the Russian Federation; LDP = Liberal-Democratic Party; WR = Women of Russia. All the independent, LPD, CPRF, and Rodina deputies were serving in the fourth State Duma. The WR deputies served in the first State Duma; the deputy labeled "various" served in different small liberal democratic parties in the first, second, and third State Dumas. Many of the women deputies could fall in more than one category; the authors chose to emphasize the deputies' occupational pursuits immediately prior to their entry into the State Duma. The category "civil society" includes active participation in building regional party organizations; both LPD deputies and one of the United Russia deputies fall into that area. The category "report contact with women's organizations" runs the gamut from women who mention that women's organizations helped provide campaign volunteers to participating in various women's forums to active participation in women's groups.
Sources: Interviews conducted in Moscow in February and March 2004.

her many years of working with children, pensioners, and veterans, coupled with her most recent position as head of education for her region, allowed her to overcome the superior financial resources of her opponent. As one woman deputy put it, "My image, my social activity, . . . speaks for itself."

The number of women in the pipeline ready to follow in the footsteps of these deputies is not large. In the late 1990s, women filled only a handful of leading executive positions at the regional level, occupying 7 of 322 policy and leadership posts.[24] Women's representation in regional legislatures also has remained quite limited. In 1997 and again in 2004, across all regions and republics of the Russian Federation, the proportion of seats held by women stood at a stagnant 9 percent. About two-thirds of these female legislators were nominated by "groups of voters" and were elected without formal party or organizational affiliations. The largest group with party affiliations, some 15 percent, were with the CPRF, which along with Yabloko was seen as the "best bet" for women, but these parties' electoral fortunes have waned since 2003. A mere 4 percent of women deputies were nominated by women's organizations, attesting to the very limited role of the women's movement in electoral politics. Most women deputies were drawn from professional administration, especially from the ranks of heads of schools and hospitals.[25]

In contrast to regional legislatures, women have played a more prominent role in local councils, constituting more than 40 percent of representatives.[26] The pattern in the region of Volgograd is illustrative: Women hold 13 percent of the regional (oblast) legislative seats, 21 percent of the seats in the large city of Volgograd, and 33 percent of the seats at the district (raion) level.[27] Yet women seem stuck at this first step on the political ladder and are unable to break through the glass ceiling to climb to higher levels. As Galina Karelova—a former first deputy minister of labor and social development and deputy prime minister—explains, "In order to go further, money is necessary, a lot of money. And they [women] don't have it."[28] Or, as Maria Arbatova, a well-known feminist and playwright, puts it: The reason for the low numbers of women deputies in the State Duma "is very simple. Women did not have and do not have money."[29]

Women's prospects appear dim when we turn to the second major route to the State Duma, the world of big business. This area is an increasingly important and distinctly post-Communist pathway to public office, yet only two of our twenty-five women followed this route to the political arena. As one of these women explained, she was well known in her region as a successful entrepreneur and launched her first campaign in 1999 on the basis of her own financial resources. Representatives of the business community were especially prominent among Unity's candidates in 1999; among the Duma candidates as a whole in 2003, the proportion of candidates with a big business background increased sharply. This sphere is one in which women are poorly represented.[30] Fund-raising for a political career is, therefore, difficult for women who have a substantial presence in small businesses that lack the financial capacity for entering the political arena.[31] For the bulk of women candidates emerging from local and regional bureaucracies, the situation was summed up by one woman deputy who remarked that she, as a "*biudzhetnik*"—a person employed on the state budget —faced limited opportunities to finance her campaign compared with some of her opponents.[32]

Aside from these two major streams to public office—the bureaucracy or *nomenklatura* and big business—civil society represents a third route. There were two women deputies who built their political careers through entrepreneurial activity in the third sector, working with new social organizations in fields like ecology and farming. LDP deputies reported extensive experience constructing their party at the local and regional levels and also had served as assistants to State Duma members. But opportunities for women to construct political careers on the basis of third-sector activism appear to be decreasing.[33]

A final avenue to public office involves academic careers. The women deputies interviewed are strikingly well educated; all have higher educations, and eight had defended dissertations at the graduate level. Nine worked at universities or at research institutes at some point in their careers; five moved virtually directly from teaching and/or research into the political realm. Russian researchers contend that university education is a significant prerequisite for women's political careers, of greater importance for women than for men. Indeed, a study of the 2003 parliamentary election showed that the most educated candidates were UR women.[34] For women to carry weight in the political arena, expertise seems a key ingredient.

The Electoral System and Parties as Gatekeepers

Turning to political factors, much scholarly literature argues that a party list or proportional representation (PR) system rather than an SMD electoral system promotes the election of women to legislatures.[35] A PR system, it is argued, provides incentives for parties to balance tickets by gender and for women to form their own parties. In the Russian electoral system until the 2007 election, half the 450 Duma deputies were selected by each method.[36] Evidence from the Russian case, however, does not exhibit a clear pattern: A total of 43 percent of the women deputies were elected through the SMD route in 1993; 67 percent in 1995; 58 percent in 1999; and 48 percent in 2003 (see table 2.1). The formation of WR in 1993 largely accounts for the strong showing of women on the party list ballot for that election. In the next two elections, more women were elected in SMD than in PR races.

Scholars have pointed to a number of factors that may help explain why PR has failed to consistently promote the election of women in Russia. Analysts of Russian politics argue that the presence of many weak, unstable parties, and the absence of any fear of a women's bloc in the electorate after the 1995 defeat of WR, undercut party leaders' incentives to recruit women candidates.[37] In most parties that did gain Duma seats, gatekeepers placed low percentages of women on party lists. The average share of women on party lists increased in 1995 in response to WR, then stabilized at 10 to 12 percent.[38] Moreover, list placement largely determines candidates' success, and most women were placed in slots below the number the party could be expected to win. In the 1993 election, for example, across all party lists (except WR), 62 percent of women were placed below the sixtieth position, and 90 percent below the thirtieth position.[39] Throughout the 1990s, the proportion of women elected in the party list vote remained well below women's proportion on the lists because "when the lists were compiled men's names were placed in the 'zone of passability' of the central list and at the top of regional lists, while women's names were relegated to the 'basement.'"[40] Though women fared better with some parties than others, successful parties constrained female candidates by gatekeeping in the nomination process. Few women were recruited to leadership positions in the major parties; they have been more prominent in minor social democratic, ecological, and other parties that fail to win Duma seats.[41] In sum, except for helping WR in the first Duma, PR did little to promote women's representation in Russia during the 1990s.

In SMD races, women performed somewhat better. In 1995 twice as many women won seats in SMD as in PR races, and in 1999 the SMD numbers remained higher. How might we explain this outcome? Some scholars propose that in the local milieu of SMD races, women's credentials—name recognition, professional accomplishment, public service, and ties to social organizations—prove to be valuable assets and thus make women attractive candidates. Parties have less control over nominations, and local reputation matters more than in PR elections. The proliferation of candidates in SMD races also lowers the threshold for representation, likely encouraging women to enter races.[42] In the end, however, the number of women elected by either method remains comparatively low. The party system is heavily focused on the "top-down" strategies of ambitious politicians rather than the "bottom-up" processes of social mobilization, a condition facilitated by the low levels of women's activism as well as the apathy and disillusionment of the public at large.

When party leaders do seek more women candidates, there is the potential for rapid change in the gender composition of the State Duma. Unlike many political systems, the Russian parliament exhibits high turnover rates. As a result of the December 2003 election, 45 percent of the women deputies were newcomers; for their male counterparts, the comparable figure was 50 percent. Again in the 2007 election, about half the elected deputies were newcomers; only 22 of the 62 women deputies served in the fourth Duma.[43] For women, the challenge of building linkages between the party system and civil society offers considerable but so far largely untapped opportunities. The construction of strong, politicized women's organizations could leverage a larger role for women's voices in the future. Instead, in the increasingly authoritarian Russian context, the growth in women's representation in the last two Duma elections has resulted mainly from administratively controlled candidate recruitment.

Does Gender Matter in Running for the State Duma?

Do the women deputies report that gender affected the recruitment process or their campaign experiences? Most of the parliamentarians denied that gender played a decisive role in the decisionmaking that led to their candidacy.[44] Typical comments include: "I think the people who asked me to run did so for my professional characteristics"; "it was important that the person [candidate] be a fighter"; "the choice had nothing to do with my being a woman but rather that I am a businessperson with strong financial resources"; and "the men of UR had confidence in me." The deputies heavily stressed their personal qualifications rather than gender as the key reason why party officials and/or governors urged them to run for the State Duma.

In a small number of cases, however, the deputies saw gender as a plus. For example, several UR women mentioned that they were selected in part because they were women, apparently by powerful governors engaged in ticket balancing for their region. One woman remarked that she was a "twofer" because she fulfilled two needs, as a female and as a member of the titular nationality of her republic. As one deputy put it, "It was the wisdom of the republic leadership which considered . . . that men and women ought to be represented." There is little evidence, however, that this recruitment was designed to advance a women's agenda; instead, the effort reflects a strategy designed to demonstrate that all groups and significant mass organizations were lined up in support of UR, a kind of symbolic gathering of societal forces.

Despite their high degree of social and political activism, the recruitment of these women deputies may perpetuate the image of the woman politician devoid of independent stature. They are tried-and-true team players, dependent on the goodwill or patronage of powerful male leaders. As Irina Khakamada, one of the most prominent woman political figures in post-Soviet Russia, puts it, "The only type of woman allowed in power is the woman-soldier. They lack personal ambition. They have no doubts. . . . On them falls the most unpleasant work."[45] Khakamada adds that women candidates often are promoted as "image enhancers" for their party and rarely have achieved political recognition on their own merits.[46]

WR sought to break this pattern. The WR leaders Ekaterina Lakhova and Alevtina Fedulova recruited women candidates who were not only familiar with women's issues—women with lengthy experience working with women's councils, trade unions, or social welfare departments—but also could advance the goal of an independent voice for women. The WR leaders felt that "it was absolutely necessary for women to have their say and to be heard," because "women have more common sense and are more sensitive to social problems, to the needs of the vulnerable." WR recognized that there was widespread discrimination against women in Russian society and sought to field a slate of women candidates with the end goal of empowering women politically, a far cry from gender balancing strategies that rested on the "decorative" inclusion of a woman.

A more nuanced perspective on gender discrimination in political recruitment was expressed by a former deputy who is a veteran of the first three Duma sessions. She held that

it's very important that I'm a woman, namely, with respect to discrimination, that is if I were a man, it would be easier. On the other hand, there is greater competition among men, but there is an informal quota . . . not written in any law that we have an advantage, a sad advantage, it has a limit. That is, we don't make decisions; if I were a man, then the issue would be only my intellect and ability to work—I feel this all the time.

On the whole, however, the women deputies reject the view that gender played an influential role in shaping their candidacies.

If the women did not perceive discrimination on the part of party gatekeepers, did they view voters as equally welcoming? The most serious complaints about voter hostility involved cases where gender overlapped with another factor, age. A CPRF woman deputy over the age of sixty met with opposition to her candidacy based on the charge that she was too old; yet, as she stated, "They don't call a sixty-year-old man old." Similar problems occurred at the other end of the spectrum, from an under-age-thirty LDP woman deputy who related that "many men looked at me skeptically. . . . They said to me, you are a girl." These comments are consistent with research findings that there is a stable trend of parties recruiting women among those age forty to fifty.[47] This pattern may stem from the perception of negative attitudes on the part of voters as well as women's life cycle experiences of childbearing and upbringing, which delay entry into the political arena.

Aside from the age issue, a few deputies mentioned minor problems like irritated men who "did not understand that . . . half of my voters are men" or a predominantly male audience at a defense plant that did not wish to listen to a woman. But the bulk of the deputies agreed that "it [being female] doesn't put them [the voters] off, only the political face of the candidate is important." Several deputies felt that though being a woman was not of decisive importance, it might have had some positive impact. A former WR deputy contended that "women voters welcomed the fact that they have a chance to elect a woman," a view echoed by a UR deputy who thought "it was very important that I'm a woman—they [women voters] hoped that I would find opportunities to resolve personal issues."

There were, however, harsh judgments and widespread stereotypes concerning women's lack of solidarity and envy of each other. One UR deputy's account of her campaign experiences especially captured this issue:

[At] headquarters, those who nominated me, . . . some of them were putting together my campaign strategy. They said—well, women will never vote for her. You ask why? Well, you understand that you women cannot create a party, though you are the majority of the population. . . . You all envy one another, one looks at another and says—you . . . always look good, dress stylishly, the appearance of a woman always calls forth jealousy, therefore they will never vote for you. That was the opinion, we argued a lot. . . . They said it was necessary to change my appearance, that I must dress in dark colors, that they would get me a suit, change my hairdo, nearly a second Margaret Thatcher!

This deputy held her ground, telling the men that they did not understand Russian women. Her personal experiences during the campaign reinforced her views on this score as she garnered warm support from women who approached her to relate how they were getting all their neighbors out to vote for her.

Yet many of the deputies did embrace such attitudes. They stressed the idea that among women there is jealousy and a sense of competition; even one of the former WR deputies noted that she preferred to rely on men in building her political career because women are more inclined to envy. One deputy stated that "we declare a women's movement, . . . but there is no solidarity, women do not work together." A CPRF deputy remarked that "women don't always support women and continue to believe men, they deceive them, but they believe. Therefore the question of women's solidarity is a burning issue, but I'm far from the thought that women should support all women." Another deputy felt that her life—having become head of a regional (oblast) department and then a Duma deputy, marrying a second (young) husband, having three children, and giving birth recently—elicited jealousy and lowered women's support for her candidacy.

Tatiana Yarygina, who was elected to the first three sessions of the State Duma and is one of the most experienced women in public service in Russia, suggests that the greatest obstacle to women having an impact on Russian politics involves their inability to join forces. As she notes, "As soon as we women start to rack up any significant successes, a unique kind of female competitiveness comes into play. It's every woman for herself, or at least for her own organization. We need to unite."[48]

The strength of women's organizations and of a women's movement varies across Russia's eighty-nine federal territories, but on the whole, women's groups exert little influence in the political arena. This diversity is reflected in the experiences of our women deputies. Some reported that they had no ties to women's groups, because there is only the Union of Women of Russia, or there are only small or weak women's organizations in their region, or because "women don't support me." One deputy responded that "I don't know how it is in other cities but in [my city], . . . they [women's organizations] always involve three to four people, not more than that. I exaggerate; maybe ten to twelve activists, and that's all." Another described the women's movement in her area as dwarflike, with women scattered and disunited. In other cases, however, deputies mentioned drawing on women's organizations, not for financial assistance but for the people power they needed for their campaigns. As one parliamentarian explained, "The main burden in the course of the campaign fell on women's shoulders." Women are the lickers and stickers—in the Russian case, the agitators, the ones arranging for the printing of leaflets, transportation, and setting up meetings.

Three of the women deputies came from regions with exceptionally strong women's organizations, and they reported quite different experiences from their colleagues. These women spoke of working closely with women's groups, of a dialogue between women's organizations and the governor, and of personal memberships in women's groups.[49] They described these organizations as united and politically active. It is striking that a woman deputy from a region with a strong women's movement could clearly articulate the importance of increasing women's representation to a minimum of 30 percent as well as other gender issues.

Unfortunately, the political parties show little interest in developing women's associations within their ranks. The current crop of leading political parties—UR, the CPRF, the LDP, and Just Russia, all of which have secured representation in the current State Duma—lack any reference on their official Web sites to women's organizations or women's issues. A party that enjoyed inclusion in the first three Duma sessions, Yabloko, does have an active Women's Council and a Gender Commission that advocates for women's equality in the political realm as well as Russian society at large.

Contemporary women deputies owe their positions largely to the goodwill of powerful governors and now increasingly to highly placed Kremlin leaders—men who operate in an environment where they are unconcerned with pressure from women's organizations or from a public eager to see more women in positions of influence. These men do have some motivation for recruiting women, given the electorate's concern with social policy and the traditional view of women as defenders of children and the elderly. Yet these circumstances contrast sharply with the experiences and outlooks of the WR deputies who served in the State Duma from 1993 to 1995. Those women were recruited by WR leaders—most notably, Ekaterina Lakhova and Alevtina Fedulova—not only to advance social welfare policies but also to give women an independent voice in public affairs.

With the change in electoral laws and the drift toward strong, centralized control, the selection of candidates for the fifth State Duma rested largely with the Kremlin leadership. Yet an early analysis of the backgrounds of the sixty-two current women deputies suggests strong continuity with their counterparts in the fourth Duma. The recruitment pathways in particular appear similar: There are only seven business women; three activists from civil society; and twelve government executives from the federal or regional level. The majority emerged from the traditional sphere of women's activism, or, as a Russian journalist put it, the "category of women bosses of the classical type."[50] Yet the new corps of women deputies echoes the Soviet past, with an updated version (no milkmaids or textile workers) of glamorous and/or famous women included among the Duma ranks. Although celebrated actresses or former cosmonauts did appear on party lists in earlier post-Soviet parliamentary elections, the fifth Duma contains a striking number of women who may prove "decorative" elements rather than serious legislators: two former cosmonauts, one Bolshoi ballerina, and five physically attractive sports champions (all UR deputies).

The Representation of Women's Interests

Comparative studies have shown that women in politics may give particular priority to social policy issues, and that they can band together across party lines to promote shared interests and goals. These studies argue that women as a constituency group are more important to women legislators than male constituents, that women deputies sponsor more legislation dealing with women's concerns, and that legislatures with higher percentages of women pass more bills relevant to women's issues.[51] Russian women were in significant respects beneficiaries of the socialist welfare state, particularly of its full employment, maternity, and family policies. Because of Russia's deep transitional recession, the end of full employment, and pressures to reduce welfare provision, in recent years women have faced the feminization of poverty, employment and wage discrimination, and the partial collapse of the welfare system that provided education, health care, pensions, and other social guarantees. Some post-Communist women's groups in Russia have also pressed issues of reproductive rights, gender equality, and gender quotas in governmental and representative institutions.

The following subsections of the chapter look at the representation of women's interests across the first four Russian Dumas. We first briefly discuss the major relevant policy positions of WR, the CPRF, and UR, as well as their ties to societal-level women's organizations. We then draw on the interviews to answer two questions posed at the beginning of this chapter: Did women legislators give priority to the interests of their female constituents, that is, did women deputies understand their roles as representing a distinct set of women's interests? Second, did women deputies band together within their parties and across party lines to defend women's interests?

Party Programs and Societal Ties

WR was formed in 1993 specifically to represent the interests of women. Although it was critical of Communism, the party favored preservation of social guarantees, especially access to the labor market and employment protections for women, profamily policies, and strong state support for the social sector. WR grew out of three women's organizations, the most important of which, the Union of Women of Russia, had its roots in the Soviet period. Its 1993 campaign "relied heavily on grassroots organization and mobilization of women's groups at the local level, which gave the party a solid political base."[52] It added to the traditional emphasis on social guarantees and the protection of motherhood a more contemporary stress on the promotion of equal opportunity for women both legally and substantively.

The CPRF, an unreformed post-Soviet party, has throughout the period focused on social guarantees, preservation of welfare, and state protections for families and motherhood. It combines a politics that is profamily in this traditional sense with a collectivist, statist, and nationalist ideology. The party remains rooted in society, mainly among older groups of activists and pensioners. It neither privileges women's issues nor focuses on gender equality or civic rights.[53]

UR is a nonprogrammatic, propresidential "party of power," formed in 2001, loyal to the president and to the policy agenda he promotes. That agenda, broadly speaking, has included liberal reforms of the welfare state and reductions in state social and labor protections that are on balance unfavorable to women. UR is subordinate to the executive and is weakly rooted in society. In response to Russia's demographic decline, UR has recently promoted pronatalist policies that provide incentives and benefits to women for childbearing. Although rhetorically committed to gender equality, it does not seek to substantively advance women's rights or equal opportunity.

Duma Deputies and Women's Interests

We wanted to know whether women Duma deputies considered women to be an important constituency group and whether these deputies saw themselves as representing specifically women's interests. We asked interviewees whether there was a distinct set of gender issues, "specific women's problems," that demand resolution, or only general socioeconomic problems resulting from the transition.

The answers showed a striking change across the Dumas. Deputies from the first and second Dumas, from WR and the CPRF, shared the view that women did have specific interests, particularly relating to employment discrimination and (though mentioned less frequently), reproductive rights, that needed to be defended. According to one statement of this view from a leader of WR, "Women are concentrated in low-prestige and low-paid jobs, their career opportunities are limited, it is very difficult to overcome prejudices. . . . Renewed economic growth can do little to resolve this problem." Such views might have been expected from WR deputies, but they were also held by women from the CPRF. According to one CPRF deputy, for example, "Yes, definitely there are women's problems. Economic growth has a very important impact, but there are also traditional factors . . . based on the privilege of men."

In contrast, deputies from UR answered with remarkable consensus that there were no specific women's issues, that problems affecting women were part of broader socioeconomic problems and thus need not or should not be addressed separately. Three responded, typically, "There are no problems specific to women; I wouldn't single out women; problems are common to society as a whole; we must cope with material conditions."[54]

Women deputies across the three Dumas identified a set of problems women face, including poverty, child care, health care, and low wages in the state sector (i.e., health, education, and culture), which disproportionately employs women. But deputies from the first two Dumas generally saw these problems in gendered terms and regarded addressing such issues as a major part of their legislative role. By contrast, most UR deputies interviewed did not express a commitment to a prowomen agenda (see table 2.3). Though a number expressed interest in social issues relevant to women, they did not see politics, or their own roles as legislators, in gendered terms.

The interviews also indicated a steadily diminishing level of cooperation among women deputies across party lines, and of collective efforts to advance policy goals related to women's interests. Leaders of the WR faction in the 1993 Duma reported a high degree of informal cooperation and support for their initiatives by women deputies (though they did not attempt to coordinate their actions formally with women in other parties). According to one respondent, there was "a sort of informal club headed by [the WR leader] Fedulova where the majority of women met once in a while. . . . Laws concerning women were supported by practically all women in the Duma irrespective of their party affiliation." WR successfully promoted legislation on child benefits and defense of women's employment rights, as well as measures to protect threatened federal guarantees to public education, gaining support from most legislative parties.[55] In sum, despite its small numbers, WR succeeded in rallying women and a critical mass of other deputies around a prowomen legislative agenda, though (as some of the deputies interviewed note) many of these measures were very inadequately financed by the government.

Table 2.3. Women deputies and representation of women's interests in the Russian State Dumas (number of women members)

Question	Women of Russia, 6	CPRF, 2; LDP, 2; Independent, 2	UR, 12; Rodina, 1
Specific women's problems that demand resolution?			
Yes	WR, 6	CPRF, 2; LDP, 1	UR, 1
No	0	LDP, 1; Independent, 1	UR, 11; Rodina, 1
Formal coordination or informal cooperation by women across party lines to promote women's interests?[a]			
Formal coordination	0	0	0
Informal cooperation			
Yes	WR, 6	CPRF, 2; Independent, 1	
None or very little		Independent, 1	UR, 5 (reelected)
If disagree with the party on issues concerning women:			
Vote for women, take own position		LDP, 1; Independent, 1	UR,[b] 4
Follow party discipline or agree with party positions	WR, 6	CPRF, 2	UR, 5; Rodina, 1

Note: CPRF = Communist Party of the Russian Federation; LDP = Liberal-Democratic Party; UR = United Russia; WR = Women of Russia.

[a] Answers from the 10 deputies who were elected to their first terms in 2003 were not included here; they are summarized in the text.

[b] Three of these 4 deputies were newly elected in 2003.

Sources: All interviews were conducted in Moscow. Interview numbers 1–8 were in February 2004; and 9–26 were in March 2004. Not every interviewee answered every question.

In the 1995 Duma, cooperation among women deputies became more limited and party discipline became more important in determining the legislative votes of women deputies. According to a deputy from WR, "In the next [post-1993] Dumas, attempts were made to form an interfactional women's group, but they failed. There were informal contacts to support particular decisions which are of concern to women." This view is buttressed by an analysis of role call voting that confirms that in the 1995 Duma women banded together to vote on a limited set of "domestic women's issues" dealing with children and family matters but divided by party on a broader set of welfare-related and other bills. The CPRF-dominated left took over defense of women's issues, promoting a traditional conception of the welfare state and women's roles that clashed with more moderate and liberal parties.[56] As a former deputy from WR stated, "In all Dumas except the first one, women were separated and could not be characterized as a united force."

Both survey and voting evidence show a further marked decline of co-operation among women deputies in the UR-dominated 1999 Duma. A majority of interviewees reported no coordination, or sporadic and generally unsuccessful attempts by groups of women to influence such major issues as the budget. Women deputies from the dominant, progovernment UR reported strong pressures to support their party's programs. One deputy, asked what she would do if faced with a conflict between a prowomen position and her party, replied that she could defend the prowomen position in the party fraction and "declare that I will vote differently, but the fraction must allow it. There is party discipline. I joined a party." Though several women from UR reported that they would vote for women or take their own positions on women's issues, it is worth noting that all but one of these were newly elected to the 2003 Duma and may have had little experience with party discipline.

Iulia Shevchenko's analysis of voting in the 1999 Duma also confirms the near absence of coordination among women deputies, demonstrating that they did not vote together on issues affecting women. She concludes,

> Women did not make a difference in the 1999 Duma. Strong party discipline minimizes the level of female deputies' commitment to the representation of women's interests. . . . The crucial role in determining legislators' position . . . is played by the government linkage. Since 1999 the right-wing electoral niche has been occupied by an electorally strong party. . . . Therefore the concerns of female constituents cease to affect roll call voting.[57]

Remarks from two CPRF women, reflecting their experience over three Dumas, vividly express these changes. A CPRF deputy noted that "in the second [1995] Duma, we joined and had very interesting relations with women of other factions. . . . Now the Duma is full of Bears [a nickname for Unity, the dominant party that formed UR]." Another deputy from the same party confirmed this view, stating that "it may be useful to cooperate in the 2003

Duma but will be just formal, because every women will vote for the policies of her faction. Unity among women is absolutely not possible."

Women's interests were weakly articulated and defended in the legislative process during the 1999 Duma, which coincided with a period of rapid economic recovery that provided a greater potential to address social and other issues. The Duma passed a broad reform program that reduced the government's obligations for social welfare. The reforms included two important changes that have been detrimental to the interests of women. The first was a revision of the labor code that reduced maternity and other protections for employed women, though some of these benefits have recently been reinstated (see below). The second was a revision of the pension system that reduces its redistributive features and is likely to seriously disadvantage women in the longer term. Welfare spending increased modestly, but programs of particular significance to women, such as child benefits and public-sector salaries, remained seriously underfunded. The United Nations Development Program, which categorizes the Putin government broadly as gender insensitive, notes that "gender issues are ignored in the Medium-Term Program of Socio-Economic Development of the Russian Federation (2005–2008)," a major planning document, and points out that the government has paid no attention to the likely gender consequences of pension reform or of planned accession to the World Trade Organization, in particular the gender-asymmetric unemployment that is likely to result from the latter.[58]

Among those interviewed, women deputies' assessments of their past influence and future prospects were quite divergent. Those who had served in the early Dumas generally saw the steady decline in women's influence that is reflected in our analysis. Women in UR, especially those who were newly elected, saw their potential for influence in more positive terms. Several spoke of a new legislative initiative (since defeated) that would prohibit gender discrimination and establish gender quotas in political and administrative organizations. Although quotas are often viewed as discredited because of their use in the Communist period, several interviewees argued that they could be useful "at least for a while" in increasing women's representation. An impressive number of deputies, including some who explicitly rejected gender politics, mentioned the leadership role of Ekaterina Lakhova and her efforts to articulate a women's platform within UR. As a WR leader who has established her authority on women's issues while party jumping, Lakhova was seen as a potential "uniting force" for women.

Women deputies have played a leadership role in some social policy issues that are of particular concern to women. In the 2003 Duma, Tatyana

Yakovleva, chair of the Duma's Health Committee, led the committee to an important advocacy role on health issues. The committee initiated legislative discussions of Russia's demographic crisis, pressing for measures to address major sources of premature mortality. It advocated state control of the alcohol market to stem the tide of accidental poisonings, and ratification of the World Health Organization's Convention on Tobacco Control. Yakovleva pressed for increased funding of medical, surgical, and obstetrical care, as well as social support for families. Lakhova, chair of the Duma Committee on Women, Families, and Children, was a vocal advocate on family issues, proposing minimal social standards for support of families and tax benefits and subsidies for child care, the cost of which has increased dramatically over the past decade.[59]

It is significant, however, that major initiatives in family policy have come not from the legislature but from the executive. Responding to Russia's declining population and low birthrate, President Putin initiated a high-profile series of measures to raise the birthrate. Some of these measures reinstated preexisting benefits, including extended maternity leaves, and pregnancy and maternity allowances. A key new initiative in early 2006 involved the introduction of "maternity capital" for women who give birth to a second child, in the form of a payment of 250,000 rubles (€7,200) to be used for housing and education or contributed to the mother's pension. This is a very large sum by the standards of most Russian citizens' incomes.

The maternity capital approach was introduced by the president with the explicit intention of increasing Russia's birthrate. Many experts on demography and childbearing trends think that it is an ill-advised incentive that fails to address either broader demographic issues or the needs of contemporary women and families.[60] Though women may welcome the increased support for childbirth, the legislation was clearly dictated and shaped by the needs and priorities of the state. It provides narrow incentives to individual women and families, rather then the broader supports for families and children that feature in the advocacy of the few leading women Duma deputies.

The Question of Quotas

Pressures for greater women's political representation in Russia have emerged from both international and domestic sources. In recent years, the Russian government has signed a number of agreements with international organizations, most prominently the Convention on Elimination of All Forms of Discrimination against Women and the European Social Charter, which commit it to gender equality. A 2001 Law on Political Parties obligates parties to "provide for men and women, who are members of a political party, equal opportunities of being represented in working bodies of the party, on lists of candidates for deputies and other elective offices."[61]

Thus far, however, efforts to legislate concrete mechanisms or quotas for gender representation have failed. A draft law proposed by the Duma's Women's Committee under Lakhova in 2001, and supported by domestic women's organizations, called for parties to limit the number of PR candidates of either gender to 70 percent of the total. The measure gained the support of only one-third of deputies, leaving the political party law without teeth.[62] A draft law on gender quotas was again discussed but failed in the Duma in 2005.[63]

Efforts to use the legal system in support of women's rights have also netted little. Women's organizations charge that the Ministry of Justice continues to register parties without regard to the Law on Political Parties. According to the Consortium of Women's NGOs, "During the parliamentary election of 2003 parties nominated only 10 to 12 percent of women in their federal lists and supported a similar amount of women in single-seat electoral districts. The Central Election Commission disregards blatant violations of the norms of Russian legislation and international agreements [on gender representation]."[64]

Conclusions and Future Prospects

The Russian case shows an overall deterioration in the representation of women's interests in the post-Communist period. Despite women's impressive educational and career credentials, during the 1990s there were significant barriers to women running for public office in terms of widespread attitudes toward women in politics and the absence of strong women's organizations and a women's movement. After the demise of WR, women's pathways to the State Duma frequently involve recruitment by regional political machines—being part of a governor's team—or recruitment by party leaders. The safe and reliable women recruited through these channels generally downplay the significance of gender differences and gender issues in society.[65] There has been a serious decline in the numbers of women deputies who are committed to the defense of interests particular to women. Indeed, our interviews indicate that few women in the predominant party, UR, even recognize such interests.

Despite the increasing numeric or descriptive representation of women in the 2003 and 2007 Dumas, the prospects for real or substantive representation of women's interests seem likely to deteriorate. This judgment is based on three factors. First, the core source of policy initiatives in Russia is now in the executive, and executive monitoring agencies on women's rights have been weakened or disbanded. The President's Commission on Women, Children, and Demography, an "institutionalized point of access within the executive branch for the women's movement," established in 1993 and chaired by Lakhova, was disbanded in 2000. The governmental Commission on Improvement of the Status of Women, founded in 1997, was dissolved, and the Round Table of Women's NGO's in the Ministry of Labor and Social Development, a channel for cooperation between women's organizations and the state, disappeared in a governmental reorganization.[66]

Second, analysts agree that the growth and empowerment of a women's movement is a critical factor in making the government more responsive on gender issues, but recent legislation that restricts the rights of NGOs in Russia seems likely to hinder even the weak existing women's movement. Policies that are beneficial to women, such as the pronatalist increases in pregnancy and child-related benefits recently announced by the president, may well emerge.[67] But they will be dictated by and designed according to the priorities of the state, not the felt needs and expressed preferences of women in Russian society.

Third and most important, the Russian political system has largely reverted to authoritarianism. The 2007 Duma election, in which the numerical representation of women increased to 14 percent of the seats, was also the first post-Communist Russian election to be judged in clear violation of democratic standards by the Organization for Security and Cooperation in Europe and the Council of Europe.[68] The election was characterized by state control of the media, newly restrictive electoral laws, heavy reliance on administrative resources to promote UR and allied candidates, harassment of opposition candidates, and allegations of voter intimidation and fraud. Of the three smaller parties that won seats, the CPRF alone stands in opposition to UR, and its support is fading.

In sum, the decline in representation of women's interests is part of the broader decline in representation of societal interests within the Russian legislature and the political system. The earlier stages of the Russian transition produced political parties—WR, the CPRF, Yabloko, and others—that, though weak, had programmatic commitments, some connections with groups in Russian society, and saw themselves as at least somewhat accountable to electoral constituencies. Those parties have been replaced, or their influence effaced, by UR, a nonprogrammatic party of power that is weakly rooted in society and accountable mainly to the executive, and by authoritarian-executive domination of the system. A second set of institutions providing societal voice, the NGOs, have developed gradually in Russia over the past decade but now seem likely to decline under governmental pressure. This movement of the political system away from democracy is mirrored in our interview and voting results, which show the detachment of UR women deputies from the role of representing women's interests, the decline in women's cooperation across party lines, and the growing loyalty of women deputies to an executive-dominated party.

Notes

1. Even among the fifteen countries that formerly made up the USSR, rather than Eastern and Central European countries, Russia stood in twelfth place in 2003 with respect to the proportion of women in its parliament, trailing countries like Turkmenistan and Belarus. See Mikhail Gorshkov, "Liudi dela: Bol'shinstvo Rossiian-Zhenshchiny, no komanduiut imi myzhchiny," *Komsomol'skaia Pravda*, November 24, 2003.

2. Inter-Parliamentary Union, "Women in Parliament in 2005: The Year in Perspective," http://www.ipu.org/PDF/publications/women06_en.pdf.

3. Two other studies of women politicians in Russia that rely on interviews as the key source of information do not focus on the State Duma. These are A. A. Temkina's study of women running for the Saint Petersburg City Council in 1994 and Ludmila Popkova's research on women politicians and activists from nongovernmental organization in the city of Samara and the Samara region in 1999. See A. A. Temkina, "Zhenskii put' v politiku: Gendernaia perspektiva," in *Gendernoe izmerenie sotsial'noi i politicheskoi aktivnosti v perekhodnyi period: Sbornik Statei nauchnykh* (Saint Petersburg: Tsentr Nezavisimykh sotsial'nykh Issledovanii, 1996), 19–32, available at http://www.a-z.ru/women; and Ludmila Popkova, "Women's Political Activism in Russia: The Case of Samara," in *Post-Soviet Women Encountering Transition: Nation Building, Economic Survival, and Civic Activism,* ed. Kathleen Kuehnast and Carol Nechemias (Washington, D.C., and Baltimore: Woodrow Wilson Center Press and Johns Hopkins University Press, 2004), 172–94. A study that does focus on the State Duma and involves interviews with many of the women who served as deputies with Women of Russia is Mary Buckley, "Adaptation of the Soviet Women's Committee: Deputies' Voices from 'Women of Russia,'" in *Post-Soviet Women: From the Baltic to Central Asia,* ed. Mary Buckley (Cambridge: Cambridge University Press, 1997), 157–95.

4. Interviews with Duma deputies were conducted by the Levada Center; interviews with former deputies from Women of Russia were conducted by an independent Russian consultant. All interviews were conducted in Moscow during February and March 2004.

5. See Jeffrey Mankoff, "Russia's Weak Society and Weak State: The Role of Political Parties," *Problems of Communism,* March–April 2003, 29–43; and Henry Hale, *Why*

Not Parties in Russia?: Democracy, Federalism and the State (New York: Cambridge University Press, 2006).

6. See Sarah Oates, "The 1999 Russian Duma Elections," *Problems of Post-Communism,* May–June 2000, 3–14; Andrew Wilson, *Virtual Politics: Faking Democracy in the Post-Soviet World* (New Haven, Conn.: Yale University Press, 2005); Masha Lipman, "In Moscow: A Facade of Democracy," *Washington Post,* December 6, 2005; and Brian Whitmore, "Russia: The New and Improved Single-Party State," *Russia's Johnson List,* April 15, 2008, http://www.cdi.org/russia/johnson/2008-78-6.cfm.

7. See Zoe Knox et al., "Parties of Power and Russian Politics: A Victory of the State over Civil Society?" *Problems of Post-Communism,* January–February 2006, 3–14.

8. For longitudinal information on public attitudes toward democracy, see Pew Global Attitudes Project, "Russia's Weakened Democratic Embrace: Prosperity Tops Political Reform," http://pewglobal.org/reports/display.php?ReportID=250.

9. See Knox et al., "Parties of Power," 11; and Vladimir Shlapentokh, "Trust in Public Institutions in Russia: The Lowest in the World," *Johnson's Russia List,* June 27, 2005.

10. On the structure and development of the Duma, see Thomas F. Remington and Steven S. Smith, *The Politics of Institutional Choice: The Formation of the Russian State Duma* (Princeton, N.J.: Princeton University Press, 2001).

11. Carol Nechemias, "Politics in Post-Soviet Russia: Where Are the Women?" *Demokratizatsiya* 8, no. 2 (Spring 2000): 199–218.

12. Anna V. Andreenovka, "Women's Representation in the Parliaments of Russia and Ukraine," *Sociological Research* 41, no. 2 (March–April 2002): 5–25. The seventeen Communist women, combined with three from the Agrarian Deputy Group and six from Popular Power, both allied with the Communists, constituted a majority.

13. The figure for the proportion of women managers comes from Zoya Khotkina, "Women in the Labour Market: Yesterday, Today and Tomorrow," in *Women in Russia: A New Era in Russian Feminism,* ed. Anastasia Poasadskaya (London: Verso, 1994), 96.

14. Temkina, "Zhenskii put v politiku," n.p.

15. For a thorough review of women's political participation during the Communist era, see Gail Warshofsky Lapidus, *Women in Soviet Society: Equality, Development, and Social Change* (Berkeley: University of California Press, 1978); Barbara Wolfe Jancar, *Women under Communism* (Baltimore: Johns Hopkins University Press, 1978); Sharon L. Wolchik, "Ideology and Equality: The Status of Women in Eastern and Western Europe," *Comparative Political Studies* 13, no. 4 (January 1981): 445–76; and Mary Buckley, *Women and Ideology in the Soviet Union* (Ann Arbor: University of Michigan Press, 1989).

16. See N. A. Shvedova, *Prosto o slozhnom: Gendernoe prosveshchenie* (Moscow: Antikva, 2002), 26–35.

17. See Lynne Attwood, *The New Soviet Man and Woman: Sex-Role Socialization in the USSR* (Bloomington: Indiana University Press, 1990), chaps. 9 and 10.

18. Buckley, *Women and Ideology,* 175.

19. See S. V. Polenina, "Zhenskii vopros i stroitel'stvo sotsialistichego pravovogo gosudarstva," in *Trud, sem'ia, byt Sovetskoi zhenshchiny* (Moscow: Iuridicheskaia Literatura, 1990), available at http://www.a-z.ru.

20. Sergei Avdeev et al., "Duma zhenskogo roda," *Izvestiia,* November 29, 2003.

21. "Survey Shows Russia Not Yet Ready for Woman President," *Johnson's Russia List,* http://www.cdi.org/russia/johnson/9085-5.cfm.

22. This question was asked as part of the survey "Woman of New Russia," conducted from December 2001 to January 2002 among 1,406 respondents, all women age seventeen to fifty years. The principal researchers were M. K. Gorshkov, N. E. Tikhonova, and F. E. Sheregi. Data were gathered from the Russian Sociological Data Archive, at the Independent Institute of Social Policy, Moscow. The data set was made available to Carol Nechemias.

23. Attwood, *New Soviet Man and Woman,* chaps. 9 and 10.

24. Elena V. Kochkina, "Women in Russian Government Bodies," *Russian Politics and Law* 38, no 3 (2000): 74.

25. S. G. Aivazova, *Gendernoe ravenstvo kak problema rossiiskikh reform: Politicheskii aspect,* excerpted in *Johnson's Russia List,* May 9, 2003. The data for the proportion of regional legislative seats held by women for 2004 were calculated from *Zhenshchiny i Muzhiny Rossii 2004: Statisticheskii Sbornik* (Moscow: Federal'naia Sluzhba Gosudarstvennoi Statistkii, 2004), 180–83.

26. Aivazova, *Gendernoe ravenstvo.*

27. Tat'iana Tarakanova, "Zhenshchiny v politike i biznese: pokolenie next," *Delovoe Povolzh'e,* July 21, 2004, http://dlib.eastview.com/searchresults/articles.jsp?art=12&id=6507493.

28. This is as quoted by Ol'ga Ivashinnikova, "Mama myla ramy, a papa chital gazety," *Moskvichka,* June 2000, 6.

29. This is as quoted by Francesca Mereu, "What Women Want: A Seat in the Duma," *Moscow Times,* September 17, 2003, http://www.eng.yabloko.ru/Publ/2003/PAPERS/9/030917_mt.html.

30. Svetlana Aivazova and Grigory Kertman, *We Elect and Are Elected* (Moscow: Consortium of Women's Nongovernmental Associations, Institute of Comparative Political Studies, Russian Academy of Sciences, 2004), 18.

31. World Economic Forum, "Meet Some Russian Women Leaders," October 2, 2003, http://annualmeeting.weforum.org/site/knowledgenaviagotor.nsf.Content/Meet percent20 Some percent20Russian percent20Women percent20Leaders_20037cef.html?open.

32. For the 1999 parliamentary election, the estimated minimal cost to run in a single-mandate district ranged from $30,000 for a Communist running in the "red belt" to $1 million in Moscow. See Aleksandr Sadchikov, "Neizvestnaiia sila," *Izvestiia,* December 16, 1999.

33. Aivazova and Kertman, *We Elect and Are Elected,* 31.

34. Ibid., 17.

35. See, e.g., Wilma Rule, "Electoral Systems, Contextual Factors and Women's Opportunity for Election to Parliament in Twenty-Three Democracies," *Western Political Quarterly* 40, no. 3 (September 1987): 477–98; V. Bogdanor, *What Is Proportional Representation?* (Oxford: Blackwell, 1982); and P. Norris, "Women's Legislative Participation in Western Europe," *West European Politics* 8 (1985): 90–101.

36. In the wake of the Beslan massacre in September 2004, President Putin pushed through changes in the political system that included the elimination of all single-mandate districts for the State Duma. In future parliamentary elections, all deputies will be elected through the party list.

37. See, e.g., Robert G. Moser, "Electoral Systems and Women's Representation: The Strange Case of Russia," in *Women's Access to Political Power in Post-Communist Europe,* ed. Richard E. Matland and Kathleen A. Montgomery (Oxford: Oxford University Press, 2003).

38. Svetkana Aivazova and Grigory Kertman, *We Elect Them—They Select Us: Gender Analysis of Parliamentary and Presidential Elections in Russia: 2003–2004* (Moscow: Consortium of Women's Nongovernmental Associations, Institute of Comparative Political Studies, Russian Academy of Sciences, 2004); http://www.wcons.org.ru/eng/ publication; Moser, "Electoral Systems and Women's Representation," 159.

39. Moser, "Electoral Systems and Women's Representation," 163.

40. R. A. Vardanian and E. V. Kochkina, "Elections: The Gender Gap," *Russian Social Science Review* 49, no. 3 (May–June 2008): 64–65.

41. Aivazova and Kertman, *We Elect and Are Elected.*

42. See Moser, "Electoral Systems and Women's Representation"; Moser and others argue that women are advantaged by the possibility to run as independents in SMD races. By contrast, Andreenkova found that women who ran independently were less likely to be elected than those nominated by a party. See Andreenovka, "Women's Representation."

43. ITAR-TASS, December 24, 2007; Marina Ozerova, "Glamur na Okhotnom Riadu," *Moskovskii Komsomolets,* December 24, 2007.

44. One LDP candidate reported earlier problems becoming head of her regional party organization, given objections to both her sex and to her young age. Once she overcame that obstacle, the road to running for the State Duma was apparently cleared of internal party barriers.

45. Larisa Kaftan, "Irina Khakamada: kak otmazat'sia ot intima s 'nachal'nikom,'" *Komsolmol'skaia Pravda,* March 9, 2006.

46. World Economic Forum, "Meet Some Russian Women Leaders."

47. Aivazova and Kertman, *We Elect and Are Elected,* 14–15. The authors note, however, that the LDP is an exception, focusing more on youth, whereas CPRF candidates, both male and female, are the most likely to be drawn from over the age of sixty.

48. Irina Rylnikova, "There Will Be No Harmony in This World until Balance Is Achieved between the Differing Worldviews of Men and Women: Interview with Tatyana Yarygina," *We/Myi,* issue 32, 2001, http://www.we-myi.org/issues/32/position .html.

49. Deputies who joined or were active in independent women's organizations should be distinguished from the handful of deputies who headed women's auxiliary groups within their political party. The UR, LDP, and CPRF have sought to increase women's involvement by creating special organizations within their party.

50. Ozerova, "Glamur na Okhotnom Riadu."

51. For a review of some of these sources, see Iulia Shevchenko, "Who Cares About Women's Problems? Female Legislators in the 1995 and 1999 Russian State Dumas?" *Europe-Asia Studies* 54, no. 8 (2002): 1201–22.

52. John Ishiyama, "Women's Parties in Post-Communist Politics," *East European Politics and Societies* 17, no. 2 (2002): 266–304; the quotation is on 287.

53. Aivazova and Kertman, *We Elect and Are Elected,* 2004.

54. One UR deputy articulated the view, also present within the broader women's movement, that state-mandated employment protections actually contributed to discrimination and hurt women in the labor market. See Suzanne LaFont, "One Step Forward, Two Steps Back: Women in Post-Communist States," *Communist and Post-Communist Studies* 34 (2001): 203–20.

55. Deputaty fraktsii "Zhenshchiny Rossii v Gos. Dumy pervovo sozyva," http:// women.centro.ru./ustav.htm; Beth Richardson, "Gender-Based Behavior among Women in the Russian Duma, 1994–1995," MA thesis, Carleton University, 1997.

56. Linda J. Cook, "Globalization and the Politics of Welfare State Reform in Russia," in *Politics Matters: Globalization and the Future of the Welfare State,* ed. Miguel Glatzer and Dietrich Rueschemeyer (Pittsburgh: University of Pittsburgh Press, 2005).

57. Shevchenko, "Who Cares About Women's Problems?" 1216. Shevchenko does find that gender plays a role in voting on issues, such as the environment, that do not tap into the left-right partisan dimension.

58. United Nations Development Program, *Russia in 2015: Development Goals and Policy Priorities—Human Development Report 2005: Russian Federation* (New York: United Nations Development Program, 2005), 60. The World Trade Organization calculates that pension reform in its current version will shift the female-to-male pension ratio from 87 percent in 2015 to 50 percent by 2050.

59. See ITAR-TASS, February 9, 2006; March 14, 2006; April 20, 2006; November 8, 2006 (from Dialog database).

60. See ITAR-TASS, April 5, 2006 (from Dialog database); October 31, 2006 (from Lexis-Nexis); *Nezavisimaya Gazeta,* August 22, 2006; *Rossiskaya Gazeta,* September 21, 2006, cited in *Current Digest of the Post-Soviet Press,* October 18, 2006; *Kommersant,* October 6, 2002; *Financial Times,* May 22, 2006.

61. Aivazova and Kertman, *We Elect Them—They Select Us,* 8.

62. Ibid.

63. Vardanian and Kochkina, "Elections," 61.

64. Consortium of Women's Nongovernmental Associations, "The Consortium News," July 1, 2004, available at www.wcons.org.ru.

65. It should be noted that President Putin introduced changes in electoral practices that took effect in 2005 that included ending the direct election of regional governors. These officials are now appointed by the president of the Russian Federation and confirmed by a vote of the regional legislature. This is part of the building of vertical power in Russia. This should have a negative impact on the emergence of strong, independent regional political machines, but there is no reason to expect changes in the recruitment of reliable women.

66. Consortium of Women's Nongovernmental Organizations, "The Consortium News"; on these executive branch commissions, see Nechemias, "Politics in Post-Soviet Russia."

67. Vladimir Putin, "Poslanie Federal'nomu Sobraniiu Rossiiskoi Federatsii," http://www.kremlin.ru/appears/2006/05/10-1357_type63372.type63374type82634.105546.shtml. Putin's speech to the Federal Assembly was delivered on May 10, 2006.

68. "International Observers Deliver Harsh Assessment of Duma Vote," *RFE/RL* 11, no. 223, part 1, December 4, 2007.

Chapter 3

Women's Representation in the Polish Parliament and the Determinants of Their Effectiveness

Renata Siemieńska

This chapter focuses on the role of women in the Polish Parliament and the ways in which women's issues have been discussed since 1989. It is based on postelection studies, analyses of documents, and qualitative and quantitative studies on the functioning of Parliament, with a special focus on the assembly elected in 2001.[1] Research conducted between January and March 2004 incorporated the opinions of fourteen female parliamentarians—members of the Sejm (the lower chamber of Parliament)—and four male parliamentarians from various political parties represented in the Sejm elected in 2001. The majority of the women interviewed were active parliamentarians who held seats on parliamentary committees. The men interviewed were heads or outspoken members of their parliamentary clubs. Many of the questions asked during these interviews were the same as those used in earlier studies. However, a direct comparison of results of the studies was impossible because the study conducted in 2004 was a qualitative one and the earlier studies were quantitative.

This chapter also includes data for subsequent parliamentary elections in

2005 and 2007. Many of the members of Parliament (MPs) interviewed in 2004 were reelected in subsequent elections, so their views are still represented in the legislature.

The "Critical Mass" Concept and the Effectiveness
of Women's Representation

The notion of "critical mass" applied by feminists was first used to express the belief that an increase in the number of women in a legistature to a certain level would bring a new quality to the formulation of women's policy. This postulate has been justified many times by the need to implement the principle of social justice, to make sure that women become MPs and influence the shape of new legislation, and the need to enrich the diversity of perspectives by articulating and examining the experiences of women that result from their social roles, which are partially different from those of men. As the discussion of this concept in chapter 1 of this volume makes clear, scholars have recently expressed doubt about the utility of such a concept. In fact, it is not really clear what number should be considered the critical mass.[2] It is also necessary to take into account the specific situation in a given country. In some countries, improvement means a higher percentage of women entering parliament; in others, it means the opposite. Theories of critical mass and its effectiveness also frequently do not take into account the wider context of the representation of women in different parties in parliament, or the changing lineup and advantage of leftist or rightist parties.

Moreover, the party type and its discipline, and the relations between the parties, which are based on rivalry but can be cooperative or hostile, are also important factors that influence the shaping of a women's lobby in parliament. The attitudes of men and women also change over time, and men and women within a single party often have very similar attitudes toward various issues. In many cases, their views do not reflect changes in male and female perceptions of the place of representatives of both genders in society but are much more conservative, especially among male parliamentarians.

Women in the Polish Parliament

Nearly two decades have now passed since the end of Communism in Poland. Several elections and successive post-Communist Parliaments allow us to analyze patterns in the ways women enter and operate within the political sphere, and the outcomes of their efforts. As table 3.1 illustrates, women's representation in Parliament in Poland has steadily increased since 1989, although it is still far from equaling the high levels that were evident under the authoritarian system. The underrepresentation of women in the 1990s and the pattern of their selection were very similar to those in other countries of the region.[3] The 2001 election brought a significant increase in the number of women in Parliament, which decreased again after the 2005 election. Nevertheless, it did not bring much change in how women's issues were discussed in Parliament. The atmosphere surrounding these issues became more traditional.

As table 3.1 and table 3.2 illustrate, the number of women elected to the Sejm has varied from of low of 9 percent in 1991 to a high of 20 percent in 2001. Ninety-three women (20 percent of the Sejm) were elected in 2005 and in 2007. Women made up from 8 to 13 percent of members of the Senat (the higher chamber of Parliament) during the period from 1989 to 1997. In 2001, women's representation in the Senat peaked at 23 percent, only to drop again to 13 percent after the 2005 elections. These figures are dramatically lower than they were during the Communist period, when 23 percent of the 1980–85 National Assembly members were women. However, during that period, women were "tokens" and had much less influence than their numbers might suggest. Moreover, women in the assembly did not represent the overall interests of women because, under the Communist system, Parliament performed a decorative function and was a rubber stamp for the decisions made by the bodies of the Communist Party (i.e., the Polish United Workers' Party).

Conditions and Mechanisms of Increasing Women's Presence in the 2001 Parliament

The increase in the proportion of women in the legislature in 2001 was due to a combination of factors that materialized between the parliamentary elections of 1997 and 2001. One of the most important of these was a change in the electoral law. During the 1997 election, left-wing parties were more likely than others to include women on their candidate lists. These patterns were consistent with election results observed in other post-Communist countries and in most Western European democratic countries, with the exception of the Scandinavian countries.[4]

The 2001 parliamentary election was a turning point for women in Parliament due to the implementation of new electoral rules. This time, con-

Table 3.1. Women deputies in the Polish Sejm during the first, second, and third terms

Name of Party or Electoral Coalition	1991				1993				1997			
	Total[a]	Percentage of Total	Women	Percentage in Party	Total[b]	Percentage of Total	Women	Percentage in Party	Total[b]	Percentage of Total	Women	Percentage in Party
Total	460		42	9.13	460		60	13.0	460		60	13.0
Democratic Left Alliance (SLD)	60	13.0	9	15.0	171	37.2	28	16.4	164	35.6	31	18.9
Polish Peasant Party (PSL)	50	11.0	1		132	28.7	8	6.1	27	5.9	—	
Freedom Union (FU)									60	13.0	9	15.0
Democratic Union (UD)*	62	13.8	12	28.5	74	16.1	16	21.6				
Confederation of Independent Poland (KPN)**	51	11.1	5	10.8	22	4.8	1	4.6				
Labor Union (UP)	4	0.9	—		41	8.9	7	17.1				
Nonparty Bloc in Support of Reforms (BBWR)**					16	3.5	—	—				
Social and Cultural Society of the German Minority in Silesia	7	1.5			4	0.9	—	—	2	0.4	—	
Social and Cultural Society of Germans in the Katowice Region					1	0.2	—	—	2	0.4	—	—
Electoral Catholic Action (WAK)**	50	10.9	6									
Civic Center Alliance (PC)**	44	9.6	1									
Liberal-Democratic Congress (KLD)1	37	8.0	—									

Polish Peasant Party–Popular Agreement (PSL-PL)**	28	6.1	1	
Movement for the Reconstruction of Poland (ROP)	6			
Electoral Action "Solidarity" (AWS)	201	43.7	20	10.0
Solidarity**	27	5.9	3	11.1
Polish Party of Beer Lovers**	16	3.4	—	
Party of Christian Democrats (PChD)**	4	0.9	1	
Polish Western Union	4	0.9	2	
For Wielkopolska Region and Poland	1		1	
Women's Alliance against Life's Difficulties	1		1	

Note: In the Sejm elected in 1997: *the parties that later became parts of the new party, the Freedom Union; **the parties, trade union, etc., that constituted Electoral Action "Solidarity."

[a] Only parties that received the highest number of seats and/or those that have women among their deputies. Twenty-nine parties or groups of various types had representatives in the Sejm. These data are from the Announcement of the State Election Commission, October 31, 1991, published in *Rzeczpospolita*, November 4, 1991.

[b] Data from the State Election Commission.

Source: Renata Siemieńska, *Nie mogą, nie chcą czy nie potrafią? O postawach i uczestnictwie politycznym kobiet w Polsce* (They have no opportunities, they do not want, they are unable, do they? About attitudes and women's political participation in Poland) (Warsaw: Scholar, 2000).

Table 3.2. Women among candidates for and deputies elected to the Polish Sejm in 2001

Name of Party or Electoral Coalition	Candidates					Elected	
	Number of Districts in Which Women Were on Lists of Candidates	Percentage of Women in Total Number of Candidates	Percentage of Women in 1st–3rd Positions on Lists of Candidates	Total	Percentage of Total	Women	Percent Women
Total		23.2		460		93	20.2
Democratic Left Alliance (DLA)[a]	41	36.3	18.7	200	43.6	50	25.0
Polish Peasant Party (PPP)	41	14.6	6.5	42	9.1	0	0.0
Labor Union (LU)*	41	36.3	18.7	16	3.4	5	31.3
Civic Platform (CP)	41	16.8	15.4	65	14.1	13	20.0
Self-Defense of the Polish Republic (SD)	39	20.3	13.0	53	11.5	9	17.0
Law and Justice (L&J)	40	17.9	12.2	44	9.6	6	13.6
League of Polish Families (LPF)	41	24.7	25.0	38	8.3	10	26.3
Social and Cultural Society of the German Minority in Silesia (GM)			16.7	2	0.4	—	—

Note: Orientation of the political parties: DLA and LU, left; CP, center-right, SD, populist; L&J and LPF, right; PPP, peasant party.
[a]The DLA and LU ran in an electoral coalition.
Source: Inter-Parliamentary Union (www.ipu.org).

stituencies were larger and had a greater number of seats, which facilitated an increase in the number of women on the lists of candidates. The reduced number of constituencies coincided with the restructuring of the local administrative structure. As a result of these changes, substantially greater numbers of women were elected to both the Sejm and the Senat. The number of women increased to 20 percent in the lower chamber and to 23 percent in the higher chamber. However, despite the increase in representation, only two women were appointed to high-ranking government positions after the last election: the minister of justice and the minister of national education and sports. The 2001 election resulted in the highest ever number of women elected for the first time. In 1997, the number of women elected for the first time was 44.1 percent, compared with 52.4 percent of men. In 2001, by contrast, the number of women elected for the first time was higher (61.3 percent) than that of men (55.3 percent).

The number of women elected depended greatly upon the number of women listed as candidates on party lists and their positions on these lists. Some women were given high positions by the party gatekeepers, who listed them in the top three slots, thereby improving their chances considerably (see table 3.2). This fact, along with the change in attitude of the general population, increased women's presence in politics in the different districts.

Attitudes toward women in politics are also changing. Increasing awareness among political elites that women should participate in politics to a greater extent—as expected by international organizations such as the United Nations and European Union—played a very important role before the election of 2001. There was also an increase in the social acceptance of female politicians. In 2001, 60 percent of women (compared with 50 percent in 1997) and 40 percent of men (compared with 28 percent in 1997) did not agree with the opinion that "men are better suited to politics than women."[5] In 2001, 46 percent of men, in comparison with 31 percent of women, voted exclusively for men, but 39 percent of men and 55 percent of women voted for men and women. Since the mid-1990s, the number of women and men who believe that women should play a greater role in public life has increased, although this has not translated into an equally dynamic increase in their presence in this sphere of life (see figures 3.1 and 3.2).

Younger people, especially better-educated women, often disagreed with the opinion that men are more suited to politics and that the best place for a woman is her home. Acceptance of the view that women should play the same role in business and politics as men followed the same pattern.[6] Re-

Figure 3.1. Percentage of women and men in a Polish survey who did not agree with the statement "Men are better suited to politics than women," 1992–2005 ($N = 1,000$)

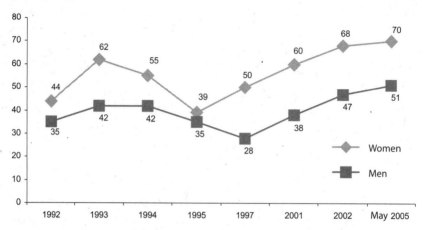

Sources: Renata Siemieńska, "Kobiety i ich problemy w Sejmie IV kadencji. Progres czy regres?" (Women and Their Problems in the Sejm of IV Term: Progress or Regression?) in *Płeć, wybory, władza* (Gender, elections, power), ed. Renata Siemieńska (Warsaw: Scholar, 2005), 40; Renata Siemieńska, Zycie publiczne: Podejmowanie decyzji (Public life: Decision making), in *Krajowy System Monitorowania Równego Traktowania Kobiet i Mężczyzn* (Warsaw: Scholar, 2006), 711.

search conducted in December 2005 after the parliamentary election found similar results.

Thus, a question arises as to whether we are dealing with a growing belief that women should be represented in politics because of the specific characteristics they will bring into this sphere of life or whether we are simply holding the view that women and men have largely similar traits and thus there are no biological or cultural deficiencies that would disqualify women from playing roles that have been perceived as suitable only for men. Women and men also have very similar ideas of what a good politician should be.[7]

A decisive majority of the women and men interviewed in 2005 believed that the desirable traits of a good politician were similar for both men and women. As time went by, the number of people attributing the desirable traits of a politician only to men decreased. The characteristics that are most often ascribed to women include honesty, frankness, intelligence, and a high degree of education (figure 3.3).[8]

When asked a series of questions about men's and women's abilities to deal more efficiently with various social and political problems, more than

Figure: 3.2. Responses in a Polish survey to the statement "Some believe that women should play the same role in business, industry and politics as men; others believe the woman's place is at home," 1992–2005 (mean percent; *N*= 1,000)

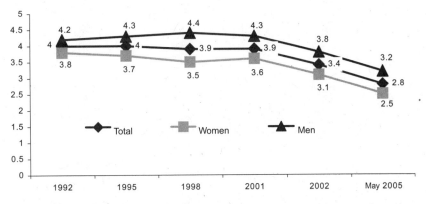

Note: Respondents identified their position using a 7-point scale, where "1" meant that women should play the same role in business, industry, and politics as men, and "7" meant that women's place was at home. The study was carried out by "Pentor" for the F. Ebert Foundation and the Center for Interdisciplinary Gender Studies of the Institute for Social Studies, Warsaw University.
Sources: Renata Siemieńska, "Kobiety i ich problemy w Sejmie IV kadencji. Progres czy regres?" (Women and Their Problems in the Sejm of IV Term: Progress or Regression?) in *Płeć, wybory, władza* (Gender, elections, power), ed. Renata Siemieńska (Warsaw: Scholar, 2005), 40; Renata Siemieńska, "Życie publiczne: Podejmowanie decyzji" (Public life: Decision making), in *Krajowy System Monitorowania Równego Traktowania Kobiet i Mężczyzn* (Warsaw: Scholar, 2006), 712.

half of all respondents stated that there was no difference.[9] For some problems, however—such as care for the elderly, providing good-quality health care, and ensuring equal rights for men and women—numerous respondents believe that women are better. Conversely, many people believe that men are better suited to deal with political issues, such as privatization and decommunization. There is a striking similarity in the opinions of men and women in this regard.

These changes in attitudes toward the roles of women in public and private life are generally taking place simultaneously among men and women. However, there is still a difference in the strength of such attitudes between the two subpopulations.

The growing strength of the women's lobby also contributed to increasing women's representation in Parliament. The women's lobby exerted more influence on political parties and on public opinion as a whole. Fifty organizations joined the Pre-Electoral Coalition of Women, an open, nonpartisan arrangement among women's organizations and groups created a few months before the election. This coalition, along with other women's

Figure 3.3. Desirable traits of politicians attributed to women and men in a Polish survey, May 2005 (percent; national random sample = 1,000)

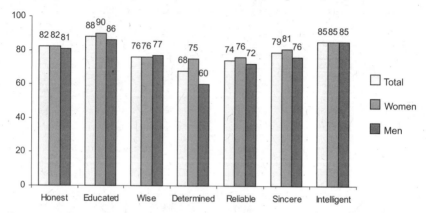

Note: Total = the percentage of all respondents who believe a given trait should be ascribed to both
women and men; women = the percentage of women who believe that a given trait should be ascribed both to women and men; men = the percentage of men who believe that a given trait should
be ascribed to both women and men.
Source: Renata Siemieńska, "Zycie publiczne: Podejmowanie decyzji" (Public life: Decision making), in *Krajowy System Monitorowania Równego Traktowania Kobiet i Mężczyzn* (Warsaw: Scholar,
2006), 714.

groups and feminist organizations, stood somewhere between the center
and the left and was supported by the Women's Parliamentary Group.
Women MPs organized a campaign called "Women Run, Women Vote" to
convince people to vote for women. The participating women belonged to
all the parliamentary parties.

In addition, some political parties introduced a gender quota. The coalition of the post-Communist Democratic Left Alliance (DLA)–Labor Union
(LU), as well as the liberal-center Freedom Union (FU), accepted the rule that
neither of the sexes should be represented by fewer than 30 percent of all candidates and that lists presented for individual constituencies should comply
with this condition. Even right-wing parties, such as the League of Polish
Families (LPF), were influenced by these changes. The LPF, pointing to its
connections with the Catholic Church, placed a substantial number of women
on its party lists for the Sejm. As in the 2001 elections, these changes occurred
despite the fact that women were rarely members of election committees (see
table 3.3). The selection of candidates was thus still made by men.

Finally, changes in the electoral preferences of society also played a role
in women's success in 2001. In that election, the DLA-LU coalition ob-

Table 3.3. Composition of election committees in the 2001 Polish Parliamentary election

Political Party	Total Number of Members	Number of Women Members
Democratic Left Alliance–Labor Union	84	16
Election Action Solidarity[a]	41	0
Freedom Union[a]	13	2
Self Defense of Polish Republic	10	2
Law and Justice	21	0
Polish Peasant Party (PSL)	16	0
Civic Platform	46	7
Alternative Social Movement[a]	4	0
League of Polish Families	10	0

[a]This party did not get to the Sejm in the elections.
Source: Author's calculations, based on Inka Słodkowska, *Wybory 2001: Partie i ich programy* (Elections 2001: Parties and their programs) (Warsaw: ISP PAN, 2002).

tained the highest number of votes, which represented a shift from right to left. This shift was important for women, because this coalition has long been willing to take women's issues into consideration in its political plans and reforms. As a result, the number of women listed as candidates was much greater than before.

The parliamentary election in the fall of 2005 occurred in a completely different political situation. The leftist parties, which had come to power earlier, lost their support. They were generally criticized for using their election success in 2001 to strengthen the financial position of their members and for creating strong, often corrupt bonds between representatives of politics and the business world. Additionally, the split of the DLA into the DLA and the Polish Social Democrats, which sought to dissociate itself from the moral sins and flaws of its mother party, weakened its election potential. This situation was conducive to the strengthening of rightist parties, particularly the Law and Justice Party (L&J) and the center-right Civic Platform (CP), which achieved almost identical results in 2005. However, thanks to a slight advantage for L&J, led by Jarosław Kaczyński, it was able to gain a majority in Parliament, together with the populist party Self-Defense of the Republic of Poland (SD) and the nationalist League of Polish Families. The CP, the DLA, and the Polish Peasant Party became the opposition, rarely undertaking any tasks in Parliament together. The position of L&J and its leader was strengthened when Lech Kaczyński, Jarosław's twin brother, was elected president of Poland in the fall of 2005.

The number of women elected to the Sejm in 2005 (20.4 percent) did not change. In the Senat, women's representation decreased from 24 to 13 percent. Women constituted 24.5 percent of all candidates. The proportion of female candidates in first place on the lists of candidates was particularly low in the nationalist LPF (7.2 percent), the conservative L&J (12.2 percent), the leftist DLA, and the Polish Peasant Party (14.6 percent each). It was significantly higher in the center-right CP (22 percent) and the populist SD (25 percent). Thus, in the 2005 election, there was no correlation between an ideology supporting the equality of women and men and the devising of candidate lists. As a result of the 2005 election, the percentage of women among the parliamentarians of the rightist parties increased by 5.4 percent in L&J and by 5 percent in the CP, which got the most votes, and by 10 percent in the SD in comparison with the election of 2001. Conversely, these percentages decreased in leftist parties by 5 percent in the DLA and by 11.3 percent in the national LPF. The Polish Peasant Party brought one woman into Parliament (3 percent of all parliamentarians). Among the thirteen women in the newly elected Senat in 2005, seven were from L&J, five from the CP, and one from the SD (table 3.4).

The next parliamentary elections took place in the fall of 2007, only two years after the previous elections. Parliament dissolved itself after the crisis with a governing coalition consisting of L&J, the LPF, and the SD. In the elections, the CP (the party that earlier had been in the opposition) received the highest number of votes. However, in order to have a majority in Parliament, it created a coalition with the Polish Peasant Party. This new coalition is more liberal. The CP is a liberal, center-right party. The Polish Peasant Party is a rather conservative one. The political orientation of the coalition and its style are more open to the West and see Poland's membership in the European Union positively.

As in the elections in 2005, women's issues were almost absent in the 2007 electoral campaign for those political parties that received enough votes to get into Parliament. The Women's Party created not long before the elections got about 1 percent of votes. The parties did not talk about quotas for women. The parties that were in the coalition after the 2005 elections emphasized a traditional role for women and the family in the electoral campaign. The number of women elected in 2007 was almost the same as in the 2005 elections. The systematically increasing number of women on candidates' lists has not caused the increase of number of elected women. Women constitute 20 percent of the total number of deputies to the Sejm: 22.97 percent of CP deputies, 22.75 percent of L&D deputies, and almost the same

Table 3.4. Share of women among parliamentarians in the Polish Sejm, 2005

Committee	Number of Women	Total Number of Mandates	Percent Women
Law and Justice	29	155	19
Civic Platform	33	133	25
Self-Defense	15	56	27
Democratic Left Alliance	11	55	20
League of Polish Families	5	34	15
Polish Peasant Party	1	27	3
German Minority		2	0
Total	94	460	20

Source: Gazeta Wyborcza, September 28, 2005.

percentage of women (22.48 percent) among L&J deputies, which shows that the political orientations of the parties and earlier commitments to promote women in elections are not reflected in the gender structures of the parties' representation in the Sejm. Women are almost absent from the Polish Peasant Party (one woman and thirty men) and are totally absent from the German Minority (see table 3.5). The number of women in the Senat was lower (eight) after the elections in 2007.

Women's Issues in Parties' Electoral Programs

The problems of the equal status of women and men, women's political participation, and other women's issues were rarely included in party programs for the 2001electoral campaign.[10] Only the DLA-LU coalition and the FU mentioned the need to change the situation of women in their programs. The DLA-LU program stressed the importance of establishing a firm legal basis for the equal treatment of men and women by legal provisions requiring

Table 3.5. Numbers of women and men deputies elected to the Polish Sejm in 2007

Party	Women	Men	Total
Left and Democrats (L&D)	11	42	53
German Minority (GM)	0	1	1
Law and Justice (L&J)	34	132	166
Civic Platform (CP)	48	161	209
Polish Peasant Party (PPP)	1	30	31
Total	94	366	460

Source: Polish Sejm data (http://www.sejm.gov.pl/poslowie/stat/stat.htm).

equal treatment in the workplace, sanctions for gender-related discrimination, granting both parents equal rights with regard to child care, and guaranteeing women options for planned parenthood.[11]

The FU's program advocated passing an act guaranteeing the equal status of women and men and establishing a commission on the equal status of women and men in the Sejm, which would be responsible for eliminating gender-related discrimination from all Polish legislation.[12] The FU was also concerned about the fact that women are forced to retire at the age of sixty years, compared with sixty-five for men. The party program stated that "this is particularly important for those women who are part of the new pension system, for whom taking away every year of work and every złoty means a lower pension."[13] The FU was less precise about the abortion issue, stating that "it is not an issue to which any party directives or programs apply. This issue is to be resolved according to one's own conscience. The FU, on the other hand, supported the idea of using national health care funds to refund contraceptive purchases."[14]

Other parties either avoided women's issues altogether or presented them in such a way as to make it easier for women to perform their traditional roles. The CP, for instance, proposed improving the care of single mothers with handicapped children. The Alternative Social Movement advocated state "remuneration for housework performed by one of the parents, at a level that would be enough not to force the mother to work outside the home, which is harmful for family life and especially for the education of children."[15]

Men and Women Members of Parliament

The basic characteristics of the deputies elected in 2001 reflect the greater variation in the age, education, professions, and class background of deputies than in previous Parliaments. The average age of women in the Sejm is slightly higher than that of their male colleagues, but age varies more by party. Members of the DLA Parliamentary Club, for instance, tend to be older—half of all men and women are between fifty and fifty-nine years of age—while in the CP or SD clubs, half of both men and women are between forty and forty-nine. In the LPF, women are clearly older than men. Women deputies are slightly less likely to be married, and they tend to have fewer children than men. In the Sejm, 27 percent of women and 15 percent of men have no children. Seventy percent of women and 92 percent of men are married. These figures have remained relatively consistent since 1989.

Women and men have approximately equal educational levels; 83 percent of women and 80 percent of men have a university education, and 12 percent of women and 14 percent of men have a secondary vocational education. The educational levels of members of the SD are substantially lower than those of parliamentarians representing other clubs. Despite the fact that most women as well as men in Parliament have pursued higher education, the educational specializations of female and male parliamentarians differ substantially. Most of the ninety-three female members of the Sejm are graduates of the humanities (twenty-one MPs) and medicine (ten MPs). Men are usually graduates of the faculties of law and administration, humanities, economics, and technical studies.

As a general rule, parties and social organizations still tend to nominate and elect women from "female" professions. The most frequent professions among women were teaching and research (one-third of the women deputies), which is consistent with the pre-1989 period. A relatively large group of women parliamentarians previously held high positions in state administration or were trade union leaders. They continue their work in parliamentary committees that reflect these values and interests but are often not the most influential bodies. Throughout the transition period, women have been greatly underrepresented in key parliamentary leadership posts.

Research conducted in 2004 and earlier studies indicate that the female members of the Sejm have better-educated parents than men and that they are often involved in social or political work (in the Communist Party or in the political opposition during the previous regime), although usually at lower levels.[16] They also often have earlier experiences in public work (e.g., as leaders of student councils, members of youth choirs, or as local government council members), which shows an early interest in civic life and demonstrates that, despite their assertions that they entered politics "accidentally,"[17] women in Parliament have demonstrated leadership abilities. In some cases, the party leaders participating in the election wanted to bring male or female professionals in specific fields, who had shown no political ambitions, into Parliament.

Women's social and cultural potential, which was decisive for the initiation of a professional career and interest in social and political issues, also played a significant role in the subsequent stages of their careers. Some female MPs underlined their patriotic upbringing ("God-Honor-Homeland," as an LPF deputy said about the educational priorities of her parents). All female MPs emphasized the role of their husband's and children's acceptance and support, an MP sometimes stating that it was her husband who came up with the idea that she should become a candidate. The children—usually grown—generally understood the aspirations of their mothers, but they rarely supported them actively, for instance, during the election campaign. A proposal from the party and support of their local environment were other factors that made the decision to enter politics easier. Usually, the offer to participate in the election was made by men. Parties, unlike relatives and friends, did not always follow up with support during the election campaign. Sometimes, as my interviews indicated, parties were eager to find previously unknown people to place on the party lists and thus avoid being accused of being reluctant to field female candidates, or of maintaining relations with people who are "close to the system" or have been entangled in various scandals. However, once they gained popularity, the party tended to push the newcomers down to a significantly lower position on the list during subsequent elections, making it much more difficult for them to enter Parliament. A large number of our interlocutors managed to get into Parliament despite occupying low positions on the lists (e.g., fourth or sixth place), outstripping or even eliminating activists from the local party structures. Some women were, however, in leading positions on the lists.

In 2005, ninety-four women entered the Sejm and thirteen women entered the Senat. Seven were from L&J, five from the CP, and one from the SD. As in the previous election, the female parliamentarians elected in 2005 were better educated than the men. Female members of all parties have a university education, except for those from the SD, in which more than half are graduates of schools of a lower level (mainly vocational secondary schools) and L&J, where 7 percent have a secondary education. In the case of men, 85.3 percent have a university education. However, in the SD, half the men are graduates only of vocational secondary schools. In the remaining parties, the number of men who do not have a university education is lower; those without a university degree are mainly graduates of vocational secondary schools. The structure of education among the Senat members is similar; all the women have a university education, as well as 93 percent of the men. The remaining men from the L&J, CP, and SD have a vocational secondary education.

Women MPs' Participation in Parliamentary Committees in the 2001, 2005, and 2007 Sejms

An MP's participation in a parliamentary committee depends upon the outcome of postelection negotiations among parliamentary clubs. As in the past, few women occupied the position of chairperson or deputy chairperson of a committee after the 2001 election. Currently, only 3 women serve as committee chairs: a DLA parliamentarian is the chair of the Committee for Social Policy and Family Affairs; an LU parliamentarian chairs the Committee on Health Care; and a parliamentarian from the SD is the chair of the Committee for National and Ethnic Minorities. In addition, 15 women serve as deputy chairs on various committees. There are no women who serve as heads of parliamentary clubs. In the Senat, in which 23 of the 100 senators are women, 2 are chairwomen, and 4 are deputy chairs of committees.

Women deputies elected in 2005 are members of all permanent committees except for the Committee for the Secret Services, and they constitute about one-third or more members of the State Control, Education, Science and Youth, Public Finance, Communication with Poles Abroad, Family and Women's Rights, Justice and Human Rights and Health committees, all of which are bodies where women are usually found (see tables 3.6 and 3.7). Six women are chairs of permanent committees (out of 28 such bodies), and 13 are deputy chairs. Almost all the female parliamentarians who occupy these positions are experienced in parliamentary work because they had previously served in Parliament for one or more terms (see tables 3.8 and 3.9). Women deputies of the seventh term have similar experience of being in the Sejm as long as men. Despite this, women are very rarely chairs of committees, as in the earlier terms.

The Women's Parliamentary Group and Its Initiatives

Almost immediately after 1989, women from the parliamentary club of the DLA and the Democratic Union undertook an initiative to create a women's bloc consisting of former activists from the political opposition. The result of their efforts was the Women's Parliamentary Group (WPG) established in 1991, which continues to exist today. Although it began as an interparty group, it later became a body consisting almost exclusively of members of the DLA and LU, as women from center and right-wing parties became less eager to join. In the 2001–5 Parliament, fifty-five of the ninety-three female deputies in the Sejm and seventeen of the twenty-three women in Senat belonged to the WPG.

According to its declaration, the WPG's main goal is to put forward legislative initiatives intended to protect the interests of women and children. One such initiative was a proposal in the early 1990s to allow single parents to calculate their income together with one of their children, as married couples do, to qualify for tax deductions. This act was meant to protect single par-

Table 3.6. Membership of women in the committees of the Polish Sejm elected in 2005

Committee	Women as Percentage of Members	Women Total	Women Chairs	Women Deputy Chairs
Permanent committees				
Administration and the Interior	37	5	—	—
State Control	17	5	1*	—
Secret Services	9	—	—	—
European Commission	43	9	—	1*
Education, Science, and Youth	39	13	1*	2**
Parliamentarian Ethics	6	1	—	—
Public Finances	43	14	1	1*
Economy	41	6	—	1
Infrastructure	40	6	—	—
Physical Education and Sport	21	3	—	—
Culture and Mass Media	29	7	—	1*
Communication with Poles Abroad	19	6	—	1*
National and Ethnic Minorities	18	2	—	—
National Defense	26	2	—	1
Environmental Protection, Natural Resources and Forestry	27	4	—	—
Constitutional Responsibility	17	2	—	—
Social Policy	38	15	—	1
Labor	17	4	—	1
Regulations and Parliamentarian Affairs	16	2	—	1*
Family and Women's Rights	26	16	1*	1*
Agriculture and Rural Development	41	1	—	—
Development of Entrepreneurship	24	3	—	—
Local Government and Regional Policy	30	8	—	—
State Treasury	27	4	1	—
Foreign Affairs	28	5	—	—
Justice and Human Rights	23	8	—	1
Legislative	23	3	—	—
Health Care	26	10	1*	2**
Extraordinary Committees				
Codification amendments	25	3	—	1
For examination of bills on amendment of the act on the National Remembrance Institute—the Commission for Prosecution of Crimes against the Polish Nation and the bill on disclosure of information on documents of the Communist secret services	17	2	—	—
For examination of bills presented by the president of the Republic of Poland, concerning the Military Counter-intelligence Services and the Military Intelligence Services, as well as legislation introducing these acts	17	—	—	—
Committee of Prosecution				
To examine the decisions concerning capital and owner-ship transformations in the banking sectors, as well as activity of the banking supervision bodies from June 4, 1989, to March 19, 2006	10	1	—	—

Note: — = none; * = one-person and ** = two persons serving a second term of office (or more) in the Parliament of the Republic of Poland.
Source: Author's calculations on the basis of data from http://www.sejm.gov.pl.

Table 3.7. Participation of women in the Polish Senat committees elected in 2005

Committee	Total Number of Members	Women Total	Chairs	Deputy Chairs
State Economy	23	2	—	—
Culture and Mass Media	12	3	1*	—
Science, Education, and Sport	20	2	—	—
National Defense	9	—	—	—
Human Rights and Lawfulness	8	1	—	—
Regulations, Ethics, and Senat Affairs	8	—	—	—
Family and Social Policy	7	2	—	1*
Agriculture and Environmental Protection	11	1	—	—
Local Government and State Administration	13	1	1	—
Emigration Affairs and Communication with Poles Abroad	26	5	—	1
Affairs of the European Union	11	3	—	—
Foreign Affairs	12	—	—	—
Legislative	6	—	—	—
Health Care	12	4	—	1

Note: — = no women; * = one person and ** = two persons serving a second term of office (or more) in the Parliament of the Republic of Poland.
Source: Author's calculations on the basis of data from http://www.sejm.gov.pl.

Table 3.8. Number of terms in the Polish Parliament of deputies elected in 2007

Party	1 W	1 M	2 W	2 M	3 W	3 M	4 W	4 M	5 W	5 M	6 W	6 M	7 W	7 M	Total W	Total M
Left and Democrats (L&D)	1	13	2	6	4	8	1	5	—	5	3	3	—	2	11	42
German Minority (GM)	—	—	—	1	—	—	—	—	—	—	—	—	—	—	—	1
Law and Justice (L&J)	10	29	17	73	5	20	1	8	—	3	—	—	—	—	33	133
Civic Platform (CP)	18	77	20	49	8	23	1	9	—	1	1	2	—	—	48	161
Polish Peasant Party (PPP)	1	9	—	5	—	2	—	3	—	6	—	1	—	4	1	30
Total	30	128	39	134	17	53	3	25	—	15	4	6	—	6	93	367
Total percentage of total number of female or male deputies	32	35	41	37	18	14	3	7	—	4	4	2	—	2	100	100

Note: W= women; M = men.
Source: Author's calculations on the basis of data from http://www.sejm.gov.pl.

Table 3.9. Chairs of the committees in the Polish Parliament elected in 2007

Types of Committees	Number of Committees	Chairs		Deputy Chairs	
		Women	Men	Women	Men
Sejm permanent committees	25	2	23	18	65
Sejm extraordinary committees	2	—	2	1	7
Sejm search committees	2	—	2	—	2
Senat committees	14	—	14	2	27

Source: Author's calculations on the basis of data from http://www.sejm.gov.pl.

ents, most of whom are women. During the second term of office of the National Assembly in 1993, the WPG was involved in amending the Family and Guardians' Code to accelerate the adoption process by withdrawing parental rights in certain situations. It had opposed sanctioning the separation of married couples that would allow couples to live apart without officially divorcing, which would allow for a new marriage, instead favoring a simplified divorce procedure by returning the right to grant divorces to regional courts.

The WPG has been actively involved in the liberalization of the abortion law. After 1956, Poland had a liberal abortion act that permitted abortions in certain situations. After a long struggle in Parliament in the early 1990s, a much more restrictive law was passed in 1993. The debates continued due to the actions undertaken by newly created women's organizations—some working for but others against the liberal law—and the law was liberalized in 1996, only to be reversed again in 1997. The more restrictive law remains in effect today.

The DLA-LU coalition government is unwilling to change the law, because it does not want to provoke a conflict with the Catholic Church. The Church's support was needed to assure the Polish public that joining the European Union was in the nation's interest and that the national culture, religion, and economic situation would not be threatened as a result of accession. Church support was thus very important to help mobilize society to vote to join the EU in the spring 2004 referendum. Changing the restrictive abortion law was not necessary in order to join the EU, because decisions in this area are left to individual states. Some women's groups in Poland have tried to get the EU to side with their cause in liberalizing the abortion law, but to date they have not been able to pressure the European Parliament to discuss the issue again.

Another WPG initiative is to pass a law concerning the equal status of men and women, which was unsuccessfully submitted several times in the 1990s and at the beginning of the 2000s, and to pass a law allowing homosexuals to legalize their relationships in order to be able to inherit property. These laws have not yet been passed. The WPG has also attempted to integrate the work of various women's organizations across the country and coordinate its work with researchers and journalists concerned with women's issues.

Opinions about the WPG vary. Women who joined it during the first term of office in 1991 pointed out that its most important functions included the ability to bring up issues that are important for women (this was the opinion of 15 percent of all the women in Parliament), eliminating discrimination in the Sejm (11 percent), and nonpolitical integration (9 percent). Those female deputies who did not like the idea of the WPG argued that it was an artificial body, because gender should not serve as a basis for an organization (15 percent of all women deputies); that their views differed from the liberal and leftist views dominant in the WPG (15 percent); that they did not like the WPG's leftist character (13 percent); or that they did not like the feminist ideas promoted by the WPG's members (13 percent). Some of them (9 percent) also stated that they did not need to seek support from an organization like the WPG because they had not experienced discrimination from their male party colleagues.[18]

The DLA and LU generally believe that the WPG plays an important role by proposing legal solutions consistent with the interests of women. However, not all female parliamentarians are members of the WPG, and even some DLA-LU MPs have not joined the bloc. Some female MPs from other parties believe that the WPG is absolutely useless and that the creation of an institutionalized platform of cooperation between women representing different parties is inconsistent with their individuality. Because the WPG is largely a DLA-LU initiative, members from other parties are reluctant to join because they do not wish to cooperate with the coalition. There are also arguments based on principle, rather than politics, such as "there is no point to create a 'ghetto for women'"; "there are no common interests of women as such, because, in fact, different groups of women have different interests"; and "it is not justifiable to talk about specific interests of women, we should talk about interests and problems of people, and these are not gender-specific." The arguments for and against the existence of WPG have remained the same from the early 1990s. However, until the 2005 election, actual membership in the WPG was determined by DLA-LU party membership. Since that election, the WPG has been led by a female MP from the CP, and its members now represent various political groups.

Problems that primarily affected women were not a high priority for the

Polish Sejm elected in 2005, except for issues associated with the family. As a result of L&J's connections with the particularly conservative wing of the Catholic Church, as well as presence of the LPF in the governmental coalition, problems of the family from the conservative point of view, with an emphasis on the role of women in childbearing and the upbringing of children, served as the basis for the act on the newborn allowance, which provides a one-time benefit payment for each woman who gives birth. This allowance can be increased by the local authority for the woman's place of residence. A decision was made to extend maternity leave and to make sure employers would not dismiss women who return after maternity leave.

The opposition protested against all these proposals. The newborn allowance was considered a waste of resources that could be used for a better purpose—to ensure institutional child care, for instance. The concept of a guarantee of employment for women was considered yet another reason for employers to be reluctant to hire women and thus for their elimination from the labor market. Neither a more liberal act on abortion nor the act on equal status for men and women made it to the Sejm—even as a discussion topic. The parties that were members of the governing coalition formed after the 2005 elections were leadership-based bodies characterized by rigorous internal discipline. Initiatives to unite female parliamentarians from different parties, even those belonging to the coalition, thus became unthinkable.

Perceptions of Women's Roles in the Sejm

Membership in specific parties determines the frames of activities of men and women parliamentarians. The leaders of clubs are in a different situation. They often enforce their opinions, sometimes very strictly, and they do not tolerate any deviations or individual initiatives. Nevertheless, when speaking about women's roles in Parliament, both male and female parliamentarians often refer to culturally determined images of women, thus diminishing women's input into parliamentary work. Perceptions about womens' roles and their views of how men perceive them are partially dependent on political orientations. In almost all cases, we can also trace some elements of the stereotypical view that women are more sensitive to social issues and less aggressive in interactions with other people. Statements by the female parliamentarians also give us an image of women known from observation of highly qualified women in other spheres of public life, who—irrespective of the political orientation of their parliamentary group—are perceived as people who are usually asked to do tedious tasks, who are eager to undertake such tasks on their own, and who usually perform them well. However, their work in Parliament seldom leads to higher positions within the organizational structure of the Sejm or to greater political influence. The argument that women do not want to accept managerial positions cannot be accepted here, given the experience and life histories of both male and female parliamentarians.

The construction in the public sphere of relationships between men and women based on submission by women, which is typical for the private sphere, determines a limited role for women in which they are legally equal. The beliefs of female and male deputies about the situation of women in Parliament are often similar across party lines.

The parliamentarians interviewed reflect these views. When asked about the role of women, a male DLA deputy noted:

> Same as men, women are sometimes more intelligent. . . . If a woman is pretty, if she is sexually attractive, she is perceived as someone who arouses [the] interest of men, because Parliament is a combination of barracks and a dorm, it is a bit like a dorm. If a woman is attractive, then men are interested and vice versa, if a man is attractive, women are interested. Perhaps . . . they are less ambitious and softer. Among the deputies, there are women who are active; they are not only interested in the "kitchen, church, and children." Even those from the LPF or the National Catholic Movement, who say women should stay at home, are not eager to stay at home or go to church. If they were, they would not have joined Parliament. A deputy's life is opposed to family life; in the case of both males and females, we need to travel a lot, we live away from home.

A male deputy from the populist-conservative SD movement asked about the role of women in the Sejm stated: "I think the role of women should be much more significant. Women not only soothe the savage breast. They are really more sensitive. I believe that the number of women is too low, both in our party and in other parties. It is not because no one wants them to be placed on the lists. Simply, they engage in less political activity, and that is natural."

When asked how women deputies are perceived, a male deputy from the conservative LPF stated:

> I look at the work of each female and male parliamentarian from the perspective of the quality of their presentations, their inventiveness when it

comes to legislation initiatives, and to me there is no division between women and men. For me, it is a personal division. . . . The role of women in the Sejm is the same as that of men! They act in accordance with the legislation on mandates of Sejm and Senat members, . . . but there are some character traits women have, . . . a different mentality, they often are able to relieve stress during a discussion, they bring in their womanhood, and if they are able to maintain these traits as Parliament members, if they are able to maintain it with dignity, with culture, I think their role is great.

A male deputy from L&J reflected the view noted above when asked whether there was an informal "division of work" in his party according to gender: "No, there are no divisions according to gender, there is only the factor of competency and diligence. I definitely more often seek opinions of women or delegate them to deal with certain acts or tasks in the name of our party, because they are competent and hard-working."

Women parliamentarians' views about their role in the legislature and how they are perceived by men also differ. A woman deputy from the LPF noted: "Women in Parliament . . . do a good job, they are very hard-working, very responsible, they are punctual, which is very important. I can see that women are much more patient, they show less emotion. I think that the ambitions of the men do not really allow them to accept the idea of women occupying the highest positions and offices; . . . it is part of the male ambition. Nevertheless, when a woman gets to occupy a position like that, she tends to do really well." A woman deputy from the PBL, however, stated that "in various ways, . . . sometimes women are perceived like decorative items."

An LU woman deputy argued that "there is great diversity, usually we do not feel any worse, although at first, as the presidium is being elected, the chairpersons or deputy chairs of commissions are being appointed, it seems that men want to get more and they only see each other. Men support men, and if a woman wants to be a chairperson, she has to get support. . . . There has to be a strong lobby supporting women. In our case, there were no problems."

However, this female Parliamentarian also pointed out problems women faced at the Sejm: "If the number of gentlemen is small, and I am talking about a problem that concerns women, they always talk very positively about women. If we are dealing with 97 percent men, and there are some circles like that, . . . I know there will be no acceptance for women's issues, because, when we are dealing with many men, they are not interested in these topics or in promotion of women. I approach men and women differently when it comes to the same issues." A woman deputy from L&J noted, "Once I thought that the fact that we are women would decrease the aggressiveness of men. But the longer I am here, the less I think so. If you are a tough woman, if you want to get what you want, sooner or later they start to treat a woman like . . . without any difference."

The interests of female parliamentarians vary greatly. Thus, women parliamentarians deal with issues ranging from finance and agriculture, to education, health care, tourism, and harmonizing Polish legislation to the *acquis communautaire*. These emphases are largely due to women deputies' professional backgrounds and experiences in a given field, but not exclusively. Other reasons include the division of tasks within political parties or personal interests. The female parliamentarians interviewed did not complain, as did women in an earlier survey, of being offered membership in committees that deal with issues that were of no interest to them, or of being prevented from participation in work of those bodies that they found interesting. There is relatively little diversity of professions among the female parliamentarians, and the fact that they usually represent heavily feminized fields may make it difficult for women to deal competently with a more extensive scope of issues; it also predetermines their perspectives. Some female parliamentarians admit they have learned about problems associated with the unequal status of women, family violence, and the existence of the glass ceiling only recently, and mainly from the media. In fact, some of them justify their lack of sensitivity to women's problems as being something they learned by working in heavily feminized fields and mainly among women. Therefore, they were unable to perceive the potential differences in treatment of women and men.

However, women deputies are often convinced that their present scope of work as parliamentarians is fully consistent with their interests. Some of them believe that getting involved in the work of a given committee would not make sense because of its composition because they firmly believe that they would be outvoted all the time. Often the parliamentary groups "assign" female and male party members to specific committees on the basis of their qualifications, or because the number of parliamentarians delegated to certain committees is too low. Of course, in this case, we are dealing with general rules of effective functioning in this environment. We can only wonder if women can choose as freely as men, and whether they are able to convince their male colleagues to admit that a given issue is important and to get the support of other party members and those outside their group.

According to female parliamentarians from the DLA, the way women are treated in Parliament depends on their position, which is based on experience and knowledge, rather than on gender. However as one of them pointed out, "I can see there are some situations, where, for some positions and functions, when there is competition, men have greater chances, because there are more of them." They stress also that women are appointed to positions that require a lot of work. "Women are often chairs of the subcommissions. . . . It is because the subcommissions are responsible for all the backbreaking work, not to mention long hours spent in meetings, the expert opinions, time needed for clarification of the changes made, step by step. This work is definitely not translated into bonuses, I am not even talking about the finances, but in general." Another female deputy from the SD believes that gender parity in Parliament is important because of women's broad experience at home and in the workplace.

On Which Issues Do Women in the Sejm Work?

Membership in specific parties determines the activities of parliamentarians. Nevertheless, personal preference also plays a role in determining the issues with which they become involved as well as their beliefs regarding tolerance within their party clubs. The justification for their involvement with certain issues often has religious, ideological, pragmatic, or even personal roots.

Rightist parties (LPF, L&J) are very concerned with family-related problems and the protection of the fetus. One woman summed it up by declaring that she is in opposition to "all deviations, which are coming into force and being enforced in the society as a norm, homosexual relationships, euthanasia." She also stressed that for her party (LPF), all issues that are not in the scope of the Charter of the Rights of the Family, issued by the pope, are unacceptable. This female parliamentarian also supports the idea of providing women with salaries for bringing up children: "Of course, it is for those mothers, who want to be responsible for bringing up their children. I am not talking here about women who want to fulfill their career ambitions. If they want to pursue careers, I have nothing against that. The problem is, then they want to have children, let's say, when they turn forty, and as we know, from the point of view of medicine, this age is not always safe for having children."

Another female parliamentarian from this party, taking a more general program ("God-Honor-Homeland") as her starting point, states that she is concerned mainly about economic problems (counteracting privatization, eliminating unemployment, protecting the national tradition). She has a

negative attitude toward liberalizing the act of abortion, the legislative solutions proposed by the DLA and the LU with regard to the rights of homosexuals, and the right of a terminally ill person to decide to end his or
her life.

Female parliamentarians from L&J identified a number of areas of focus. The scope of these issues depends mainly on the drafts presented by
the government. Thus, one female parliamentarian noted that she has dealt
with a protest against the act proposed by the government that would eliminate the alimony fund. A woman parliamentarian from the Civic Platform
emphasized the variety of interests of its female members: "Women deal
with such issues as public finances, . . . health care issues, . . . agricultural
affairs, . . . the act on cosmetics." She believes that many of problems should
have been solved before the enlargement of the European Union: "We are
now joining the EU, and we are like fish trying to breathe on the shore, one
more thing, one more thing. Now we will defend the homosexuals, now we
will talk about abortion, now this or that. Some matters need to be regulated
and dealt with, but not now, when the whole state is collapsing. . . . Or this
act on equal status of women and men. It is identical in 90 percent with the
content of the labor code. . . ." On the other hand, a critic of women's organizations could say, "[It is] a method to get money from the state budget,
money for women's organizations, [nongovernmental organizations], as a
special favor."

A woman deputy from the LU noted: "I am primarily interested in the issues of education, because I am a teacher. . . . The other committee for which
I work is also a regulation committee associated with our activity and the
scope of our mandates, functioning of the offices, the highest positions, financial affairs of the Sejm Office, as well as civil services. . . . I am now in
my second term of office in the presidium of the Women's Parliamentary
Group."

Another deputy from the DLA stated: "Of course, I am involved in the legislation devised by the Committee on Social Policy and Family, that is, legal
regulations pertaining to social assistance, benefits, the act on socially beneficial and volunteer organizations, all of the pro-social (initiatives). I am also
a member of the Committee on Education. I have managed to establish a permanent subcommittee for the affairs of children and youth within the Committee on Social Policy and Family. . . . I work for the committee established
to examine the civic legal bill on counteracting violence in the media."

Her colleague, also from the DLA, noted: "I am a chair of the subcommittee for the act on equal status of women and men. . . . The other one is

the law on the bar, a very difficult one. . . . I have completed work on the
act of the subcommittee dealing with freedom of conscience and religion,
. . . and I find working on the act on access to information and media very
difficult. . . . I also prepare reports concerning the bill on detention and its
coordination with the penal code."

Representation of Interests of Specific Groups

Female parliamentarians often identify themselves with their own professional group (e.g., teachers). However, a different group or part of society
can serve as a basis for identification. The identification can have also ideological character. For example, a female deputy from the LPF said: "I represent people whose opinions and backgrounds have been disregarded, . . .
who are absolutely honest, with Catholic backgrounds. To me, a woman is
a person who achieves her objectives in the family. I do not see, like feminists, a special world only for women." Some female deputies (also some
from leftist parties) become interested in women's issues because of their
family experiences. For instance: "I am not a struggling feminist or a person perceived in this way, a revolutionary. . . . As my child is reaching adult-
hood, and I look at myself and everything that is going on in Poland, I think
that the issues of women, starting from politics and ending with various relations at work, with abortion, . . . I am convinced they should be dealt
with." The belief that there are no problems that concern only women is
shared by several female parliamentarians from different parties. Therefore,
some female deputies of the L&J and DLA stress the interests of the regions
or constituencies that they represent. A female parliamentarian of the L&J
says: "I represent the people of my constituency—farmers, craftsmen, small
merchants, the unemployed, many people, who have been harmed by various institutions, people who feel lost." A female member of the DLA ad-
mits her interests in social activities: "I definitely represent a group of social activists in the literal sense, those who are involved in public work. . . .
I feel very closely associated with [nongovernmental organizations], I identify myself with them."

Some female deputies are engaged in an implementation of promises
given to women in the programs of their parties before the election. As one
woman stated, " providing mammography for women, encouraging them to
undergo medical examinations in the period of menopause, to consult good
gynecologists, oncologists. . . . Young girls came from small villages to undergo such tests." Another female deputy stressed the work of her party to

get the labor code to take into account the protection of women during pregnancy, maternity leaves, prohibition of shift work, as well as issues of sexual abuse.

Reasons for the Lack of Cooperation among Women Deputies

There are various reasons for the lack of cooperation among women in the Sejm: party discipline, differences in political orientations, and personal animosity, sometimes rooted in the past. These barriers to cooperation, of course, also influence the work of men. As noted above, the interests of women parliamentarians are very diverse, and some of them demonstrate a strong emotional commitment to the issues mentioned. Many of these interests are determined primarily by the professional background and experience of each parliamentarian, but some also reflect the results of women's appointment to particular committees by the management of parliamentary clubs. The female parliamentarians interviewed did not complain that they were offered positions in committees in which they were not interested or that they were not allowed to participate in certain commissions. It also interesting that some of the female parliamentarians found out quite recently, after they had already been elected to Parliament, and mainly from the media (for instance, a woman deputy from the rightist party Polish Peasant Bloc) about such problems as the unequal status of women and men, domestic violence, and the glass ceiling. In fact, one parliamentarian explains that her lack of sensitiveness to women's problems is due to her work experience. As a teacher, she always worked among women. Therefore, she was unable to notice the differences in treatment between women and men. We may conclude that this type of experience makes it difficult for women to deal competently with a broader range of matters, and it enforces a point of view determined by the experiences gathered in the "ghetto of women."

Conclusion

In recent years, the number of women in the Polish Parliament has increased. However, the Polish case shows clearly that an increase of the number of women in Parliament in itself does not automatically mean that greater attention will be paid to problems that are particularly important to women or that there will be greater effectiveness in resolving them. During Parliament's 2001–5 term and the beginning of its 2007 term, women's issues were not discussed frequently in Sejm debates. They were not often subject to legislative initiatives, and even less often were such initiatives successful. After the 2005 elections, the parties in the governing coalition focused primarily on issues related to women's status as mothers.

Poland's 2004 accession to membership in the European Union has influenced its national legislation concerning women. One of the early examples of the country's standardization of its situation in relation to conditions in the EU is the principle of wage equality for men and women.[19] The Polish initiative was enacted for economic reasons, but it can also be regarded as the beginning of the country's European-oriented social policy, in response to its low female labor participation rate and in an effort to narrow its gender gaps in both wages and unemployment.

These trends reflect conditions that are both external and internal to Parliament. The post-Communist government, which sought to lead Poland into the EU, needed the support of the Catholic Church to achieve this goal. Therefore, the government avoided dealing with problems that the Church would not accept. The Church has been influential in Polish politics for a long time, and it was particularly successful in mobilizing rural voters for the referendum on EU accession.

Conversely, an increase in the representation of the right-wing, populist, and centrist parties in the Sejm, which strongly opposed liberalizing the abortion law, made it difficult to pass the act on the equal status of women and men (which included the creation of a ministry for these issues). It is also necessary to remember that even within the ruling coalition, there was no unanimity in these matters.

An analysis of behaviors and debates for the MPs in office from 2001 to 2005, as well as the term initiated in 2005, shows that consideration of certain issues by the Sejm is not correlated (or is only weakly correlated) with the number of female parliamentarians. It would be too simple to expect such a correlation. Much more important is the context: the types of parties in Parliament and relations between them. If the parties impose strict discipline on their members, speaking of certain issues or methods of solving problems becomes difficult, or even impossible, if the views of the party leaders with regard to a given matter or their political priorities are totally different. Relations between parties also influence the possibilities of cooperation between women from various parliamentary groups. If these relations are hostile and any attempt to reach understanding is treated as betrayal, it is very difficult to propose initiatives that would require the support of representatives of various groups.

The value of the concept of "critical mass" is based on pointing out the significance of bringing more women into legislatures. If their number is greater, they may play an important role in considering problems that are important for women; however, it depends on the existence of permanent, stable, and democratic relations, based on cooperation among parties, simultaneously with any rivalry among them.

Is the increase of the number of women in the Sejm a sign of success, even though their views range from radical rightist and clerical to radical leftist? I believe that the answer is definitely yes. Studies of attitudes toward the presence of women in public life in 1992 (when Hanna Suchocka was the prime minister) and 2002 (after the increase in the number of women in Parliament elected in 2001) have shown that the presence of women in politics leads to a higher level of acceptance of women as actors in public life.[20]

Most parliamentarians are aware of the fact that Poland's accession to the European Union will change the perception of its situation and the role of women. Although legal harmonization lies in the hands of individual EU member states, the frequency of economic, political, and cultural contacts will accelerate changes in attitudes with regard to the position and rights of women in society. Women deputies to the Polish Parliament differ in their responses to this change—some see it as a reason to be happy, while others believe that it is a cause for concern.

Notes

1. Renata Siemieńska, *Kobiety: Nowe wyzwania—Starcie przeszłości z teraźniejszością* (Women: New challenges—clash of the past and the present) (Warsaw: Instytut Socjologii-Uniwersytet Warszawski, 1996); Renata Siemieńska, "Women's Political Participation in Central and Eastern Europe: A Cross-Cultural Perspective," in *Women in Post-Communism,* ed. Barbara Wejnert, Metta Spencer, and Slobodan Drakulic (London: JAI Press, 1996), 63–92; Renata Siemieńska, "Consequences of Economic and Political Changes for Women in Poland," in *Women and Democracy: Latin America and Eastern Europe,* ed. Jane S. Jaquette and Sharon L. Wolchik (Baltimore: Johns Hopkins University Press, 1998), 125–52; Renata Siemieńska, *Nie mogą, nie chcą czy nie potrafią? O postawach i uczestnictwie politycznym kobiet w Polsce* (They have no opportunities, they do not want, they are unable, do they? About attitudes and women's political participation in Poland) (Warsaw: Scholar, 2000); and Renata Siemieńska, "Women in the Polish Sejm: Political Culture and Party Politics versus Electoral Rules," in *Women's Access to Political Power in Post-Communist Europe,* ed. Richard E. Matland and Kathleen A. Montgomery (Oxford: Oxford University Press, 2003), 217–44. See also Renata Siemieńska, "Kobiety i ich problemy w Sejmie IV kadencji: Progres czy re-

gres?" (Women and their problems in the Sejm of IV term: Progress or regression?) in *Płeć, wybory, władza* (Gender, elections, power), ed. Renata Siemieńska (Warsaw: Scholar, 2005).

2. Drude Dahlerup, "The Theory of a 'Critical Mass' Revisited," paper presented on the Annual Meeting of the American Political Science Association, Washington, 2005.

3. Wejnert, Spencer, and Drakulic, *Women in Post-Communism;* Jaquette and Wolchik, *Women and Democracy,* 125–52; Marilyn Rueschemeyer, ed., *Women in the Politics of Postcommunist Eastern Europe,* rev. and expanded ed. (Armonk, N.Y.: M. E. Sharpe, 1998); Matland and Montgomery, *Women's Access to Political Power.*

4. Joni Lovenduski, Joni Hills, and Jill Hills, eds., *The Politics of the Second Electorate: Women and Public Participation* (London: Routledge, 1981); Joni Lovenduski, *Women in European Politics: Contemporary Feminism and Public Policy* (Amherst: University of Massachussets Press, 1986).

5. Siemienska, "Women in the Polish Sejm," 239.

6. See www.monitoring.rownystatus.gov.pl.

7. Siemieńska, *Nie mogą, nie chcą czy nie potrafią?*

8. Ibid.

9. Ibid.

10. Inka Słodkowska, *Wybory 2001: Partie i ich programy* (Elections 2001: Parties and their programs) (Warsaw: ISP PAN, 2002).

11. Ibid., 25.

12. Ibid., 74.

13. Ibid., 64.

14. Ibid., 69.

15. Ibid., 193.

16. These earlier studies include Renata Siemieńska, "Elites and Women in Democratising Post-Communist Societies," *International Review of Sociology* 9, no. 2 (1999): 197–219.

17. Some female members of the Sejm declare that the beginning of their careers in politics were accidental—that they began to be politically active to solve a specific problem, and only later did they find that they were interested in this kind of work.

18. Siemieńska, *Kobiety: Nowe wyzwania.*

19. This EU principle is based on Council regulations EEC No. 1612/68 (7, 2) and EEC No. 1408/71 (3), Article 235 of the EEC Treaty, and Council Directive 76/207.

20. Siemieńska, *Kobiety: Nowe wyzwania.*

Chapter 4

What Difference Do Female Deputies Make in the Slovene Parliament?

Milica G. Antić

Women's political representation cannot be regarded as satisfactory, nor was it so during the socialist period. There were many promises but little realization from the Communist Party and leading politicians who, on the one hand, regarded women as serious political actors in the processes of modernization and the democratization of society as they understood it, but, on the other hand, did not take steps to realize their equal representation in politics (especially high-level politics). Slovene women were visible in politics through different periods in history; they contributed to the movement of national awakening in the nineteenth and early twentieth centuries, as well as to the Anti-Fascist Movement during World War II, but their role was always undervalued and quickly forgotten afterward, and women were again pushed to "where they belonged"—in the home and with the family. Women were never seen as serious and powerful political actors in high politics. They received their full voting rights only after World War II, when women became visibly active in some women's party organizations.

There were few strong women working for women's issues in the Communist Party and, as in many other socialist regimes at that time, women were declared to be equal and emancipated, especially in the field of economic and social life. But in the field of politics, there was no space for democratic dialogue outside the Communist Party. There was no room for opinions other than the party line for anyone, including men. There was also no room for special women's demands and activities outside class demands and activities to improve the position of the working class. Namely, under socialism, a common understanding of the women's question was that it was a part of the class question. This question was going to be solved by the activity of the Communist state and its agencies, and no special engagement of women was needed for that. The only special women's organization, the Anti-Fascist Women's Front, was dissolved soon after World War II; that is why some Slovene feminist writers say that this was a period of state feminism, or feminism from above.[1]

We should not, however, neglect the major changes during this period in the position of women. Women were given equal access to schooling and equal access to paid jobs; they were supposed to be equally paid for equal jobs. Discrimination on the basis of sex was prohibited in different spheres of life. Paid maternity leave for employed women was introduced, and there was a legal right to abortion, to list only the most important of these changes. As Rueschemeyer notes, "During the Communist period, the more skilled the woman was or the more involved she became in her profession, the more she identified with the place were she worked, the more interested she was in keeping her job and the more reluctant she was to become a full-time homemaker."[2] Such women were also more interested in public life and politics.

During the socialist period, women were active primarily in the Communist Party. They followed the goals put forward by this organization and not special goals concerning women as a separate social group. There were some strong party politicians whose task it was to work with and for women who ultimately did a lot for them.[3] But in general, there was no special analysis by Slovene leaders or scholars concerning women's political activities as women; nor did women hold a special status as a political group before the 1980s. These studies suggest that the share of women in politics did not correspond to their level of participation in the national economy, where there were almost as many women as men. The reason for this disparity was in part the widespread conviction that women's emancipation follows from economic emancipation, and in part the unfavorable influence of tradition in private life.[4] Despite the fact that the Communist Party declared equality between women and men, and despite the fact that there were quotas for women, workers, and youth, women did not reach a critical mass in political bodies during socialism. Women's share of party members reached 30 percent only in 1977.[5] Similarly, women's share of the Socio-Political Chamber of the Slovene Assembly exceeded one-fourth only in the 1970s and later: in 1974, 26 percent; in 1978, 28 percent; in 1982, 26 percent; and in 1986, 24 percent.[6]

The Slovene transition from state socialism had many particularities because it paralleled the process of state building. Fortunately, Slovenia's dissolution from its previous federal state was the "easiest" in Yugoslavia, with "only" ten days of clashes between the Federal Yugoslav Army and Slovene territorial defense units and police. In this period, national consolidation was the main aim in Slovenia. In this situation, women's issues did not come to the forefront. Rather, issues such as the survival of the endangered Slovene nation, the creation of a market economy, and returning to Europe were among the most important goals. In this period of systemic transformation, women's role in politics did seem to change somewhat. There was a strong belief that democratization and liberalization would bring solutions to all sorts of problems, from the market economy to political representation and gender equality. Women were present in large numbers in the activities of civil society and in the party opposition rows.[7] As the transition progressed, however, their role began to diminish and, paradoxically, consolidation did not result in the stabilization of women's political participation.[8]

Slovene society went through a so-called negotiated transition process. The reform Communist Party was open to systemic change and started negotiations with the newly formed opposition groups. The second half of the 1980s was described as "the most beautiful years of our lives"—during this period, the League of Communists gradually relinquished power, and the leaders of the party allowed many different political actors (women's groups included) to be active.[9] Talks and negotiations with the opposition started in the spring of 1989. The old political elite accepted the rules of the democratic game and was included in the process of democratic transition.[10]

Despite the fact that the first multiparty election in Slovenia in 1990 was held for the old three-chamber Assembly and that systemic political changes occurred only in the beginning of the 1990s, this founding election was very important and paradoxical in several respects. The electorate gave a majority of the vote to the anti-Communist parties (the DEMOS Coalition), but the individual party that received the best result was the former Communist Party —today's United List of Social Democrats. Similarly, in the first presidential election the previous Communist leader, Milan Kučan, received more votes than the DEMOS candidate, the prominent dissident Jože Pučnik.

During the transition, women in Slovenia were more politically active in nongovernmental organizations and much less so in the newly formed parties. The most relevant move was the demand of the women from the former youth organization for a Women's Ministry at the end of 1980s. The goal was not met immediately, but after the second multiparty elections in 1992, a Parliamentary Commission for Women's Politics was established and soon after that the Governmental Office for Women's Politics. But conservative ideology had also been strengthened and was visible in political debates. Slogans about family values and the traditional female role in society, as well as maternity and family as values, were stressed and put in opposition to women's public role.

Women and Politics

In the realm of politics, the first democratic election in 1990 demonstrated the change that had taken place. Women's political representation dropped dramatically (see table 4.1). Women did not get ministerial positions; nor were they present in the leadership of the parties. The prevailing environment was certainly not "female friendly." Gender did not appear on the political agenda. Nor was it part of the public discourse.

At first glance, women did not gain but rather lost as the result of the democratic changes, at least where political representation is concerned. The large number of parties and their fragility did not help female participation. Party formation started in the late 1980s, but the party system is still unstable; parties merge, dissolve, rename and form. But the largest one remained the same: the Liberal Democracy of Slovenia (LDS) became stronger from one election to the next. Its support grew from 14.5 percent in 1990 to 36.2 percent in 2000.[11] From 1990 to 2000, it formed a wide coalition government of four parties, with parties from the left and right of center. However, it lost the election of 2004.

As table 4.1 shows, female representation in the Slovene National Assembly was the lowest after the 1996 election; it increased 5 percentage points after the 2000 election and remained the same after the 2004 election, but it is still very low. In the 1996 election, the relatively large electoral failure of the United List of Social Democrats (Združena lista socialnih demokratov, ZLSD) resulted in the absence of their female representation.

Table 4.1. Women deputies in the Slovene Parliament, 1990–2004

Year of Election	Number of Women	Percent Women
1990	27	11.25
1992	12	12.3
1996	7	7.8
2000	12	13.3
2004	11/12[a]	12.2/13.3[a]

[a]After the establishment of the government, one more woman came in.
Sources: National Assembly of Slovenia (www.dz-rs.si) and the author's own calculations.

But conversely, the strongest party has numerically the strongest women's presence in Parliament, and the majority of female members of Parliament (MPs) come from the left-wing parties. Female representation in Slovenia thus depends mostly on the parties of the left. In contrast, right-of-center parties the see women's role more at the backstage of politics and not at the forefront. Women members in these parties themselves are mostly comfortable with this role. It is not surprising at all, therefore, that the two biggest parties from this ideological spectrum, the Slovenian Democratic Party (Slovenska demokratska stranka) and the Slovene People's Party (Slovenska Ljudska stranka), have had no female MPs for some time. Yet left-of-center parties have not made a significant step forward in supporting women's equal engagement in politics. Two parties (LDS and ZLSD) have formal or informal quotas for internal party bodies and national election slates, but the share of women among MPs is still relatively low; after the 2004 elections, LDS had three women MPs among twenty-three parliamentarians, and ZLSD had two out of ten (see table 4.2).

The reason for this state of affairs is the fact that politics is still considered as a man's field. Parliament is a strong political body in Slovene politics, and being an MP in the Slovene Parliament is still considered a prestigious man's political post. The party apparatus, which is predominantly male, and which serves as the gatekeeper for women on their way to political positions, is not ready for changes resulting in more opportunities for women.

Dissatisfaction with the situation among women and men who were active supporters of women in politics led to an effort outside the parties to obtain a national law to promote gender equality by, for example, introducing quotas for the national election. A nationwide network, the Coali-

Table 4.2. Women deputies in the Slovene Parliament by party, 1992, 1996, 2000, and 2004

Party	1992		1996		2000		2004	
	Number	Percent	Number	Percent	Number	Percent	Number	Percent
LDS	2	9.1	1	4.0	5	14.7	3	13.4
SKD	2	13.2	1	10.0	—	—	—	—
ZLSD	2	14.2	—	—	3	27.2	2	20
SNS	2	16.6	1	25.0	1	25.0	1	16.6
SLS	2	20.0	1	10.0	—	—	—	—
SDS	—	—	1	6.2	—	—	3	10.3
DS	1	16.6	—	—	—	—	—	—
ZS	—	—	—	—	—	—	—	—
DeSUS	—	—	1	20.0	—	—	—	—
NSi	—	—	—	—	2	25.0	2	22.2
Other	1		1		1		1	
Total	12	13.3	7	7.8	12	13.3	12	13.3

Note: — = none; LDS = Liberal Democracy of Slovenia; SKD = Slovene Christian Democrats; ZLSD = United List of Social Democrats; SNS = Slovene National Party; SLS = Slovene People's Party; SDS = Social Democratic Party; DS = Democratic Party; ZS = Greens of Slovenia; DeSUS = Democratic Party of Pensioners; NSi = New Slovenia.
Sources: National Assembly of Slovenia (www.dz-rs.si) and the author's own calculations.

tion for Parity, was established in 2001. Nearly two hundred well-known women from different political backgrounds and some influential male allies set a common goal of achieving "equal representation" for women in all political decisionmaking bodies. The coalition worked closely with some female MPs and some prominent male political leaders to introduce changes into Slovenian legislation and to improve the situation of women in politics.

These activities culminated in the signing of a proposal by more than two-thirds of all the MPs requesting a constitutional change that would allow the enactment of positive measures in politics. The amendment was enacted by Parliament in July 2004. The first positive change was the introduction of a binding 40 percent gender quota for the European election, which resulted in the election of 42.9 percent of women (three out of seven) Slovenian members of the European Parliament. The second was the amendment to the electoral law for local election—starting with 20 percent gender quota and raising it 10 percentage points at each next election until it reaches 40 percent.[12] And the third positive change was electoral law for the national election, which defines gender quotas for 35 percent, but starting with 25 percent for the 2008 election.[13] The proof of how quotas can be effective can be seen in the last local election; after 20 percent (starting) quotas for the election in 2006, the share of female city councillors almost doubled (from 13 to 21.5 percent). It is hoped by proponents that a similar trend is going to occur in the next parliamentary election in 2008.[14]

Slovenia's Complicated Electoral System

In addition to party gatekeepers, the Slovenian electoral system is often mentioned as an inhibiting factor with respect to female representation. The newly established parties in the early 1990s agreed to adopt a variant of proportional representation.[15] The country is divided into eight geographically, historically, and societally determined constituencies. Each constituency is further divided into eleven voting units. For each full electoral quota, the party receives one seat from that constituency. Seats remaining when all full-quota seats have been awarded are distributed in a second tier, using the d'Hondt formula, a highest-averages method for allocating seats in Parliament. Two seats are reserved for Hungarian and Italian minorities and are allocated according to a majoritarian first-past-the-post system. In addition, since the 2000 elections, there has been a 4 percent electoral threshold. From the perspective of women's electoral chances, there is an important "deviation" from the "pure" proportional representation system that forces Slovene political parties to behave as if they were in a majoritarian system. In each electoral constituency, the parties submit eleven candidates, but they are not presented as a complete list as in most proportional representation systems. Rather, as noted, constituencies are divided into eleven voting units. Voters do not see the entire party list, but choose a party through the choice of a single candidate put forth by the party in their voting unit. The votes given to candidates in each voting unit are aggregated to determine how many seats the list/party is entitled to receive in the given constituency. This practice was designed with the aim to limit "partitocracy" and assure an MP-voter linkage, but it has some strange implications.

Under these circumstances, party gatekeepers must choose one candidate for each of eighty-eight electoral units. This requirement fundamentally alters and undermines the logic of ticket balancing in a proportional representation system. If the party chooses a woman, she will be the party's only candidate in that voting unit, rather than being part of a party list. This fact, combined with the fact that women in politics are generally unpopular in Slovenia, makes party gatekeepers more hesitant to nominate women. Nevertheless, overall, we can clearly draw the conclusion that parties serve as gatekeepers for women's entrance into parliamentary office and that parties more decisively influence women's representation in institutional politics than the electoral system itself.[16]

Women in the Parliamentary Arena

The Slovene Parliament consists of the National Assembly and the National Council. The National Council is the upper house, which represents social, economic, and local interests and has forty representatives. The National Assembly consists of ninety deputies selected from among the citizens of Slovenia who are not, according to the Constitution, bound by any instructions. The way in which the National Assembly works has changed considerably from the early 1990s. Parliamentary work is in the process of normalization, with fewer irregular sessions, fewer committees and working bodies, more experienced MPs, and committees and commissions that have become more important.

From the gender perspective, there have been both negative and positive changes. On the negative side, there is no longer a special commission for gender equality as there was in the previous two terms. After the 2000 election, this committee was incorporated into the larger Committee for Home Affairs, and after the election in 2004 into the Committee for Petitions, Human Rights, and Equal Opportunities, which means that female MPs lost one important channel for their legislative work and one power position or channel for the realization of their interests. The Act on Equal Opportunities of Women and Men was accepted in June 2002 without major difficulties, and the proposal for change in the Constitution to provide a legal basis for positive discrimination laws in the field of politics and especially for elections was supported by a two-thirds majority of the MPs, to mention only some of the most important changes. Conversely, however, since the ideological turn in government (to the right of the center) in the 2004 election,[17] there has also been some backlash in the field of women's presence in politics. There is once again only one woman in a ministerial position in a newly formed government, and the ruling center-right coalition promotes family values.

Who are female deputies in the National Assembly? As a rule, women MPs come from the capital or larger urban centers. On average, women politicians in Slovenia are older than male politicians, a conclusion that is in harmony with those of numerous foreign researchers.[18] The data also show that women MPs have on average fewer children than male MPs (our count includes children who are economically independent as well as dependent children).[19] The formal qualifications of women MPs are generally higher than those of male MPs. The greatest number of male as well as female MPs come from the fields of the humanities, social sciences, and economics (see table 4.3).

Data on the numbers of male and female politicians occupying leading positions in the National Assembly confirm the thesis that politics is still a man's domain, as well as the rule according to which "the bigger the concentration of the political power, the smaller the number of women involved in politics." Women have never held the position of president of the National Assembly; this position is reserved for male politicians from the strongest political parties. The highest position that has been achieved by a woman MP is vice chair. During the last two periods, this position was twice occupied by women MPs from the ruling coalition, but in the current term all are men. A similar situation prevails in parliamentary groups: No woman MP has ever been the leader of a parliamentary group.

The National Assembly has standing commissions and committees that cover the area of ministerial activities, which can differ from one parliamentary term to another. In the 1996–2000 term,[20] there were no women

Table 4.3. *Female members of the Slovene Parliament by party and by occupation, 2000–2004*

Female Member	Party	Occupation
Sonja Areh Lavrič	SNS	Commercialist / pensioner
Silva Črnugelj	ZLSD	Higher librarian / director of a library
Lidija Majnik	LDS	Schoolteacher / director of a library
Irma Pavlinič Krebs	LDS	Lawyer / head of public administration
Majda Potrata	ZLSD	MA in Slovenian literature / assistant professor at a university
Marija Pozsonec	Representative of the National Communities	Schoolteacher
Danica Simšič	ZLSD	Journalist /editor at state television
Majda Širca	LDS	Art historian / editor at state television
Marija Ana Tisovic	NSi	Stomatologist / pensioner
Cveta Zalokar Oražem	LDS	Teacher of the Slovene language / mayor
Majda Zupan	NSi	Lawyer / manager in a bank

Note: SNS = Slovene National Party (Slovenska nacionalna stranka); ZLSD = United List of Social Democrats (Združena lista socialnih demokratov); LDS = Liberal Democracy of Slovenia; NSi = New Slovenia (Nova Slovenija).
Source: Data from the National Assembly of the Republic of Slovenia (http://www.dz-rs.si).

MPs among the twenty chairs of the eleven commissions and nine committees. Thus, in spite of greater representation (growing from 7.8 percent in 1991 to 13.3 percent in 2000), women MPs do not advance to leading positions within the National Assembly's working bodies. This situation can be attributed in part to the fact that the number of commissions and committees was reduced, so that competition for these positions increased. Another reason is that MPs with longer parliamentary experience are in a better position when candidates for important positions are chosen. Women miss this opportunity, because just one woman MP had been in Parliament for more than one term. As noted, women are found only in vice chair positions. In the current term, there are two women vice chairs, one from the opposition and the other from the governmental party, of twenty-four committees and commissions, and five deputy chairs, three from the opposition and two from the governmental parties.

In the previous term, there were several changes in women MPs' roles in committees and commissions. Because the number of committees and commissions has been reduced, women MPs sat on average on a lower number of committees. And because the issues that were originally handled by the Commission for Gender Equality have been relegated to the Committee for Home Affairs, because the Commission for Gender Equality was abolished, it is understandable that women MPs (seven) are concentrated in the Committee for Home Affairs. Most women MPs have chosen to work in two committees that deal with traditionally gender sensitive areas (professional segmentation)—the Committee for Health, Labor, Family, Social Policy, and the Disabled; and the Committee for Culture, Education, Youth, Science, and Sports—even though women do not chair these committees. The share of women in the Committee for Home Affairs, the Committee for Health, Labor, Family, Social Policy, and the Disabled, and the Committee for Culture, Education, Youth, Science, and Sport oscillates between 27.2 and 38.8 percent, which means that if they acted as a group, women would have considerable power, because they have almost achieved, or exceeded, a critical mass.

In the 2004 term, the situation did not significantly change. There were still more women members of the committees for health, culture, and the family. The two committees that deal with issues that have some connections to women's issues are the Committee for Petitions, Human Rights, and Equal Opportunities, and the Committee for Work, Family, Social Affairs, and the Disabled. The first has seven members and it is chaired (opposition party) and vice chaired (governmental party) by women. There are four women members in the second, which has sixteen members; men hold both leadership positions. In the last committee, some important laws that concern women's social situation were passed or are still being debated, despite the fact that there are few women members.

Evidence: Women Deputies' Views

We conducted face-to-face interviews with all twelve female MPs who served in the previous term and a corresponding number of male MPs from the same party parliamentary groups (twenty-four interviews in total were conducted; see chapter 10 for one interview). Social characteristics (age, education, profession) of male and female MPs interviewed were similar to those of the National Assembly as a whole.[21]

From the quantitative analysis of their work (speeches) in Parliament (in the last two terms), we found that female MPs most frequently discussed issues pertaining to labor, family, and social matters, followed by health care issues and culture. The least frequently discussed areas were defense and international relations. When MPs were asked about their legislative priorities and about their successful work in Parliament, we found a clear-cut difference between male and female MPs. The female MPs primarily listed laws and issues connected with questions on gender equality (the law on equal opportunity, change in the Constitution for equal gender representation, greater gender sensitivity in the use of language) among their successes, whereas the men's answers were more scattered. The male deputies, for example, never mentioned matters related to gender equality, which is why we conclude that male and female deputies thus have different policy priorities; women MPs clearly pay more attention to gender-sensitive issues.

The most important commitment of all parliamentarians regardless of their gender is the party. Women MPs are also very committed to their occupation or profession, and they often refer to their original occupations, such as the fact that they are doctors or lawyers, when they speak in Parliament. Being a member of an ethnic minority (Italian or Hungarian) is very important as well, because there is only one MP for each minority (see table 4.4).

We were also interested in differences among MPs belonging to different parties. To evaluate these differences, we asked the MPs about their opinions about women in politics. There is a high degree of consensus among Slovene MPs (almost 90 percent) that there should be more women

Table 4.4. Members of the Slovene National Assembly by party and gender, 2000–2004

Party	All	Number of Men	Number of Women	Percent Women
LDS	34	30	4	12
SDS	14	14	—	—
ZLSD	11	8	3	27
SLS+SKD	9	9	—	—
NSi	8	6	2	25
DeSUS	4	4	—	—
SNS	4	3	1	25
SMS	4	4	—	—
Representative of Hungarian and Italian minorities	2	1	1	50

Note: LDS = Liberal Democracy of Slovenia; SDS = Slovenian Democratic Party (Slovenska demokratska stranka); ZLSD = United List of Social Democrats (Združena lista socialnih demokratov); SLS+SKD = Slovene People's Party + Slovene Christian Democratic Party (Slovenska Ljudska stranka + Slovenska Krščanska Demokracija); NSi = New Slovenia (Nova Slovenija); DeSUS = Democratic Party of Pensioners of Slovenia (Demokratska stranka Upokojencev Slovenije); SNP = Slovene National Party (Slovenska nacionalna stranka); SMS = Party of Slovene Youth (Stranka Mladih Slovenije).
Source: Data from the National Assembly of the Republic of Slovenia (http://www.dz-rs.si).

in politics; and even more important, there is no female MP who thinks that this is not a problem. The differences among deputies who come from different political parties come to the surface when the question turns to the methods, tools, and actors needed to address this problem and whether special measures (including quotas) are needed. These differences appear among women as well: two-thirds of women deputies would support special measures (from the left-wing parties), and one-third would not (mostly from the right-wing parties). For the last group, quotas have negative connotations, and they generally understand quotas as a way to force women to enter politics and not as a means with which female candidates would only have equal chances to stand for election. One of the deputies, for example, said that he would support quotas only if the woman herself decides to enter politics. Similarly, 60 percent of males would support these, and the rest would not. But even in the left-wing parties, MPs are not unanimous. Opponents of using special measures to ensure greater participation of women in politics can be found among both genders on both sides of the ideological spectrum. These differences are greatest among the MPs of the parties on the right. However, because men have a majority in the National Assembly, no decision can be made without their consent.

Cross-party connections and discussions on the part of women deputies were influenced by their small numbers in Parliament. The fact that women representatives have not reached a critical mass affected the degree of difference that might otherwise have characterized their legislative work, as well as links between women representatives, and their joint actions. In the last two Parliaments, women were few not only in parliamentary groups (one woman per parliamentary group), but in the National Assembly as a whole (seven and twelve respectively). In the present National Assembly, their numbers rose slightly, but they worked jointly only within the LDS parliamentary group, in which there were five women. The overall impression is still that of an atomized group. Women deputies work primarily within parties, and because there is generally only one woman in any party's representation, they have little opportunity to work with other women. Our study did not find cross-party women connections. Allegiance to the party, its ideology, and politics is an important factor in women deputies' work (at times a constraining one), and it has an impact on their preferences and the decisions they make. Women parliamentarians have not yet formed a group, at least not officially, and only half support women's networking within Parliament.

Networking by women deputies with women's organizations and associations outside Parliament is also low. Only half the female MPs are members of any women's group. It is most often women from the left-wing parties who state that they are members of their parties' women's groups or wider coalitions (e.g., the cross-party Coalition for Equal Representation of Women in Public Life). These groups serve primarily as discussion or consultation groups rather than as pressure groups.

We found no significant difference between male and female self-proclaimed party obedience. The majority of deputies, regardless of gender, think that they are as obedient as the average MP. But women MPs see themselves as slightly more obedient than average, and male MPs see themselves as slightly less obedient than average. When their vote is in question, there are many fields where men and women deputies vote differently, and there is no significant gender difference—they often vote differently in the fields in which they are experts, either from their previous political or professional or life experiences (regional or local politics) or from their current political engagement.

We found that women voted in a more disciplined way and were highly loyal to their parties. The exception to this rule was evident in the case of the strongest women's group, LDS. The five women MPs from LDS form a circle that often sticks together. They harmonize their positions and then often appear en bloc toward their party group on the issues they consider important, including women's issues. But, on the whole, women MPs do not act in this way, but rather follow party ideology, priorities, and guidelines; women's issues are not high on these scales. Women deputies see themselves as "more disciplined" or disciplined to "the same degree" as their colleagues. When asked about voting differently than their party, only one female MP declared that she "often" voted differently from her party group.

The majority of women deputies got the impulse for their political career from their partners or husbands (private individuals), and male MPs were most often invited by their party leaders (public ones). Conversely, when women have an impact on male political careers, they appear as individuals (mothers or wives); in female careers, women as a social group appear as a stimulative factor. Women MPs were often supported by women as a group (coworkers or women in the party). Many female MPs said that their decision to enter politics was supported by their colleagues at work, by women's party groups, or by members of some other civil society groups, which means that women as a social group (an organized collectivity) had an impact on their activities.

There are also differences in the routes men and women take to Parliament and in the length of time it takes them to get there. It is most common that women develop their career from the local to the national level step by step, and that they have to work hard to be recognized as trustworthy. Male MPs developed their political careers more quickly than their female colleagues. The average period between the onset of one's political career and entrance into Parliament is 5.2 years for a male MP and twice that, 9.75 years, for a female MP.

What seems to concern women in politics the most is their treatment by some of their male colleagues, which shows that they do not see them as equal. MPs from the right of the political spectrum in particular would, in their informal conversations, often refer to women leaders as they are as women (young, nice, or beautiful) and less as they are as politicians with their own political positions, priorities, and options. They would also sometimes make sexist remarks in commenting on their points of view, revealing the impact of male sexual ideologies. Women deputies also criticize their male colleagues for not creating an environment in which they will not face hostility, sexism, or even hate speech. An environment in which all opinions will be respected—irrespective of whether they are expressed by a male or female, from "my party," or from the others—is still to be created.

With respect to the European level, some MPs (mostly from the left-wing parties) think that the period of the adaptation of Slovene legislation to the

European directives has had some positive results. These include the incorporation of paid nontransferable father's parental leave into national law, serious treatment of sexual harassment at work, and acceptance of the national Equality Law. In part, the 40 percent gender quota for the European Parliament has also been accepted, due to the pressure of European politics and politicians.

Conclusion

The position of women in Slovenia, including their socioeconomic situation, is not that bad in comparison with other countries that enter the European Union. The employment rate for women is 61 percent, which places Slovenia eighth among EU states, whereas the unemployment rate for women in 2007 was 8.9 percent and for men 6.1 percent; the average monthly gross earnings of women is 7 percent lower than that of men. The number of women studying at the tertiary level grew significantly—in 2006, the share of women graduates at the tertiary level was almost 62 percent.[22] The result of a prolonged education and the difficulties women have finding a first job is that young women prolong birth to a later age. Women also spend more time doing the work for their family members, both at home and outside it. From the research that has been done on these issues, we can assume that there is an effect on their decision to enter into politics.

Discussing more precisely the presence of women in Parliament, one can see that they still have not reached equal representation or the critical mass necessary to enact specific legislative decisions from which women can benefit. The fact that women representatives in the Slovene National Assembly have not reached a critical mass has affected the degree of difference that could otherwise characterize their legislative work, links between women representatives, and their joint actions. Women deputies still give the overall impression of being atomized individuals inside their parties and in Parliament. Thus, our study did not find cross-party connections among women deputies. Allegiance to the party, and to its ideology and politics, is an important factor and at times a constraining one in the work of women deputies, and it has an impact on their preferences and eventual decisions. Women parliamentarians have not yet formed a network, and only half support women's networking within Parliament; their networking outside Parliament with women's organizations and associations is more prevalent among these from left-wing parties and is still at a low level. Women's inability to introduce essential changes in parliamentary work in Slovenia is attributable not only to their low representation and modest representation in the hierarchical structure of Parliament, but also to the fact that they are mostly newcomers in Parliament, although not completely without political experience.

It is frequently expected that women in legislatures will pursue different priorities than men. If we take as evidence the types of commissions and committees in which women MPs in Slovenia participate (education, health care, culture), the types of questions they pose (education, health care, labor, family, social policy), and the types of bills they propose (education, health care, labor, family, social issues, environment, home affairs), we can conclude that women do have different priorities and that their legislative work is concentrated in the areas that significantly affect women. It is also significant that the Parliament elected in 2000 passed several bills that will very likely affect the quality of women's lives, among these the Employment Act, the Parenthood and Family Earnings Act, the Marriage and Family Relations Act, the Health Care and Health Insurance Act, and last but not least, the Equal Opportunities Act. It would therefore be wrong to claim that the changes we have witnessed—despite the fact that they are modest—are negligible, because even the minimal increase in the percentage of women in Parliament has produced greater awareness about the significance of gender equality and women's equal representation in politics.

However, in the last few years, there have also been some changes that can have a promising effect on women's position in society and in politics. In 2007, a new president of the state was elected, Danilo Türk, whose orientation comes from the center-left. Despite the fact that the president does not have executive power, he can play an important role; his moral judgment is very important in politics. In the same year, the LDS, one of the parliamentary parties, had a woman in the leading position—Katarina Kresal. In the election to the National Assembly in the autumn of 2008, all the parties are obliged to put at least 25 percent of women on their candidate lists—which (if they put them into the electoral units in which party has good chances) can help voters to elect more women. The fact that Slovenia held the Presidency of the Council of the European Union in the first half of 2008 also prevents some traditional parties from their goal of introducing (as promised in the last election) changes in the regulation of family life and demographic policy, same-sex marriages, violence against women, and the like.

Since the 40 percent quota for women in the European Parliament was introduced, 42 percent of the members of the EU from Slovenia have been women; after the 20 percent (starting) quotas for local elections, the share of women city councillors almost doubled (from 13 to 21.5 percent). If the trend on quotas continues, there are additional possibilities of improving the situation of women in politics in Slovenia with the next parliamentary election in the autumn of 2008, when the 25 percent quota was to be introduced.

Notes

1. Vlasta Jalušič, "Socially Adapted, Politically Marginalized: Women in Post-Socialist Slovenia," in *Women, Society and Politics in Yugoslavia,* ed. Sabrina P. Ramet (University Park: Pennsylvania State University Press, 1999), 51–66.

2. Marilyn Rueschemeyer, "Introduction," in *Women in the Politics of Postcommunist Eastern Europe,* rev. and expanded edition, ed. Marilyn Rueschemeyer (Armonk, N.Y.: M. E. Sharpe, 1998), 6.

3. Vida Tomšič was one of them: a party leader who dealt with the so-called woman's question under socialism, was the most important figure in changing the public image of socialist women to a more enlightened, liberal, and political one. For more information, see Milica G. Antić and Ksenija H. Vidmar, "The Construction of Woman's Identity in Socialism: The Case of Slovenia," in *Women's Movements, Networks and Debates in Post-Communist Countries in the 19th and 20th Centuries,* ed. Edith Saurer, Margareth Lazinger, and Elisabeth Frysak (Cologne: Bohlau Verlag, 2006), 291–307.

4. For more information, see Vida Tomšič, *Ženska, delo, družina, družba* (Women, work, family, society) (Ljubljana: Komunist, 1978); Maca Jogan, *Ženske in diskriminacija* (Women and discrimination) (Ljubljana: Delavska enotnost, 1986); and Tanja Rener, "Uveljavljanje žensk v delegatskem sistemu," in *Ženske in diskriminacija,* ed. Maca Jogan (Ljubljana: Delavska Enotnost, 1986), 114–29.

5. Jogan, *Ženske in diskriminacija,* 31.

6. Ibid.

7. For more about women in public life in the period of transition, see Eva. D. Bahovec, ed., "Gender and Governance: The Civic and Political Participation and Representation of Women in Central and Eastern Europe," Faculty of Arts and Society for Cultural Studies, Ljubljana 2005.

8. Rueschemeyer, *Women in the Politics of Postcommunist Eastern Europe,* 6.

9. Milica G. Antić and Eva D. Bahovec, "Feminizem, liberalizem, demokracija," in *Meje demokracije,* ed. Darko Štrajn (Ljubljana: Liberalna akademija, 1995), 171.

10. Danica Fink-Hanfer and Miro Haček, *Demokratični prehodi I* (Ljubljana: FDV, 2000), 294.

11. Danica Fink-Hafner and Milica G. Antić, "The 2002 Presidential Elections in Slovenia," *Electoral Studies,* no. 23 (2004): 143–82.

12. See http://www.uradni-list.si/1/objava.jsp?urlid=200572&stevilka=3215.

13. See http://www.uradni-list.si/1/objava.jsp?urlid=200678&stevilka=3401.

14. For more about quotas in Slovenia, see Milica G. Antić and Maruša Gortnar, "Gender Quotas in Slovenia: A Short Analysis of Failures and Hopes," *European Political Science* 3, no. 3 (2004): 73–79, and Milica G. Antić and Lokar Sonja, "The Balkans:

From Total Rejection to Gradual Acceptance of Gender Quotas," in *Women, Quotas and Politics,* ed. Drude Dahlerup ed. (London: Routledge, 2006); and www.idea.int.

15. These emerged from compromise and negotiation among transitional actors. In the negotiations among the ruling government in 1990 and the newly established parties, the former supported a majoritarian system. The latter favored some form of proportional representation. Because no actor had a clear majority, the 1990 elections were held with three different systems for the three chambers of parliament. In the aftermath, most of the numerous small parties preferred a clear proportional representation system; others favored some sort of mixed system that would preserve elements of direct MP-voter linkage and overcome the perceived weaknesses of proportional representation. Because the final rules required a special two-thirds majority, the electoral system that emerged was a complex version of proportional representation with elements of majoritarianism mixed in. Also see "Franc Grad, The New Electoral System," in *Making a New Nation: The Formation of Slovenia,* ed. Danica Fink-Hafner and John R. Robbins (Aldershot, U.K.: Dartmouth, 1997), 172–81.

16. Vlasta Jalušič and Milica G. Antić, *Ženske-politike-možnosti: Perspektive politike enakih možnosti v srednji in vzhodni Evropi* (Women-politics-equal opportunities: Prospects for gender equality politics in Central and Eastern Europe) (Ljubljana: Mirovni inštitut, Inštitut za sodobne družbene in politične študije, 2001).

17. For more, see Danica Fink-Hafner, "Slovenia," *European Journal of Political Research* 45, nos. 7–8 (2006): 1260, 1265.

18. See Richard E. Matland and Kathleen A. Montgomery, eds., *Women's Access to Political Power in Post-Communist Europe* (Oxford: Oxford University Press, 2003), 23.

19. For more, see Milica G. Antić and Gabriella Ilonszki, *Women in Parliamentary Politics: Hungarian and Slovene Cases Compared* (Ljubljana: Peace Institute, 2003).

20. See ibid. for research on women's activities in the National Assembly in the previous term.

21. For more detailed information, see ibid.

22. See http://www.stat.si/doc/pub/dejstva_zenske_moski.pdf.

Chapter 5

Women in Parliament
in the Czech Republic

Sharon L. Wolchik

After the end of Communism in what was then Czechoslovakia, expectations about the impact this change of regime would have on women's status and opportunities were mixed. On the one hand, some expected that the end of the Communist Party's monopoly on power and the repluralization of politics that rapidly ensued would provide new opportunities for women to articulate political views, band together with others to form new political parties and nongovernmental organizations (NGOs), run for office, and pressure political leaders to take action on issues of interest to them.

On the other hand, the new opportunities to be active in the economic sector—as well as the decrease in public spending, price liberalization, and the end of government subsidies for many previously low-cost services, together with the newly competitive nature of politics and the freedom not to

The author thanks Petra Rakušanová and her colleagues at the Institute of Sociology of the Czech Academy of Sciences for their help in conducting the interviews and providing some of the background materials on which this analysis is based.

be involved—were seen as factors that might well create barriers for women interested in becoming political leaders. The end of real, if unofficial, quotas that had maintained a certain level of women's representation in the effective as well as symbolic elites during the Communist era also was seen as something that would be likely to lead to a decrease in women's representation in political leadership. In fact, as the pages that follow reveal, the picture is more complicated than either one of these sets of expectations implies. As more optimistic observers expected, the change in political regime did indeed open new opportunities for women. Nevertheless, there are still very real obstacles for women in reaching positions of leadership and using these positions to make a difference in women's lives once they achieve them.

The discussion that follows focuses on the experiences, perceptions, and activities of those women who have achieved positions of political leadership. In addition to publicly available information concerning the composition of Parliament and its various bodies, it draws in part on background materials provided by Petra Rakušanová and other analysts at the Institute of Sociology of the Czech Academy of Science and in part on in-depth interviews conducted in the spring and summer of 2004 with thirteen women members of the Chamber of Deputies, the lower house of the Czech Parliament. The deputies interviewed were drawn from all the parties represented in Parliament at that time.

Women Leaders: Numbers

In Czechoslovakia and, after 1993, in the Czech Republic, as elsewhere in the post-Communist world, the number of women in Parliament decreased in the early elections after the fall of Communism. Women's representation among the national parliamentary elite fell from between 16 and 23 percent during the Communist era to 10.7 percent after the June 1990 parliamentary elections. In June 1992, there were twenty-six women deputies (8.7 percent of the total) in the Federal Assembly and twenty-two (10.7 percent) in the Czech National Council.[1] Women comprised 15 percent of legislators (thirty) in Parliament in June 1996. There were thirty-four women in the Parliament elected in 2002, when they comprised 17 percent of the total number of deputies in the lower chamber and ten women in the Senate, where they account for 12.4 percent of all senators. In 2006, women made up 15.5 percent of deputies in the lower chamber and 13.5 percent of members of the Senate.

As in the Communist era, when women in both the symbolic govern-mental elite and the effective Communist Party elite had higher levels of turnover and lower tenure in office than their male counterparts,[2] there is a high degree of turnover among women deputies. Approximately 40 percent (twelve women) of the women in Parliament in 2006, for example, were newly elected. Ten were elected for the first time in 2002, four in 1998, and three in 1996. Only two women have served longer than 10 years. One, a member of the Christian Democratic Union–Peoples' Party (CDU-PP), was first elected to Parliament under the Communists in 1986. Women parlia-mentarians' average tenure is 4.4 years.

Women in Parliament: Social Backgrounds

Although the number of women in legislative office decreased in the first decade after the end of Communism, this decrease in and of itself cannot be equated with a decline in women's role in political leadership. First, the na-ture of the positions themselves has changed. After 1989, legislators were not merely members of a body that was largely a rubber stamp for decisions made by the Communist Party but rather members of the country's effec-tive elite. The women elected to Parliament after 1989 also differ from their predecessors in many other important ways.

One of the most important of these was in the area of education. All the women deputies and senators in the Czech Parliament for whom informa-tion was available in 1997 had higher educations. Many had advanced de-grees; 5 had medical degrees, 7 had law degrees, and 4 had PhDs.[3] Educa-tional levels appear to be similarly high among women deputies elected in 2002; 6 women deputies have law degrees, 1 has a medical degree, 5 have engineering or scientific degrees, and 6 have other advanced degrees.[4]

Table 5.1. Women deputies in the lower house of Parliament, Czech Republic, various election years

Election Year	Number of Women	Percent Women
1996	30	15.0
1998	30	15.0
2002	34	17.0
2006	31	15.5

Source: Czech Statistical Office (http://www.czso.cz/eng/redakce.nsf/i/home).

Twenty-five of the 33 women deputies elected to Parliament in 2002 (75.8 percent) had university degrees, compared to 85.6 percent (143 of 167) of male deputies.[5] There are important differences in the educational levels of both men and women deputies from different political parties. All the women deputies of the CDU-PP and 90 percent of those from the Social Democratic Party (SDP) had university degrees, as did 75 percent of women members of the Civic Democratic Party (CDP). Two-thirds of the Communist Party's women deputies and 75.8 percent (25 of 33) of the party's male deputies have university degrees.

Women elected to Parliament after 1989 also differ from their Communist predecessors in another important way. Rather than comprising a disproportionately high number of those who were workers or agricultural workers compared to their male counterparts, who were overwhelmingly drawn from the state and party apparatus,[6] women leaders elected after 1989 have had occupations far more similar to those of their male counterparts. In the early years after 1989 in particular, these occupations differed in important ways from those typically found in the legislatures of more established democracies in Europe and the United States. Thus, in 1990, women parliamentarians included several writers, numerous doctors, an economist, and several other academics. However, the career paths and occupations of these women leaders' male counterparts also were not standard-issue parliamentary backgrounds. Male deputies in that year included creative artists, writers, engineers, doctors, state officials, and former dissidents.[7]

What is important here is less the fact that men's and women's occupations differ than the fact that, although different in many cases from those found in more established legislatures, the occupations and careers of the women deputies elected since 1989 have provided them with skills and experiences that have been as relevant (or as lacking in relevance) to the process of governing in a democratic state as those of the men elected to Parliament since that time. Coupled with their educational levels, the women in the Czech Parliament are thus currently in a better position than their predecessors to have an influence on policymaking.

As a result of these trends, women parliamentarians have had skills and tools for wielding influence that have been much closer to those of their male counterparts than did women during the Communist era. They also have come from professional backgrounds that, although they reflected the large degree of occupational segregation by gender in the labor force, also more closely resemble those of their male counterparts.

Age differences among men and women parliamentarians are relatively small. The average age of the women deputies elected in 2002 was forty-seven years. The oldest two women were fifty-eight and the youngest was twenty-three. Gender-related age differences varied to some degree by party and were greatest among deputies affiliated with the right-of-center Freedom Party–Democratic Union (FP-DU), where there was an approximately fourteen-year difference in the average age of women deputies and all deputies. Differences are significantly lower among deputies from other parties. The average age of women elected to the Chamber of Deputies in the June 2006 elections was forty-eight. The oldest woman was sixty-three, and the youngest was twenty-six when elected.

Party Affiliations

As is the case for most legislators in the Czech Republic, most women deputies and senators are members of political parties who are elected to Parliament as part of a party list. In the Parliament elected in 2002, the women deputies were fairly evenly distributed among the SDP (eight), the Communist Party (seven), and the CDP (six). One woman, who has been in Parliament since 1986, was elected on the slate of the CDU-PP. Taken together, there were considerably more women deputies in left-of-center than in right-of-center parties at that time. This tendency for women to be better represented among deputies of left-of-center parties is similar in many other post-Communist states and may reflect the fact that these parties were not as affected by the backlash against the whole idea of women's equality that occurred soon after the end of Communism.[8] It also reflects the fact that the SDP has a 25 percent quota for women candidates, although the party did not field that many candidates in 2002.

However, in the Czech Republic, there has been a fair degree of fluctuation in this respect. In 1990, women accounted for 21.9 percent of deputies of the Communist Party, compared with 14 percent of all deputies to the Czech National Council. Although this tendency continued in Slovakia after the breakup of the joint state, most women deputies elected in the Czech Republic in 1992 ran on the lists of the right-of-center CDP. In 1996, women constituted the highest proportion of deputies in the extreme-right-wing Republican Party (five of nine, or 55.5 percent) and the Communist Party (five of eighteen, or 22.7 percent). The largest number of women deputies was found in the SDP, although they accounted for a somewhat smaller percentage. In the 2006 elections, women accounted for 50 percent of deputies of the Green Party, compared with 15.5 percent for the entire Chamber of Deputies. The CDP and SDP sat the largest number of women deputies (nine each), although women represented only 11 and 12 percent, respectively, of all deputies seated by those parties in the Chamber of Deputies (table 5.2).

Women's proportion of candidates for the lower house of Parliament increased from 20.2 to 26.1 percent between the 1996 and 2002 elections. However, the proportion of women candidates who were elected decreased from 72 percent in 1996 to 65 percent in 2002.[9] In recent elections, women have formed the highest proportion of candidates of those parties that have not received enough votes to gain seats in Parliament. In the 2002 elections, there were more women candidates in nonparliamentary parties in nine of the fourteen voting districts.[10]

Committees, Activities, and Cabinet Positions

Women deputies sit on a broad range of committees, from those dealing with foreign affairs and defense to those responsible for social policy and health care. They also serve as chair or vice chair of a variety of committees, including the Mandates and Immunity Committee, the Constitutional and Legal Committee, and the Committee on Science, Education, Culture,

Table 5.2. Women deputies in the Czech Republic by party, 1996–2006

Party	1996		1998		2002		2006	
	Number	Percent	Number	Percent	Number	Percent	Number	Percent
CDP	7	10.29	7	11.11	8	13.79	9	11.11
SDP	11	18.04	11	14.87	10	14.29	9	12.16
KSCM	5	22.73	6	25.00	12	29.29	8	30.77
KDU-CSL[a]	2	11.11	3	15.00	4	12.90	2	15.38
SPR-RSL	5	27.79	—	—	—	—	—	—
US	—	—	3	15.78	—	—	—	—
SZ	—	—	—	—	—	—	3	50.00
Total	30	15.00	30	15.00	34	17.00	31	15.50

Note: — = none; CDP = Civic Democratic Party; SDP = Social Democratic Party; KSCM = Communist Party of Bohemia and Moravia; KDU-CSL = Christian Democratic Union–Czech People's Party; SPR-RSL = Rally for the Republic–Republican Party of Czechoslovakia; US = Freedom Union; SZ = Green Party.
[a]In 2002, KDU-CSL ran in a coalition with US-DEU.
Source: Czech Statistical Office (http://www.czso.cz/eng/redakce.nsf/i/home).

Youth, and Sport. However, the largest number of women deputies elected in 2002 was found on the Committee on Science, Education, Culture, Youth, and Sport. Four of the women deputies also served on the Standing Commission on the Family and Equal Opportunity. It is also important to note that most committees have from three to five vice chairs.

In comparison with their percentage of all members, women deputies elected in 2002 were less likely to be members of the most prestigious committees, including the Budget Committee and the Committee for the Economy (on which there were no women), as well as those that deal with defense and security, European affairs, foreign affairs, and foreign policy.[11] Both men and women deputies see those committees on which men predominate as the most prestigious. Women deputies are more likely to consider all committees, aside from those that deal with education, youth, culture, and sports, and the Mandate and Immunity Committee, as significant.[12] In 1995 and 1997, the Budget Committee, the Foreign Affairs Committee, and the Committee for Science and Education passed the highest number of resolutions. There was little difference in the frequency of meetings between committees with varying proportions of women deputies during this period.[13]

Most women deputies interviewed were satisfied with their committee assignments. One woman who served on the budget committee noted, "I was afraid that I would be put on the committee on labor and social affairs, as this is traditionally seen as a position for women. However, I got my wish to serve on the budget committee, and I am very happy to do so." Those women who serve on committees generally thought to deal with issues of special concern to women also appear to be happy with their assignments and see their work in those committees as a way to make a difference, though they do not necessarily see themselves as women's advocates.

Since 1990, women have held ten positions as ministers in the Czech government. Women have headed the ministries of Commerce; Trade and Tourism; Justice (two women); Health (twice); Transportation; and Education, Youth, and Sport. There were two women ministers in the Czech government formed after the 2002 elections. Petra Buzková, a lawyer who is a member of the SDP, was minister of education, youth, and sport, and formerly served as the deputy speaker of the Chamber of Deputies. Marie Soucková served as minister of health until her resignation in the spring of 2004. Both Buzková and Soucková also served as vice chairs of the Czech SDP. There were four women in the government formed in 2007 after seven months of negotiations following the June 2006 elections. One of these continued as minister of defense until late January 2009, when she became deputy prime minister; a second woman served as minister without portfolio in charge of human and minority rights until late January 2009. A third woman served briefly as minister of culture but resigned two weeks after her appointment over a conflict about a vice minister; and another served briefly as minister of education. In late January 2009, Daniela Filipová was named minister of health (see table 5.3).

Women's Routes to Political Office

Most of the women deputies interviewed for this project were what we might call "accidental" deputies, at least the first time they stood for election. Thus, although most had been active in some form of public life at lower levels, and several had served as party activists at higher levels, many of the women interviewed noted that they decided to pursue a political career after their party or others suggested that they run. The response of a deputy elected for the first time in 2002 reflects this path to higher office: "I had been active in party and municipal politics and then I was offered the chance to run for Parliament. I had the confidence of the membership of the party." Another deputy who had been active in the NGO sector and was asked to run by a coalition of center-right parties noted,

> I was asked to run. They said I needed to be involved and could not remain aloof from politics. I thought about it for two days and was very anxious. Then I decided that I had been leading up to political engagement my whole life, although I kept myself apart from it [in the NGO sector].

Other women deputies interviewed highlighted their desire to have an impact on policymaking or to continue the work they had pursued on lower levels in Parliament as their main motives for running for office.

Table 5.3. Women in government in the Czech Republic, 2009

Name	Portfolio
Vlasta Parkanová	Deputy prime minister
Daniela Filipová	Minister of health

Source: "Czech President to Appoint New Ministers on Friday," *Ceske noviny* (http://www.ceskenoviny.cz/tisk_clanku_view.php?id=355758&BACK=/news/index_view).

Despite the somewhat happenstance nature of many women leaders' initial decisions to run for office, many in fact had had substantial political experience before running for Parliament. Several had been members of their parties since shortly after the end of Communism in 1989 and the rebirth or founding of their political parties in 1990. One had been active as a student in the Communist-era youth organization and had been a member of the party for twenty-seven years. Several of the deputies began their activity at the local level as members of their municipal councils and worked their way up the ladder of political office before being tapped by their parties to run for Parliament. As a deputy from the center-right CDP put it, "After the [1989 Velvet] Revolution, I first joined Civic Forum and then the CDP. I went though all its functions at all levels: basic membership, local, district, regional functions, the central committee of the party. All levels. Completely all. And at the same time I also worked in the area of politics and became a member of the municipal council and later vice mayor of my town—so all kinds of functions."

Perceptions of Political Roles

Most of the women interviewed identified discussion of pending legislation and participation in the work of their committees as their most important task as deputies. Several also noted their work with constituents, including holding office hours in their districts and trying to resolve issues raised by individual constituents, as an important part of their responsibilities. As one indicated: "Like all deputies, I attend meetings of my committee and Parliament and participate in the work of my committee. Since I have a wide spectrum of experience, I take positions in areas of my expertise." Another stated: "I would divide it into two things. I give close attention to lawmaking activities. I am a teacher, so I follow education and public administration. I am part of a deputy's club. I also take part in the preparation of laws and then I work for my own region on local issues. . . . I also am in communication with the mayors of my region. . . . I also work for women and children, and in the area of sport and culture, and for handicapped people."

All but two of the deputies interviewed perceived themselves as representing the interests of citizens in their electoral district rather than as advocates for women or for some other social group. Two, including one from the Communist Party, saw themselves as representing the interests of a particular social group. One of the women who identified herself as a representative of all citizens in her district nonetheless noted that, because women are a large part of the population in her district, she also represents women's interests. As the quotation above illustrates, another woman deputy identified work for women and children as among her most important activities.

Most women felt that they were respected in Parliament by their male counterparts. "I would say yes [that women are equally respected]. I don't see a problem. There are cases in which women don't speak up, but there are also men who don't. When a woman is active, it is not a problem," a deputy who came to Parliament after working in the NGO sector noted. However, many agreed that there were special issues women deputies faced that their male colleagues did not. "We are respected to the same degree," a woman deputy born in 1965 stated, "but there is a physiological difference. If a woman deputy has children and a household. . . . It's not a question of professions but the division of labor that makes the difference."

Relationships with Parties, Constituents, and Interest Groups

Not surprisingly, as the lower house of the Czech Parliament is elected using a closed list system, most women deputies claimed close relationships with their parties. All but two women (including one who was an independent who ran on the Union of Freedom list) indicated that their party had actively supported their campaign. Most also stated that their parties' ideologies or programs were important factors that helped them win their elections. High levels of loyalty to their parties were also evident in women's responses to questions concerning the extent to which they agreed with their parties' positions on issues of special concern to women. As a member of the SDP stated, "My party is generally good on women's issues. I don't have any disagreements with them on this." Another, who was critical of her party's position on gender issues, nonetheless noted that she generally voted with her party on policies that had a particular impact on women. An SDP deputy, however, indicated that she had broken with her party's position in a vote on social support to allow women with small children to work limited hours.

Most women deputies felt that they had some influence on their party's decisions, although the area varied. Most also indicated that they had frequent interactions with others in their parties and their parties' clubs in Parliament. Women leaders were much less likely to have frequent contact with deputies from other parties aside from those on their committees. Similarly, most deputies indicated that they had limited contact with other women leaders, aside from those in their parties. Several, however, indicated that they worked closely with women deputies on their committees and frequently discussed issues that came before the committee with them. One deputy laughingly noted that she often talked to other women deputies in the ladies' restroom. When asked what they discussed, she indicated that their conversations generally dealt with family or personal issues, but sometimes included issues before the committees or Parliament.

Attitudes Concerning Issues of Special Concern to Women and Gender Equality

As noted above, very few women deputies view themselves specifically as advocates for women. Only one of those interviewed indicated that she had spoken in plenary session in support of a law to forbid discrimination against women. One woman indicated that her party had delegated two other women parliamentarians to speak on the issue. Another, a Communist Party deputy, indicated that she did not speak but supported the law. Still others, however, who were members of center-right parties, indicated that they opposed the antidiscrimination law. Several women deputies mentioned their opposition to what they termed "positive discrimination," or affirmative action, in this connection. "I think some measures should be adopted to prevent discrimination," a deputy first elected in 2002 noted, "but on the other side, it is not good to create positive discrimination because it causes reactions (against women)." A deputy from the center-right CDP, who saw a great deal of discrimination against women in many areas and saw herself as an advocate for women, stated, "The issue is rather to create the same conditions for men and women. I don't think women should get preference; this is not good. It is simply enough for women to have the same conditions."

At the same time, however, several women deputies indicated that they had been active on issues of particular interest to women, including maternity allowances, labor law, and domestic violence. Another indicated that she had worked to get a law allowing midwives to work independently through Parliament (see chapter 11 for an additional perspective). Several deputies stated that they had not been active at all on "women's" issues.

When asked to identify the most important problems facing women in the Czech Republic at present, most women deputies identified unemployment and the employment problems of women over fifty years of age as critical problems. Several also identified the lack of services to support working women, the need for equal reward for equal work, regulations governing adoption, and services as important issues. A deputy first elected in 2002 identified discrimination in obtaining jobs and in some political parties, and equal pay for equal work, as key issues.

Most deputies stated that it was necessary to approach issues facing women as part of larger social issues, rather than by themselves. As one SDP deputy put it, "We have to deal with these issues generally, because women's issues and other issues come into this." Another deputy who came to Parliament after years of working in the NGO sector noted, "We can't separate women's issues from other issues: in the area of civic rights, there is no difference between men and women." This same deputy also shared an example from her own experience to illustrate her perspective: "I am on the commission on the family. There was a woman who divorced a husband who had a high position in the police and two children. So there was a problem of how this woman should be protected. But this was not a woman's problem, but a society-wide problem. It was a problem of how the police functioned." A Communist Party deputy, however, stated that women's issues need to be addressed separately if they are to be resolved.

When asked what is necessary to achieve equality between men and women, deputies frequently referred to differences in men's and women's roles in the family as critical. One deputy stated that "equality won't ever occur, because there is a physiological difference that can't be overcome. We can do something in women's favor, but we can't ever do it [achieve equality]." Another, who reported that she had a great deal of influence on her party's positions on women's issues as well as on other decisions within her party, stated: "I am someone who built her own career and I don't need anyone and I don't think I need any help or protection or that I've been discriminated against."

Other deputies, however, mentioned the need for women to organize, more attention to services, and change in men's and women's attitudes. A deputy with a background in the NGO sector noted, "I haven't thought of this. But . . . I think this question is difficult. Laws can't do it. . . . Women have to set forth their demands more forcefully. We need to do it ourselves, not by legislative means, or antidiscrimination legislation. We can't strengthen women's equality this way. There should be a change of consciousness in the future, but that it can be legislated, no, I don't think so. Financial support for young women and mothers should help."

Women leaders identified several measures needed to increase the number of women in high political positions. These included changes in women's views of their roles; the creation of better possibilities for women to balance work and family; and more attention to attracting women candidates on the part of political parties. The response of a deputy who was a member of the SDP was typical: "What would be necessary? Better domestic arrangements. Women still have responsibility for the household. Young women can't go into politics. Young men can do it, as most of the household is cared for by the wife. What is necessary? Services, so women can do it. And good partners." Another deputy also referred to women's domestic situation: "The problem is women and their families. Not everyone can risk it [a political career]. If you have someone good like a grandmother to help you, it's OK; if not, it's hard." Still another responded that it was "time and emotional demands. Women's can't do it because of the conflict between politics as a profession and their children. It is always a sacrifice for women. I don't know what is needed, really. I think politics is for people over fifty, and this is true two times for women, after they have raised their kids." These responses parallel the identification of loss of time with family as one of the greatest disadvantages women deputies see in being parliamentarians.[14]

The Impact of Women's Representation on Policy and Factors That Affect Women Deputies' Influence

As the above analysis indicates, the number of women among parliamentarians in the Czech Republic has increased. Although they are still less often found in positions of leadership within the body or elevated to positions as ministers, women leaders have the educational and occupational backgrounds needed to participate in policymaking effectively. Analysis of the voting records and speeches in Parliament of women deputies indicates that many women are making good use of their opportunity to question government ministers, submit legislative proposals, and participate in debate within the chamber on significant issues of national import.

Women leaders report that they have varying degrees of influence within Parliament and in determining their parties' positions. Most feel that they can make a difference at least some of the time, either through their work on committees in formulating and revising proposals for laws or as advocates for their constituents. Many identify the ability to gain a broader perspective on public issues, have access to more information than most citizens, and influence policy as the most gratifying aspects of their jobs.

Some women deputies are also developing links to women's groups and other advocates for women outside Parliament. A recent example of this cooperation occurred in the area of legislation about domestic violence. In this instance, a coalition of women's groups and interested women parliamentarians worked together to increase public awareness of this problem and affect public policies that deal with it.[15]

However, there are also limits to the influence women deputies can exert, particularly with regard to serving as advocates for women. The first of these reflects the fact that, although their level of representation in the national legislative elite is equivalent to or better than that of women in many European Union member countries and other developed nations, numbers do seem to count. At 17 percent of the total number of deputies in the lower house after the 2002 elections and 15.5 percent after those of 2006, women are still a minority of deputies. As discussed in chapter 1 of this volume, scholars have recently questioned the utility of the concept of "critical mass"—the notion that there is a certain threshold in terms of the proportion of total members, often set at 30 percent, that is needed to allow members of minorities or other disadvantaged groups to air issues of particular concern to them or have the ability to get controversial items onto the legislative agenda. Some scholars, in fact, have argued that increases in the numbers of women can lead to hostility toward women deputies and feminist objectives; others have suggested that solidarity among women deputies, and the likelihood that they will work together on issues of particular concern to women or serve as advocates for gender equality, may be greatest when there are fewer women in a legislative body rather than a greater number. Still others have linked the effectiveness of quotas for women in public office, and hence an increase in the numbers of such women, to strong links to women's organizations.[16] The experience of women in the Czech legislature cannot be used to test the impact of large numbers of women legislators on policymaking or the nature of interactions in the legislature as a workplace, because their numbers remain small. The relatively small proportion of women deputies in the legislature has not, however, led them to seek solidarity with each other, as some scholars have hypothesized might occur.

There are also other factors that limit the influence women deputies can have on policy outcomes. These include legislative procedures. The fact that most bills the Czech legislature considers are introduced by the government rather than by individual deputies further limits the influence of women parliamentarians.[17]

The party recruitment system is another barrier to greater influence on the part of women in Parliament. An electoral system that relies on party lists could theoretically be more favorable to higher levels of women's representation, because parties could, by placing women high on their lists where they are sure to be seated in Parliament if the party receives enough votes to meet the threshold requirement, ensure that women are well represented in Parliament.[18] The ability of party leaders to manipulate the slate of candidates is one reason why some in the Czech Republic and elsewhere in the region have once again called for the use of quotas to ensure that women are adequately represented in political leadership. At the same time, the party recruitment system, by placing control of political recruitment in the hands of the party leadership, means that the women, as well as the men, who run for office are dependent on the party for support (as well as for information and resources while in office), and for election. Coupled with the tradition of strong party discipline in the Czech Republic that dates back to the interwar period, the position of the party as the electorate of first resort can limit women's ability to focus attention on issues of particular interest to women, particularly if the parties on which they are dependent have well-defined stands on these issues. A party-based recruitment system and a closed-list proportional representation electoral system also limit women deputies' ability to cooperate across party lines.[19]

The Standing Committee on the Family and Equal Opportunity, to which several women deputies belonged in 2006, offers a mechanism for overcoming the divisions among women deputies that result from their integration into the apparatuses of their own parties. Working with NGOs and experts on women's issues from the universities and the Academy of Sciences, this committee has the potential to raise issues of particular concern to women. In theory, it can also serve as a forum for women deputies to air their views independently of their parties, particularly on issues of special salience to women. However, to date, there is little indication that it has done so.

Political attitudes are a final barrier to greater influence by women parliamentarians. At the mass level, women's ability to be influential leaders is limited by lingering perceptions and beliefs that politics is still not quite an appropriate arena of activity for women. The image of the old Communist Party woman functionary seems to be fading, particularly among younger groups of voters, but there are still those in Czech society who see politics as too dirty for women, not of critical importance for women, or somehow the proper domain of men. Most men and women also feel that men have greater opportunities to succeed in politics than women.[20] These attitudes, of course, are less important for the day-to-day work of women parliamentarians once they achieve office than they are in depressing the total number of women in office. But even in Parliament, they are reflected to some extent in the low representation of women deputies in the committees perceived to matter most and women deputies' limited representation in parliamentary leadership and cabinet positions.

Women parliamentarians' activities are also influenced by popular attitudes concerning gender roles and women's equality. As the Czech historian Hana Havelková notes, popular attitudes toward gender equality are complex and difficult to take at face value.[21] Nonetheless, it is significant that most women still see politics as an aberrant activity for women, and few want to run for public office. Women as well as men are less likely to support women who run for office, and there is little popular support for viewing women's issues apart from those of society as a whole.[22] In these circumstances, there is little popular pressure for women deputies to present themselves or act as champions of women's interests or advocates for gender equality.

Elite political culture also limits the extent to which women can advance in leadership positions or become active advocates for women in the policy-initiating and policymaking arenas. Surveys of women political leaders conducted in the mid-1990s found that many were reluctant to see or portray themselves as advocates for women. As is the case with many of their male counterparts, these women preferred to see themselves as advocates for all citizens, not just one group of citizens. They also did not feel that their positions were secure enough to take on the parties' bureaucracies on these issues.[23]

A final barrier to greater advocacy by women members of Parliament for women's issues arises from the limited contact that those political leaders who obtain their positions through partisan channels have with NGO leaders. The limited ties between NGOs focusing on women's issues and political leaders in part reflect the third sector's general distrust of politics. Political leaders in turn, sometimes feel that the NGO sector, which does not have the responsibility to govern, can distort public debate and take too strong an advocacy position. This mutual distrust and the perception that the two areas have very different missions have limited cooperation between women leaders and NGOs working on issues of special concern to women or related to gender equality until fairly recently. In the case noted above focused on domestic violence, a coalition of women politicians and activists from a variety of women's NGOs worked together to raise awareness of the issue and encourage political leaders to formulate and enact legislation making domestic violence in the home a criminal act and extending the protections of the state to victims of domestic abuse.[24]

The Czech Republic's accession to the European Union has also influenced women deputies' roles in Parliament. As part of the accession process, Parliament adopted laws that prohibited discrimination based on sex as part of the Labor Code and Act on Employment. It also included a provision prohibiting sexual harassment in the workplace in the Labor Code in January 2001. However, very few cases have been brought to the courts on the basis of these measures.[25] The need to adapt Czech law to EU norms before accession triggered another round of intense discussion of family roles and responsibilities, and of the public impact of sexual orientation, and has also been reflected in research on how to increase the representation of women in politics.[26] It also focused attention on the extent to which women legislators can or should pay special attention to their common interests as women and roles as women's advocates, and highlighted the question of how women leaders can balance these concerns and their broader roles as citizens' representatives and members of political parties. Few of the women deputies interviewed, however, identified the EU as a significant source of support for gender equality. The potential influence of the EU's focus on issues related to gender equality, therefore, has yet to be realized, beyond the adoption of those measures necessary for accession. As integration proceeds, however, and as more deputies gain experience in EU-related activities, the role that EU support for gender equality plays in legitimizing public and elite discussion of issues related to such equality can be expected to increase.

Conclusions

The role of women deputies in the Czech Parliament is quite different from that of their predecessors in the Communist era. Not only is the role of the legislature itself markedly different in the current political system, but the kind of women who become members of the legislature is also very different. Equal to their male counterparts in education and professional accomplishment for the most part, these women deputies have the skills and experiences needed to act as forceful and effective legislators. The numbers of women in the legislature have also increased since the first free elections of 1990, particularly in the lower house, where women's representation among all deputies has increased from twenty-two to thirty-one (11 to 15.5 percent). Women's representation among senators has remained at the same somewhat lower level since 1998, when the upper house was established (nine to eleven women; 11 to 13.5 percent).

At present, there is little evidence that the increase in the number of women leaders has resulted in increased advocacy for women's interests in the legislature. Most women deputies see themselves as representatives of all citizens rather than primarily of women. Party-based recruitment systems and the strength of party discipline within the legislature inhibit cooperation among women across party lines, and the lack of a mobilized women's movement and limited contacts between women leaders and women's NGOs mean that women deputies are not subjected to much pressure to act as women's advocates.

At the same time, there are signs that these patterns may change somewhat in the future. Certain women deputies clearly perceive the problems women face in operating as effective leaders within Parliament, while others express an interest in finding ways for women to cooperate across party lines on issues of special concern to women. Women's groups outside Parliament are becoming increasingly aware of the importance of working with and putting pressure on legislators, including women deputies. With the Czech Republic's accession to the EU, both those inside and outside Parliament who want to push for more concerted action on issues that affect women now have access to an outside agency with a stated commitment to eliminating all forms of discrimination against women and ensuring gender equality. The impact of this factor, which was clearly evident in the adoption of a number of legal measures guaranteeing women's equality in the preaccession period, in ensuring actual enforcement of regulations on the books or in supporting new legislation now that the Czech Republic is an EU member remains to be seen. Deputies interviewed for this project had varying degrees of awareness of the EU's impact on women's issues and differing evaluations of the importance of its influence. However, at the least, the EU's policies regarding gender mainstreaming provide women's advocates both inside and outside government with a set of mechanisms for drawing greater attention to issues of special interest to women, and to gender equality.

Notes

1. Sharon L. Wolchik, "Gender and the Politics of Transition in the Czech Republic and Slovakia," in *Women and Democracy: Latin American and Central and Eastern Europe,* ed. Jane S. Jaquette and Sharon L. Wolchik (Baltimore: Johns Hopkins University Press, 1998), 168.

2. For discussions of women's situation in Czechoslovakia under Communism, see Sharon L. Wolchik, "The Status of Women in a Socialist Order: Czechoslovakia, 1948–1978," *Slavic Review* 38 (December 1979): 583–602; Hilda Scott, *Does Socialism Liberate Women? Experiences from Eastern Europe* (Boston: Beacon Press, 1974); and Alena Heitlinger, *Women and State Socialism: Sex Inequality in the Soviet Union and Czechoslovakia* (London and Montreal: Macmillan Press and McGill–Queen's University Press, 1979).

3. Wolchik, "Gender and the Politics of Transition," 169.

4. For more information, see http://www.psdp.cz/cgi-bin/eng/sqw/detail.sqw.

5. Petra Rakušanová, "Zeny na kandidatkách výbraných politických stran a srovnání se zahranicim," in *Volby do poslanecké snemovny 2002,* ed. Lukas Linek et al. (Prague: Sociologický ústav akademie věd České republiky, 2003), table 5.

6. Wolchik, "Status of Women"; Sharon L. Wolchik, "Women and the Politics of Transition in the Czech and Slovak Republics," in *Women in the Politics of Post-Communist Eastern Europe,* ed. Marilyn Rueschemeyer (Armonk, N.Y.: M. E. Sharpe, 1994), 3–27.

7. For more information, see www.volby.cz.

8. See Jaquette and Wolchik, *Women and Democracy;* Wolchik, "Women and the Politics of Transition"; Steven Saxonberg, "Women in East European Parliaments," *Journal of Democracy* 11 (April 2000): 145–58; Steven Saxonberg, *The Czech Republic before the New Millennium: Politics, Parties and Gender* (Boulder, Colo.: East European Monographs, 2003); and Jírina Šiklová, "Feminism and the Roots of Apathy in the Czech Republic," *Social Research* 64, no. 2 (Summer 1997): 258–80.

9. Rakusanová, "Ženy na kandidatkách," table 6.

10. Ibid., 38.

11. Ibid., table 7.

12. Ibid., table 8.

13. See Zděnka Mansfeldová et al., "Committees of the Chamber of Deputies of the Czech Republic," in *Committees in Post-Communist Democratic Parliaments: Comparative Institutionalization,* ed. David M. Olson and William E. Crowther (Columbus: Ohio State University Press, 2002), 69–92.

14. For a recent study of why women politicians leave political life, see Petra Rakušanová and Lenka Vaclávíková-Helsušová, "Odcházení: Politický odcházejicí z politické sceny a jejích zkušeností," *Gender / rovné priležitostí / výzkum* 9, no. 1 (2008): 17–25.

15. Interview with Petra Hejnová, Prague Gender Studies Center, Prague, November 26, 2001.

16. See Michele L. Swers, *The Difference Women Make* (Chicago: University of Chicago Press, 2002). See also the symposium in *Politics & Gender* 2 (2006), noted in chapter 1 of this volume, that addresses this debate. See also Kathleen Lyn, "Power and Influence in State Legislative Policy-Making: The Interaction of Gender and Position in

Committee Hearing Debates," *Political Science Review* 88, no. 3 (1994): 560–76. For analyses that emphasize strong links to women's organizations as key, see Irene Tinker, "Quotas for Women in Elected Legislatures: Do They Really Empower Women?" *Women's Studies International Forum* 27, nos. 5–6 (2004): 531–46; and Irene Tinker, "Assumptions and Realities: Electoral Quotas for Women," *Georgetown Journal of International Affairs,* Winter–Spring 2009, 7–14.

17. For further discussion of the role of the government and individual legislators, see Jana Reschová and Jindriska Syllová, "The Legislature of the Czech Republic," in *The New Parliaments of Central and Eastern Europe,* ed. David M. Olson and Philip Norton (London: Frank Cass, 1996), 82–107.

18. Richard E. Matland and Kathleen A. Montgomery, eds., *Women's Access to Political Power in Post-Communist Europe* (Oxford: Oxford University Press, 2003).

19. See Veronika Sprincová, "Pomohou si strany samy? Uloha ženských sdružení uvnitr politických stran zastoupených v Poslanecké sněmovne Parlamentů ČR," *Gender / rovné příležitostí / výzkum* 9, no. 1 (2008): 26–32.

20. Centrum pro výzkum veřejného mínění, Sociologický AV ČR, "Diskrimináce v zaměstnání a role práce, partnerškych vztáhů a společenskéh výžiti v celkové spokojeností se životem," May 14, 2003; and Centrum pro výzkum veřejného mínění, Sociologický ústav AV ČR, "Srovnání postávení mužů a žen na trhu práce," May 14, 2003.

21. Hana Havelková, "Abstract Citizenship? Women and Power in the Czech Republic," in *Gender and Citizenship in Transition,* ed. Barbara Hobson (New York: Routledge, 2000).

22. See Wolchik, "Women and the Politics of Transition," 3–27, 116–41.

23. On women leaders, see Hana Maříková, "Ženy ve vrcholových politických pozicích," *Sociologický časopis* 33 (1997): 435–43. For the results of a study of men and women leaders in politics and business in the Czech Republic, see Sharon L. Wolchik, "Gender Differences among Political and Economic Elites in the Czech Republic," paper presented at the Conference on Determinants of Women's Representation in Parliament in Central and Eastern Europe, Bergen, Norway, May 28–29, 1999.

24. Interviews with Petra Hejnová, Prague Gender Studies Center, Prague, May 2001, and Washington, May 2002.

25. For further discussion of the impact of the EU on Czech legislation affecting women, see Open Society Institute, *Monitoring the EU Accession Process: Equal Opportunities for Women and Men* (Budapest: Open Society Institute, 2002), 144–46; and Lean Seppanen Anderson, "Regulating Women and the Family: Czech Policy Making Since 1989," paper presented at the Thirty-Fourth National Convention of the American Association for the Advancement of Slavic Studies, Pittsburgh, November 21–24, 2002. See also Hana Hašková, "Czech Women's Civic Organising under the State Socialist Regime, Socio-economic Transformation and the EU Accession Period," *Sociologický časopis / Czech Sociological Review* 41, no. 6 (2005): 1077–1110.

26. For a recent example, see Petra Rakusánová, *Česka politika: Ženy v labyrintu mužů?* (Prague: Forum 50%, 2006).

Chapter 6

East German Women in the
Parliament of Unified Germany

Marilyn Rueschemeyer

In contrast to the five other countries in our study, the transformations after
the end of the Communism in the former German Democratic Republic
(GDR; East Germany) were shaped by unification with West Germany. That
is not to say that relationships with the West, especially economic ties, did
not exist in the other countries. They did, though in different forms; and they
were important for many of the political responses and initiatives that developed even before the end of the Communist period. The GDR, however,
was incorporated into the Federal Republic of Germany (West Germany),
adopting its Constitution as well as its economic, political, and social institutions. The East's industries were privatized through the Treuhand, its
unions were incorporated into the West German union structure, and its par-

The author thanks the Wissenschaftszentrum Berlin für Sozialforschung (Social Science
Center) in Berlin, the Watson Institute for International Studies at Brown University, the
Rhode Island School of Design, and the Woodrow Wilson International Center for
Scholars in Washington for their support and encouragement of this project. She is also
indebted to Edward Wagner who, at the Watson Institute, was her very impressive re-

ties were integrated into the West German party system. These steps were enthusiastically embraced by many in the East's population because of their hopes for economic betterment and a more open, less authoritarian milieu.

Some of the transformations had begun to take place a decade earlier in the GDR. In addition to independent peace and environment groups as well as innovative cultural creations and performances that sprung up, a critical conversation was taking place in a number of leadership circles and in industry. However, as in most of the other Central and Eastern European countries where the transformation process also was initiated earlier, the development after the end of Communism was internally shaped by past commitments and loyalties varying in their endurance.[1] This engendered difficulties in responding to opportunities as well as to pressures created by the economic, political, and cultural systems of the Western countries. Ethnic and nationalist developments created perhaps more difficulties in some of the other former Communist countries than they did in Germany. But the unification process led to a number of specific tensions and very difficult problems in the former GDR, though it also offered opportunities and supports for East Germans that were not available to the other post-Communist countries.

This chapter focuses on the experiences and the political goals of East German women who became members of the lower house of the German Parliament, the Bundestag, though I also had extended interviews with male parliamentarians from the former GDR as well as with male and female "West" German members of Parliament.[2]

I begin with a brief overview of the position of women in the former GDR and then turn to the early transformation years after the end of Communism. This historical background will help us to understand both the life experiences of the women parliamentarians and their political concerns and

search assistant—and colleague—while preparing for the interviews of this chapter; to Gero Neugebauer, who answered all sorts of inquiries from Berlin before the author arrived; and especially to the members of the Bundestag who, with their staff, took so much time and care during our talks there despite enormously pressured weeks during the period the author was working in the Parliament. The representatives she spoke with were Cornelia Behm, Iris Gleicke, Antje Hermenau, Petra Hess, Jelena Hoffmann, Renate Jaeger, Angelika Krueger-Leissner, Gesine Loetzsch, Christine Lucyga, Maria Michalk, Petra Pau, Cornelia Pieper (and a member of Pieper's professional staff, Daniela Zehentner), Christa Reichard, Christel Riemann-Hanewinckel, Silvia Schmidt, Gisela Schroeter, Margrit Spielmann, Marlies Volkmer, Barbara Wittig, Waltraud Wolff, Peter Hettlich, Andreas Weigel, Antje Blumenthal, Kirstin Griese, Rita Pawelski, Thomas Doerflinger, and Anton Schaaf.

goals. The main part of the research for this volume was completed before Chancellor Gerhard Schröder called for an election in 2005 that he narrowly lost. I returned to Berlin two more times for discussions with social scientists and repeat interviews and refer throughout the chapter to a number of new developments under the new Christian Democratic–Social Democratic coalition government. Interestingly, nearly two-thirds of the East German parliamentarians were reelected in 2005. Of the twenty-seven parliamentarians I interviewed in this study, twenty were reelected.[3]

Women in the German Democratic Republic

The historical background of the Central and Eastern European countries has given a special shape to developments after 1989–90, to the situation and problems of women as well as to the emerging democratic politics and the new role of women in politics. The place of women in society had profoundly changed during Communist rule. For our inquiries, however, it is important that the education that women received during the period of Communism, their participation and position in the workforce, and their status differed in the countries of Central and Eastern Europe. Even the newly initiated quota system—to which we will return several times in this discussion—varied in its development, as did the actual participation of women in political life and their assessments of these experiences. It is also true that policies affecting the participation of women in the labor force and in the public sphere were different in East Germany and West Germany and that these differences were important for developments both before and after unification.

By the time the Communist regime in the GDR ended, nearly 90 percent all East German women eligible for employment were participating in the labor force or studying. Women contributed 40 percent of the family income. Seventy percent of all women had completed an apprenticeship or advanced vocational training, and women forty years of age or younger had achieved the same educational level as men. They represented about half of all students in higher education.[4] Women have had, even with limited political autonomy of social and political institutions, considerable participatory experience in the workplace; in unions, especially in union work collectives; and in their neighborhoods.[5] Approximately a third of the deputies in the Volkskammer (the People's Chamber—the GDR's unicameral legislature) were women. Women were members of local and regional governments, and by the late 1980s women occupied half of the city council seats in a number of cities.

During the first years of the Communist regime in the GDR, after the end of the Nazi period and World War II, there were complex reasons for supporting women's participation in the labor force and their training to enter it. But even if one important goal in these years was to make use of women's labor—with socialist ideology and egalitarian conceptions of gender relations playing a less significant role—women's participation in the labor force and in other social and political institutions still had important consequences for GDR women's self-understanding.

Policies affecting the participation of women in the labor force were different in East Germany and West Germany. In the West, politicians and church leaders tended to advocate a return to "normalcy" after World War II, and for many years most women in the West maintained their roles as homemakers or as wives supplementing the family income with their work. But there was nevertheless a trend toward greater female labor force participation. In 1985, 45 percent of West German women were in the workforce; by 1990, nearly 60 percent were. Yet this was still less than the percentage of women working in East Germany at that time.

In both Germanys, the participation in the highest executive positions remained low, less than 4 percent. The percentage of women in the middle levels of management was higher in East Germany, though still less than that of their male colleagues. About a third of these positions were filled by women.[6]

The supports for both men and women to participate in the workforce, not surprisingly, were stronger in East Germany than in West Germany, and the issues revolving around the differences are still salient and will be discussed later in this chapter. In the GDR, day care for children was comprehensive. Though in the 1950s and 1960s, the state support for child care was meager; by the 1970s, most children were in day care; and in the 1980s, more than 85 percent of children between the ages of one and three were in day care centers, and nearly 90 percent of those between three and six were in preschool kindergarten. During this last decade of the GDR, working parents had a guarantee of forty days per year of paid time off from work to care for sick children fourteen years or younger, and after childbirth a parental leave was granted until the child was a year old, at 75 to 90 percent of net pay with a guarantee of return to the job at the same level of employment. With two or more children, this leave was extended to eighteen months. In the last years, the leave could also be taken by the spouse or grandmother.[7]

By the mid-1980s, women in West Germany had a fourteen weeks' maternity leave, with a stipend and employer's supplement that together were equivalent to their wage or salary. Only 3 percent of children under the age of three were in public day care centers. Before unification, a mother could take five paid days a year to care for a sick child of eight years or younger.[8]

Developments after 1989–1990: The Early Unification Years

Many women in East Germany had an interest in politics and were prepared to enter political life, yet they did so only in limited numbers after 1989–90. Women initiated projects and groups. An independent women's movement was formed. Women were included in roundtables and in the democratic political negotiations that took place. A number of women played a significant role in citizen movements and in political parties. Indeed, several of the women now in the Bundestag had been active in new organizations and political parties during the transition years. In the election to the Volkskammer of then-still-separate East Germany in March 1990, more than 20 percent of the newly elected representatives were women.

Yet the participation of women was far from equal to that of men, women were underrepresented among elected representatives, and women's issues were not particularly salient. In part, this had to do with politicians' assessment of the most important issues that had to be addressed in the transformation of the economy and politics; in part, it was due to declining supports in health care, education, and especially child care, which of course was crucial to women's participation in the labor force. The uncertainty of conditions affected policy decisions, but so did the existing power relations. Defining the most important needs was part of the political game and reflected established economic and political inclinations.

Indeed, in the first election in unified Germany, the East handed a major victory to the Christian Democratic Party (CDU/CSU), which, together with the much smaller Free Democratic Party (FDP), was able to co-opt the corresponding "bloc parties" that had existed in the GDR under the dominance of the communist Socialist Unity Party but addressed different concerns and different social groups. The Social Democratic Party (SPD), which at the time of this research was the majority party in the ruling coalition, received only a bit more than half the votes of the CDU. The Reformed Communist Party (the Party of Democratic Socialism, PDS), and the Alliance 90 / Greens, an eastern-western organization of environmental activists during the transition period, also won seats in the new Parliament. In the federal elections in 1994, the CDU maintained its lead in eastern Germany but lost votes in four of the new German states; in Brandenburg, the SPD became the strongest party. The PDS gained in all five eastern states and Berlin; its support in the West was negligible. Women held 21 percent of the seats in the Bundestag in 1990 and 26 percent in 1994. Table 6.1 indicates changes in party support in the eastern and western part of the country from 1990 to 1998.

It could be expected that during the very early transition years, eastern German and western German women would work intensively together to pressure local and regional parliaments as well as the national Bundestag to address issues of common concern. But though some of these early meetings were interesting to a number of eastern women, there were also tensions that reflected different understandings of feminism, different emphases on the kind of issues that had to be addressed, and differences in self-understanding. Of course these differences also existed within East German society, some well before the preparation for unification.

Unemployment in eastern Germany rose dramatically after unification, and women, especially those in certain age and occupational categories, were especially affected. In 1992, the second year of unification, the unemployment rate—if one includes the "hidden unemployed" in short-term employment (which was typically limited), in retraining programs, and in early retirement—came close to 40 percent. At the end of June 1992, 63.6 percent of the unemployed in eastern Germany were women. Women's greater responsibility for the care of the children as well as for negotiating a new school system and new health and insurance systems during this extraordinarily difficult period left very limited time for either social and political engagement or for the search for employment.

By 1997, the participation of women in the labor force in eastern Germany was 81.3 percent (men's participation rate was 79.7 percent); the employment rate of women was 62.6 percent (men's was 67.1 percent), with 21 percent of the employed women and 3 percent of the employed men working part time. The unemployment rate for women was 23 percent, and that for men was 17.8. In western Germany, by 1997, the labor force participation rate for women was 65 percent, compared with 80.5 percent for men; and the employment rate was 59 percent for women, compared with

Table 6.1. Election results in the eastern German and western German federal elections, 1990–1998 (percent)

Year or Comparison	CDU/CSU[a]		SPD		FDP		A90/G		PDS		EXR[b]	
	West	East	West	East	West	East	West	East	West	East	West	East
1990	44.3	41.8	35.7	24.3	10.6	12.9	4.8	6.3	0.3	11.1	2.6	1.6
1994	42.1	38.5	37.5	31.5	7.7	3.5	7.9	4.3	1.0	19.8	2.0	1.2
1998	37.1	27.3	42.3	35.1	7.0	3.3	7.3	4.1	1.2	21.6	2.8	5.0
1998/1990[c]	−7.2	−14.5	+6.6	+10.8	−3.6	−9.6	+2.5	−2.2	+0.9	+10.5	+0.2	+3.4
1998/1994[d]	−5.0	−11.2	+4.8	+3.8	−0.7	−0.2	−0.6	−0.2	+0.2	+1.8	+0.8	+3.8

Note: CDU/CSU = Christian Democratic Party; SPD = Social Democratic Party; FDP = Free Democratic Party; A90/G = Alliance 90 / Greens; PDS = Reformed Communist Party; EXR = parties of the extreme right wing.

[a]In eastern Germany, only CDU.

[b]EXR, parties of the extreme right wing: 1990, die REPublikaner (REP); 1994, REP; 1998, Deutsche Volksunion, National Democratic Party, REP.

[c]Change in 1998 compared with 1990 in percentage points.

[d]Change in 1998 compared with 1994 in percentage points.

Sources: Richard Stöss and Gero Neugebauer, "Die SPD und die Bundestagswahl 1998," table 5, Free University of Berlin, http://www.sowifo.fu-berlin.de/osi/start_frame.html. This table originally appeared in slightly different form in "The Return of Left-Oriented Parties in Eastern Germany and the Czech Republic and Their Social Policies," by Marilyn Rueschemeyer and Sharon Wolchik, in *Left Parties and Social Policy in Postcommunist Europe,* ed. Linda J. Cook, Mitchell A. Orenstein, and Marilyn Rueschemeyer (Boulder, Colo.: Westview Press, 1999), 116; it has been reprinted by permission.

73 percent for men. Forty percent of women worked part time in western Germany, compared with 4 percent of men. In western Germany in 1997, 10.9 percent of women and 11.4 percent of men were unemployed.[9] Interestingly, despite the greater unemployment in the east, a higher percentage of eastern women are in the labor force. It is important to remember that even with comparatively generous benefits for the unemployed in Germany, those without work in eastern Germany often are withdrawn from friends and former colleagues. Certain groups of women are isolated more generally, for work meant some degree of social integration.

One contentious issue in the early transition period was abortion. A new law for both the east and west was to be created by 1992. Though abortion during the first three months of pregnancy, with contraceptives distributed free of charge, had been legal in East Germany since 1972, West Germany's penal code outlawed abortion unless women met certain criteria, usually defined as medical reasons. A few years later, after much controversy, the new regulations allowed abortion without punishment during the first three months of pregnancy, preceded by mandated counseling. The pressure to maintain unity was strongest in the CDU, according to Rita Suessmuth, former speaker of the Bundestag, who noted the importance of support of eastern German women for the success of this legislation.[10]

In some cases, policies that were important to eastern German voters were initiated by western German politicians. These included an increase in the number of days allowed off work with full pay to care for a sick family member; the age of a sick child, for whom such a leave was granted, was raised especially to meet the needs of single parents. A number of issues with respect to women in the workforce were addressed more concretely during the last two Parliaments.

One important development at the time of unification was the movement toward a quota system in party organizations and in parliamentary politics in West Germany. In much of the political discussion in post-Communist societies, any quota system was dismissed as a product of Communism that brought in women who were not really qualified for the job. In addition, political figures in many of the post-Communist countries who opposed the participation of women in the labor force also advocated women's return to their "natural" roles, as housekeepers and mothers. Because the West German Green Party and the western SPD had previously initiated a quota system, the PDS, the Alliance 90 / Greens, and the eastern SPD offered similar opportunities. The consequences of these initiatives were particularly impressive in the last three elections held in West Germany. Interestingly, a few of the members of Parliament I had interviewed from the former East Germany mentioned that they, too, had been against the quota, believing that it was not necessary and that they could fulfill all their goals without help. We will return to their subsequent reflections later in the chapter. They are now convinced that without it, far fewer women would be sitting in the Bundestag. This change of view on the importance of the quota is shared by many of the eastern women representatives.

Getting Elected to the Bundestag

In eastern Germany, it has been suggested that women more often than men have been nominated to safe seats in the Bundestag, the lower house of Parliament.[11] Yet during the 1998 Parliament, out of a total of 44 women from the former GDR, 16 were elected directly, as constituency candidates, while 28 won as list candidates. In western Germany, including Berlin, out of a total of 155 women, 57 were elected directly as constituency candidates, while 98 won as list candidates. With a representation of 31 percent, women were nearly a third of the members of Parliament. Brzinski notes that after the 1998 election, women seemed to have a better chance of getting elected in the east than in the west; eastern women held 36.4 percent of seats for their region and western women 29 percent.[12] That appears to be mostly a result of differences among parties and their relative strength in east and west. Thirty-five percent of the SPD representatives were women, 57 percent of the Green representatives (their smaller coalition partner), 19 and 11 percent of the CDU/CSU representatives,[13] 21 percent of the FDP representatives, and 58 percent of the PDS representatives.

In the Parliament elected in 2002, the focus of this study, the overall representation of women, 195, in the 603-member Bundestag had increased from 31 to 32 percent.[14] Women headed six of the thirteen federal ministries. The SPD, with a 40 percent quota goal, had 40.5 percent representation of women on its party lists and had increased its proportion of elected women to 38 percent; the smaller Green Party, with its 50 percent quota goal, had 48 percent on its party list and increased its share of women in Parliament to 58 percent. With 34 percent, the CDU filled its quota of a third of women on the party list; nearly a quarter of the CDU representatives are women. The CSU has no quota for women, but 30.2 percent of the candidates on the party lists were women; 21 percent of those elected were women. The FDP, also without a quota for women, had a 21 percent representation of women on its party lists, and 21 percent of those elected were women. The PDS, with a 50 percent quota, did not succeed in gaining the 5 percent of the vote it needed for proportional representation and to form a formal party organization in Parliament; two women were directly elected and sat in the Bundestag until the 2005 election, when the number elected to Parliament increased.[15]

Thirty-five women representatives from the former GDR were elected in 2002. The representation of women among all the eastern members of the Bundestag was approximately the same as the 32 percent representation of women in Parliament as a whole.[16] One hundred and nineteen women in the 2002 Bundestag were elected through party lists (62 percent); 38 percent were directly elected. It is significant that in the former GDR, this proportion was nearly reversed; 57 percent were elected "on their own," as it were. In this 2002 election, twenty women from the former GDR were directly elected, while fifteen were on party lists (table 6.2).

Beginnings of Political Involvement and Party Support

As mentioned above, not only were women in the former GDR prepared to enter politics, but a number had also been active in local and regional organizations, in unions, in professional groups, and in the East German Parliament, even if their power or autonomy to create or amend policies was limited. Whether enthusiastic, passive, or very critical, most of these women had participated in the official youth group, the official union organizations, and the like. Aside from the two PDS women directly elected

Table 6.2. Members of the German Bundestag elected in 2002, by party and gender

Party	Number of Members	Number of Women	Percent Women
Social Democratic Party (SPD)	251	95	37.8
Christian Democratic Party (CDU)	190	44	23.2
Christian Democratic Party (CSU)	58	12	20.7
Alliance 90 / Greens	55	32	58.2
Free Democratic Party (FDP)	47	10	21.3
Reformed Communist Party (PDS)	2[a]	2	
Total in the Bundestag	603	195	32.3

[a]Directly elected.
Source: Frauen in Führungspositionen, Abgeordnete, Bundestag, 2002.

to the 2002 Bundestag, a few other representatives had also been active in official GDR organizations.

However, most of the women from eastern Germany in the postunification Parliaments had very different backgrounds, and they emphasized these differences. In fact, it was their expressed lack of participation in the official GDR apparatus that made them more acceptable. The new "eastern" SPD was jokingly described as a party of religious ministers. A few SPD activists were indeed ministers. In Parliament itself, there were two women from the former GDR who had studied theology; one became a Protestant minister before entering politics. Several women mentioned their Protestant backgrounds. Some of these women joined the CDU. Others identified themselves as religious Catholics; while some joined the CDU, others became members of the SPD, a decision to which we will return. These "counterregime" identities were not only mentioned in our talks but also in official printed summaries of the education, career, and social involvement of the Bundestag's members. Only one eastern woman mentioned in her background summary that she was an atheist.

Aside from religious commitments and a reluctance to participate in the official GDR apparatus, other difficulties were noted. One woman—who in her official, printed summary mentioned that she had been a member of the Communist Party for eight years—referred to her stand against the stationing of atomic rockets, which brought her difficulty (including exclusion from the staff of the GDR Academy of Sciences), her subsequent stay in Britain, and her return in 1989.

It is impossible to probe the deepest instincts for political involvement and activity, but it seems fair to mention especially the decade of the 1980s as one in which people in East Germany gathered in a variety of ways, in peace and environmental groups, in women's and church groups, and in a variety of new cultural creations and activities and acted within official organizations in the GDR to help transform, open, improve, and, for a number, radically change the society. Many of the women in Parliament were involved in these activities, hopeful that they could begin modest transformations. A number were elected to the first independent GDR Volkskammer before unification. Not surprisingly, a few women said they had no intention of getting involved with any political party.

With unification and political organization taking on the structures of western Germany, it became clear to a number of activists that the most sensible way to realize political goals was to take part in political parties. Indeed, potential candidates had a better chance of party support if they were active in forming and developing the new party in their locality or district. There were some comments about being encouraged by the parties to become, in turn, active in unions, professional associations, and churches. But that sometimes met with reservations. One of the representatives said that although she participates in some of its activities, she refused to join the church in her community, even after a request by the pastor. "Everyone would know that I did it for political reasons."

Because nearly all women were in the labor force in the GDR, their professional backgrounds were also helpful to the parties in defining the expertise of potential candidates, the extent of their general education and experience, and the connections that these brought to the communities where they lived and worked. The professional backgrounds of nearly all the women in Parliament were extensive and, for a number, included fields usually thought of as "male," such as engineering; two of the engineers among the women members of the Bundestag specialized in agriculture and construction (see table 6.3).

How did the women decide on a party? For those with particular social commitments and professional involvement—for example, for women with environmental interests—the now Alliance 90 / Greens (a coalition of transition movements and Greens) was an obvious choice, even with its limited support in the east. Those who had been involved in East German organizations and committed to building a decent communist society typically chose the PDS; at the time of the 2002–5 Bundestag, this party had very limited support in the west. A number of women who were religiously committed joined the CDU, which in the early Parliaments formed the government. At the same time, precisely because this party had been one of the bloc parties in the former GDR, representing a particular constituency and interests, yet under the dominance of the Communist Party, it was rejected by those women who wanted to support a party without connections to the old regime. (One woman representative who identified herself as Catholic refused to join the CDU because "it didn't stand for social justice.") The FDP was also a bloc party in the former GDR and had more support in the east in the early years than it does now. In the early years, both the CDU and FDP, as well as the PDS, had established political constituencies that they could call on for support. At the same time, the PDS continued to be divided by an "orthodox" wing that was more critical of the federal state and international market economy. The SPD and Alliance 90 / Greens, however, had to establish political organizations and supportive constituencies in the east.

Table 6.3. The occupations of eastern German women members of Parliament, 2002–2006

Party	Occupation	
Social Democratic Party (SPD)	Engineer (3)	Social worker
	Construction engineer	Mayor
	Teacher/instructor, teachers college	Parliamentary staff member
	Special education teacher	Accountant
	Foreign language teacher	Doctor
	Administrator	Principal
	Clerical worker (2)	Nursery school teacher / economist / administrator
	Biotechnologist	
Christian Democratic Party (CDU/CSU)	Veterinarian	Businesswoman
	MA, philosophy / academic instructor	Tax consultant
	Physicist/cabinet member, chair, CDU 2000	Chemist, judge
	Engineer / cabinet member	Engineer
Alliance 90 / Greens	Agricultural engineer	Interior designer
	High school teacher / administrator	Clerical worker
Free Democrats (FDP)	Translator	
Reform Communists (PDS)	Philologist / university assistant	Teacher

Source: Author's data.

The SPD had been incorporated into the Socialist Unity Party in the late 1940s, during the early years of the regime, and so did not exist as a bloc party. In principle, especially the perceived Scandinavian version of social democracy was very attractive to many people in the former GDR. It stood for a commitment to democratic governance, an openness to the market but with an enduring regard for the weaker groups in society.[17] Some of the women who joined the SPD spoke of their difficulties in understanding its philosophy and workings. Though the eastern party remained somewhat separate with respect to its membership, its relation to other political parties (including the PDS), and its political strategies—especially on the local and regional levels—the West German SPD provided technical and financial support and basically shaped the structure and basic policies of the East German party.

Good professional qualifications and "acceptable backgrounds" during the Communist period allowed women who were interested in political activity to become involved in political parties. But there is a big jump from participation in a local or state party organization to being selected for a party list that is being created to bring representatives into the national Parliament. Essentially, the parties without an inherited organizational base did not always have much of a choice. They had to take people with experience in the community, and if the candidates were able to organize successfully and prove their distance from the regime, they had access to political opportunities that are amazing to follow and that were amazing to those elected. Actually, despite the access of practically everyone in eastern Germany to western German newspapers and television, and despite the meetings between active party members in the East and West, many of the women and men who entered the Bundestag had only a limited understanding of what the Federal Republic was about, a limited feel for decisionmaking in the parties themselves, and a limited knowledge of how negotiations in the Parliament take place. Most important, they entered with a number of ideas of their own, some of which were affected by earlier orientations.

Entering Parliamentary Work

Most newcomers in any Parliament enter with excitement and some sense of trepidation. That was true as well for the women I interviewed. Most were uncertain of how Parliament functioned and uncertain if they had enough knowledge and experience. They were sensitive to their general position as former citizens of the GDR. The representatives from eastern Germany meet at regular intervals, usually once a month. Although they belong to different parties, relations with other parties on the local and regional levels are somewhat more cooperative than in the west, and that to an extent carries over into their work in the Bundestag. As are all representatives, they are responsible and involved with their constituencies, and they need to respond to the problems, interests, and hopes of the people who elected them. On a number of pressing issues in the former GDR, there is support from all the eastern parties.

It seems that even with the perceived differences and cleavages that will be discussed, the effects of long discussions and debates within the parties and in Parliament, as well as among individual representatives, are having a strong effect on the members of Parliament from the former GDR. The complexity of the issues they are dealing with, the necessity of negotiation, and the—by now—years of experience with the political parties on all levels have given most of the representatives much more confidence than they had when first beginning their work in the Bundestag. A few also noted that their colleagues in the west are listening to their experiences as well.

Nevertheless, a certain solidarity that existed among the eastern representatives from the beginning of their work in Parliament clearly persists. Although one or two representatives observed that this is weakening, others stressed the differences between the western and eastern representatives and their parties. One male member of Parliament who moved to the east for his work and was then elected there thought that the representatives from the east were more like colleagues than those in the west: "We 'easterners' disagree, we discuss intensely, but we are more harmonious with each other than the western representatives." Several of the women representatives agreed with this assessment. The women also commented on the different manner of talking of "typically male" representatives from the west: "They speak a great deal, often embellishing without end. Not one western male would give up the opportunity to speak, even if the hour were very late." "We are used to speaking simply and to saying what we want to say, and then finish. We are not used to this kind of debate." "Eastern men are more practical and come quickly to the point; they are all used to speaking with us in a different way; Western men speak a lot, also about how great they are." Western parties are still seen as parties of the west. According to one representative, the differences between east and west are less extreme in the SPD than among the Greens. "But the Greens changed some in the last few years and now relate more to reality." Yet according to another, "the western Greens sit, embroider, and utter intellectual sentences."

One of the eastern male representatives did disagree with his many women colleagues who spoke about the differences in harmonious relations between the representatives coming from the east and west: "In Parliament, there is only competition, even if people want harmony. How do you think anyone gets elected? They compete with each other for candidacy or in the elections. That doesn't change after entering Parliament; any discussion of a great community is nonsense."

The party system in Germany tightly controls its members. There are discussions, debates, and working groups that address specific issues. In the latter cases, proposals or reactions to a particular issue are agreed on; they are then discussed on the next level of the party organization until a common position is reached. Sometimes, this process can be difficult for those involved. The issues may be very complicated, and there may be strong divisions within the party—a more leftist-oriented wing, a conservative wing, differences among the younger members who are organized, and so on.

Parliament has committees (Ausschuesse) with representatives from the various parties who express interest in the issues being discussed. In this Bundestag, twenty-one committees were set up.[18] Eastern women were represented on nearly all of these, though the eight committees (of twenty-one) headed by women were all headed by western German parliamentarians. I interviewed women on a variety of committees, as well as male and western German members of the Committee for Family Affairs, Senior Citizens, Women, and Youth.

When the entire Parliament gathers to vote, there is strong pressure on party members to vote with the party, with the majority. Only on rare occasions—for instance, in the vote on stem cell research or the earlier vote on abortion—are members of Parliament encouraged to vote "according to their conscience." But when there is disagreement, members may be engaged in talks with party members, "experts, with more experience," according to a few of the representatives, who try to convince them of the rationale behind the party's decision and emphasize that the majority of party members have expressed a strong preference for a particular course of action: "I think our problems will last for a generation. I didn't vote with the party when it decided to support an enterprise using new technology. Of course I had to take the voters in my constituency into account, and they wanted the facility to remain. In any case, it went through."

In the discussions on social reforms initiated by the governing coalition, a number of members of the SPD were opposed to certain of the proposed changes. Fearing the resignation of the chancellor and the fall of the government, which had only a narrow majority in Parliament, they supported most of them. There were several complaints from the eastern members of Parliament about the lack of policies informed by solidarity: "When the situation is bad, you just can't cut social supports." "When the enterprises introduce technology and the workers are let go, I understand it, . . . but where is the solidarity?" One eastern representative commented: "If we discuss cuts, the easterners are angry. But most recognize that the state finances are not in good shape. It is not clear that the Greens will support cuts. If you lose the state, you cannot solve economic questions, and that potential problem is recognized by the eastern Greens."

Critical Issues for Social Reform

Although legislation has been initiated during all the periods of the Bundestag, the representatives elected in 2002 faced major new legislation on the government's proposed social reforms. These reforms sought to cope with a long-lasting recession, but, above all, also with a looming crisis of the welfare state due to rising pension and health care costs. This involved extended negotiations with the unions, protests from various segments of the population, and differences within their own parties—and within the ruling coalition. Even with an impressive staff, the representatives were responsible for carefully reading the literature on each proposal, engaging in ongoing party and parliamentary debates, and acting responsibly toward their own constituencies and to the nation as a whole. This section will include a few examples of the reforms initiated by the governing coalition and is followed by a discussion of the issues especially important to the women members of Parliament who were interviewed.

Under one new law, unemployment benefits were reduced to twelve months and unemployment aid (subsequent supports for the unemployed given after paid-for unemployment insurance runs out) was merged with welfare benefits. As part of an effort to reduce unemployment, this measure was complemented by a reorganization of the Labor Office, which was renamed the Federal Job Agency and had the responsibility to manage unemployment benefits and find placements for those without work. The law required companies to inform the office if an employee has been given notice and to free up employees for job hunting so they can find work before becoming unemployed.

Another new measure eased the restrictions for laying off workers for smaller companies. Cuts in benefits for those who refuse jobs or training complemented the restructuring and development of job centers. Though most of the SPD and Green representatives in Parliament supported the measures, several of the eastern representatives were very hesitant about their implementation. One measure initiated to fight youth unemployment, pushed by left-oriented groups, was a law requiring companies with more than ten employees to have at least one apprentice slot for every fifteen workers. Companies falling below the minimum would pay a levy into a training fund, whereas companies above the minimum would receive payouts from the fund.

Other reforms were considered to preserve Germany's social security system, such as raising the retirement age and reducing benefits. There have been reforms in health care that would force patients to pay more for treatment (co-pay for doctor visits and prescriptions) and reduce public health insurance coverage for such services as dentures and health spa visits. An important issue was a proposed elimination of the government's "sick pay."

The policy had been that after one week of illness, Germany's public health funds cover wages up to six weeks. Under the new law, people would be required to take out separate policies for illness-related wage losses. A law was also passed to reduce monthly payments for the national health care system from 14.3 percent of an employee's income in 2004 to 13.6 percent in 2005 and 12.15 percent by 2006. These contributions are split between employers and employees. The reductions aimed to reduce nonwage labor costs and thus to help encourage new employment.

To stimulate economic growth, the third stage of tax reform had been pushed ahead one year to 2004. Citizens were to receive an average income tax cut of 10 percent. That also means a shrinking of federal spending. More tax relief was to be given to those groups with lower incomes. The small business sector, especially one-person companies, was to also receive extensive tax relief under the reform.

A Sudden New Election

In 2005, in the middle of his second term, Chancellor Schröder called for new, early elections. The so-called Hartz IV reforms of the labor market that had been initiated had not met expectations; unemployment remained very high, and there were frustrations among those without work and among employers who wanted increased flexibility. Furthermore, Schröder had problems with left-wing colleagues who were against continuing the reform agenda. In state elections in May 2005, the SPD faced extensive defeat. In the national election campaign, the CDU had an early 20-point lead over the SPD in the polls; its lead diminished, however, and in the days before the elections, the differences between the support for the two parties narrowed considerably. (The CDU was associated even more than the SPD with unpopular reforms.) The end result was only slightly more favorable for the CDU. The SPD lost votes to the new Left Party (Die Linke), which was formed by an alliance of the post-Communist PDS and a small west German party (Wahlalternative Arbeit und Soziale Gerechtigkeit) created by disaffected SPD members, including Oskar Lafontaine, a former SPD leader. This Alliance was formally constituted as a unified party only in 2007. Because the SPD was unable to form a coalition only with the Greens and was unwilling to join with the new Left Party, the SPD, after extensive negotiation, entered into a coalition with the CDU/CSU. Angela Merkel became chancellor in 2005, the first woman and the first person from the former GDR to hold this office.

Merkel advanced very rapidly in the new politics of unified Germany. She became chair of the CDU in 2000 (again, the first German woman to do so). She had previously served as federal minister for women and youth,[19] as well as federal minister for the environment, protection of nature, and reactor security. Her background is rather unusual; she was born in West Germany, and her family moved to the former GDR. Her father was a Lutheran pastor and her mother was a teacher. She studied physics at the University of Leipzig and then worked at the Central Institute for Physical Chemistry at the Academy of Sciences in East Berlin. She became politically active in East German politics during the transition period.

In 2005, women headed five of the fifteen federal ministries: Family, Senior Citizens, Women, and Youth (CDU); Education and Research (CDU); Justice (SPD); Health (SPD); and Economic Cooperation and Development (SPD). In Parliament, the representation of women remained stable: 32 percent of the members are women (table 6.4). Of the 115 members of the 2005 Bundestag from the former GDR (including the former East Berlin), 36.5 percent were women. In 2002, the SPD had the highest percentage of eastern women in the Bundestag. But that changed in 2005; the new Left Party now has a higher percentage of eastern women in the Bundestag than the SPD. Because the Left Party had gained more than 5 percent of the vote, it was proportionately represented in the Bundestag. Table 6.5 indicates the overall differences between eastern and western German political preferences in this most recent 2005 election. The support for the new Left Party was far greater in the east than in the west. In the spring of 2006, Petra Pau, one of the two PDS politicians directly elected as members of the Bundestag in 2002 (when the party did not reach the necessary 5 percent for a PDS bloc in Parliament), was elected to represent the new Left Party among Parliament's vice presidents.

Table 6.4. Members of the 2005 German Bundestag, by party and gender

Party	Number of Women	Number of Men	Percent Women
Christian Democratic Party (CDU/CSU)	45	181	19.9
Social Democratic Party (SPD)	80	142	36.0
Free Democratic Party (FDP)	15	46	24.6
Left Party	25	29	46.3
Alliance 90 / Greens	29	22	56.9
Total in the Bundestag	194	420	31.6

Source: Deutscher Bundestag (www.bundestag.de).

Table 6.5. Election results for the 2005 Bundestag in western and eastern Germany (percent)

Party	West	East
Christian Democratic Party (CDU/CSU)	37.5	25.3
Social Democratic Party (SPD)	35.1	30.4
Free Democratic Party (FDP)	10.2	8.0
Left Party	4.9	25.3
Alliance 90 / Greens	8.8	5.2

Source: Der Bundeswahlleiter, Bundestagswahl 2005 (http://wahl.tagesschau.de).

In the months following the early elections, issues revolving around re-forms continued to be intensely discussed in the new coalition government. There were not only strong disagreements between the CDU and SPD members, but there were also tensions between the right and the left within both parties. Merkel ended up having to form a coalition with the SPD because her strong advocacy of reform was unpopular with many voters. The coalition parties disagreed on measures that would loosen the rules governing Germany's labor market, with the SPD opposing conservative initiatives making it even easier to lay off staff during an economic downturn. The CDU advocated flexible company-based collective bargaining and making it easier for companies to opt out of sectorwide wage agreements.[20] There was legislation to increase the incentives for unemployed people to search for work, do retraining, and to make unemployment compensation more difficult to get after unemployment insurance ends. Unemployment insurance was to be paid partly out of general revenue to reduce indirect wage costs and make hiring less costly.

Changes in contributions to health care were also in discussion. The CDU wanted a flat contribution so that everyone who has public insurance pays the same fee, delinking the fee from wages.[21] The SPD advocated graduated fees related to income to be paid by all, including those with higher incomes, who are now privately insured. The contributions would be partly paid out of general revenue, such as the value-added tax (VAT), to reduce the costs of hiring labor. By the summer of 2006, coalition leaders agreed on approximately half a percentage point increase in premiums paid by workers and employers at the start of 2007. From 2008 on, tax revenue would be used toward medical care coverage for children. Among the coalition decisions was an agreement that a central fund, rather than the separate health insurers, would administer the pooled contributions of employers and workers.

These discussions are related to the decision to increase the VAT (from

16 to 19 percent), which took effect in January 2007. The higher VAT has resulted in considerable controversy. There were worries about dampening the economy and complaints about having to pay more for all sorts of things. However, many hoped that the tax increase would prevent cuts in important social supports. Still others believed that the increased VAT would help to reduce the budget deficit.

Other Issues of Particular Importance to the Women Representatives

Not surprisingly, the issues that were most important to the women representatives related to the major difficulties in eastern Germany, especially the ongoing problem of unemployment. At the time of my last visit in late 2007, unemployment was 6.7 percent in the west and 13.7 percent in the east.[22] "It is better to reduce the work week to 35 hours even if the pay is lower because there will be more workplaces," one woman member of the Bundestag argued. "There is competition with Eastern Europe and firms moving there, which affects on our salaries, and there is competition within Germany, with firms moving from the west to the east." Related issues concern the further reduction of security of employment and the problems of pensions for certain segments of the population: for women, for example, who were forced to retire at age fifty-five after unification or have become unemployed and after a few years give up the search or take on part-time work. This situation has improved with legislation providing that for those working part time and earning less than the average salary, the average be taken as the base when calculating the pension. In an article on pension policy in the European Union, the authors note that women moving in and out of the labor force often lose pension benefits whether the pension plans are public or private. The expansion of "labor market flexibility" puts more workers at risk of getting inadequate pensions. Several analysts have advocated monitoring the contradictions related to traditional caregiving obligations of women and their increased participation in the workforce.[23]

One issue that is being discussed again and again and addressed by the SPD—as well as by the current minister for family affairs, seniors, women and youth, Ursula von der Leyen (CDU)—is how to encourage women to engage in work outside the house as well as in family life. In addition to responding to the European Union's agenda on equality between men and women (see the European Parliament member Constanze Krehl's comments in chapter 12 of this volume),[24] the German government is attempting to address the issue of the low birthrate. Approximately 40 percent of women who are highly qualified never have children.

One policy measure encouraging women to have children was enacted earlier. It includes a monthly payment for each child as well as a leave from work with payment and a guaranteed return. There is flexibility; the leave may be shared by both parents, one may take the full year or, if the employer agrees, work part time for a longer period. A new parenting benefit, which was in preparation by the SPD before the 2005 elections and then put into effect by the current minister for family affairs, von der Leyen, began in January 2007. In part, it compensates for the loss of income due to having a child; it also encourages fathers to become more involved in taking care of their children. The benefit replaces 67 percent of the previous net income of the parent staying at home to care for the child up to a maximum amount of €1,800 (roughly $2,250 at the time) a month. The coalition has proposed that two bonus months be added if the parent not usually staying home (usually the father) reduces outside work hours or a takes a work break during that period to care for the infant. Nonworking women and women in jobs with low pay receive €300 (then $375) a month after the birth of a new child.

A number of politicians in the earlier 2002–5 Parliament were already responding to the expectations of eastern German women and the demands of many of their western voters. For eastern representatives, it was of crucial importance to maintain some of the supports they had come to take for granted, including child care, so that men and women as well as single parents can take part in the workforce. All-day child care, federally subsidized but state sponsored, had been voted on in Parliament, though the CDU had fought for choice and flexibility with respect to funding these day care programs. One suggestion was to give the family the money and let the parents decide what to do with it. Some of the states governed by the CDU attempted to subvert the legislation and not develop the all-day program. More recently, after the 2005 election, the CDU and SPD advocated establishing free preschools for children aged three to six by 2009. In the spring of 2006, the priority for day care was again emphasized, especially for preschool children under three. The goal is to increase all-day child care for 230,000 additional families by 2010. If, by 2008, more than 10 percent of the communities do not offer this, there will be a legal right to request day care from the child's second year on. Furthermore, parents can deduct two-thirds of financial outlays for care provided for children up to the age of fourteen from taxable income. The maximum deduction is €4,000 per year per child. If only one parent works outside the house, it will be possible to deduct child care costs for children between the ages of three and six.

Interestingly, during the initial transition period after 1990, women from the west came to the east to explain the philosophy and workings of the different political parties. One of the eastern representatives remembered that the western women cautioned them to make certain that the child care facilities were not taken away. "We paid 30 East German marks a month for food; otherwise we paid nothing. Our system of child care was much better than in the West," noted Cornelia Behm, an Alliance 90 / Green representative in the last Parliament. She emphasized the importance of nonworking women having access to child care "because without it, it is very difficult to look for work." "Some communities create child care programs only for employed women; in principle, it is to be there for all children."[25]

Part-time work is available, but very few families have both parents working part time. If there is a child, either can stay at home or both can share the care. But when it is the husband who is working full time, it may be financially disadvantageous for him to cut back (though this issue has been partially addressed by the new benefit, as mentioned above). There were additional conditions established to support people working part time. If a woman (and it is mainly women who make this decision) decides to work three or four hours a day, she may be able to combine her professional life with the care of children. The employer cannot turn her down without explanation but may not hire her in the first place because of the future possibility of this benefit.[26]

As mentioned above, a large number of professional women have made the decision not to have children. One eastern woman maintained that western German society is unfriendly to children: "I wanted kids and had three. Here in the west, women want careers and no kids. In our party, there are two young women with kids. One sometimes brings the baby to our meetings; the other's husband stays at home and she sees the baby once a week."

One issue mentioned by at least two of the representatives with whom I spoke that will be familiar to a number of western parents was the "future of children in a society oriented toward consumption." "You need music brought into the schools and aesthetics taught; children should not spend hours watching television or working on the computer." Developing these programs as well as a number of others was to be an important enrichment of the expanded school day.

Of particular importance, some of the issues that disturb representatives relate to party policy. The one eastern woman representative from the FDP, who also served as vice president of the national organization of FDP women, was concerned about the absence of a women's quota and the inadequate active participation of women. Twenty-three percent of the members of the FDP are women, down 3 percent since 1996. Of the young members who came into the party in July 2003, only 20 percent are women.[27] The FDP is also against encouraging part-time work through legislation and sees negative consequences for women between twenty-five and thirty-five, a fear of hiring women, and concern about having legal difficulties if it seems that they are acting beyond the law. The party is uneasy about payments for women bringing up children and believes it is too expensive for the government.

Even within the SPD, with its quota and supports for women, there are differences about what should be legislated. As one member puts it: "We have pushed for the balance of men and women in public service organizations and in that sense, the SPD regulations are good. But the party is divided about the private economy. One side maintains the party should force to have women in leadership positions; the other side maintains that should be voluntary."[28] More generally, there has been disappointment expressed about the difficulty of implementing the legislation that has already been passed. One such legislative initiative concerns the programs for the chronically ill, people with breast cancer or diabetes, for example, for which the states are responsible. Although some doctors participate in the program, a number of others do not; they are hesitant because the legislation "reduces their freedom."[29]

Finally, the involvement of women representatives with women's groups varied enormously. Some participated in the SPD's women's organization with great interest; others expressed a lack of interest and even disdain. Where women's groups were active in the community or state where they were elected, the representatives kept in contact with them. A few of the representatives believed that women's groups lost influence: "Women came into leadership positions in other ways and also had disagreements among themselves." "I will never forget that at the party meetings, the Women's Council [Frauenrat] had a table. A woman in men's pants attacked me after I explained why I accepted second place on a party list. She doesn't know how different we are."[30] There are interparty women's initiatives in some other parliaments and community councils, such as in the Berlin Parliament, where the SPD has been in coalition with the PDS.[31] In the national Parliament, women from the east and west and in various parties worked together for abortion rights. Individual (rather than party) voting was encouraged in the Bundestag plenum on abortion.

It is important to keep in mind the many obligations of the parliamentarians in their own district as well as in Parliament. The myriad of social reforms that have been initiated both in previous Parliaments and in the current Parliament demand enormous concentration. Parliamentarians also have tensions addressing issues in their personal lives; some have had great support from their husbands, but others have had very little help. One woman noted that "there are tensions between my work and the family, but only doing politics and not having the family would be terrible." A few of the women are single parents; still others are divorced. When our talk was interrupted by calls to come to the Bundestag plenum, I often walked with the parliamentarian to the meeting. There were at least two occasions when the woman I walked with was in tears.[32]

Summary Observations

The representatives interviewed are in a difficult situation. First, their constituencies are often in difficulty; the unemployment rate in some areas of the east is extraordinarily high. Second, there are conflicts within the parties; these were especially intense during the 2002–5 Parliament in the SPD, when the reforms were initiated, but they are now also salient in the CDU and in the new Left Party, which has succeeded in entering state parliaments not only in the east but also in the west (in the 2007 and 2008 elections in Bremen, Hessen, Lower Saxony, and Hamburg), thus continuing the tensions that became apparent earlier.[33] Third, the women have internalized a number of values from their earlier years in the GDR that at times are at odds with decisions made within their own party, even though they understand the economic problems in contemporary Germany that have to be addressed and they sympathize with many of the political strategies of their parties. These commitments revolve around notions of solidarity: Politics as the art of solidarity, the readiness not to exclude the other, the effects of social policy on the entire society. I have heard this again and again from women in the former GDR.

Less problematic are their commitments to older professional goals, and women who have worked outside the home all their lives talk and care about these. There is some pride and a feeling of being different in their upbringing, taking for granted that the supports they had were crucial for what they attained, even if equality was not fully established between men and women.

For some, there is a feeling of lack of expertise and experience, especially among the newcomers. There are the difficulties of keeping up with all the proposed legislation, as well as tensions about the outcomes. At the same time that east-west differences are noted, it seems that the intense discussion results in both east and west listening seriously to each other, more now than earlier. The eastern representatives feel that some of what they had to say was taken seriously and even appreciated. One eastern representative summed up these discussions: "We want to keep what we have and they want to get what they did not have." But even with the change that several perceive in the atmosphere, expertise, party position, and being able to make your case are important. Here, the comparatively new entrance of GDR women into the Bundestag affected their position in the Bundestag as a whole as well as in the parliamentary committees and in the parties.[34] And as discussed above, the parties, with very few exceptions, put great pressure on members to support their official position in Parliament.

Most important, however, the women members of Parliament with whom I spoke in 2007 are becoming even more confident and increasingly knowledgeable of how political goals are achieved. Their close contact with and support for groups and organizations in their district, and their efforts to convince colleagues in their party to support local goals and to collaborate with colleagues in other parties with similar aspirations, have considerably increased.[35]

The political concerns of the women who represent eastern Germany in the unified Parliament tend not to be feminist in the "Western" sense, though there is of course variation among them. Most are indeed interested in policies affecting women, but their issues are generally embedded in their overall political orientation, which finds expression in their choice of party. As mentioned above, their identity as "easterners" shapes their positions as well. Their past experiences—both their professional backgrounds and their experience with the social support for families in the former GDR—strongly influence their views of what needs to be achieved now in unified Germany.

Although the difficulties of their political work, outside obligations, and desires may be overwhelming, these eastern German women parliamentarians take enormous pride at being part of it all, and at exerting some impact on the shape of their society. These women face many issues that confront them not only as lone individuals and not only as members of a political party but also as part of a group that has experienced an intense past—a past that has shaped much of what they are about and what they hope they can accomplish.

Notes

1. See, e.g., Michael Dauderstadt, Andre Gerrits and Gyorgy G. Markus, *Troubled Transition: Social Democracy in East Central Europe* (Bonn: Friedrich Ebert Stiftung, Wiardi Beckman Stichting, and Alfred Mozer Stichting, 1999); Janos Kornai, Stephan Haggard, and Robert R. Kaufman, eds., *Reforming the State: Fiscal and Welfare Reform in Post-Socialist Countries* (Cambridge: Cambridge University Press, 2001); and Linda J. Cook, *Postcommunist Welfare States: Reform Politics in Russian and Eastern Europe* (Ithaca, N.Y.: Cornell University Press, 2007).

2. There is also an Upper House or Senate, the Bundesrat, which represents the governments of the states (Länder). It was not included in the research project because the representatives in the Bundesrat act on instruction of their respective state governments.

3. The interviews lasted about an hour to an hour and a half, and sometimes longer, but then were occasionally interrupted because of parliamentary meetings and votes. The procedures could be seen in the plenum itself or on the internal parliament screen. I spoke with twenty of the thirty-five East German women in Parliament: thirteen were members of the Social Democratic Party, the larger party in the "red-green" coalition; two were members of the Green Party (their coalition partner in the Bundestag); two were members of the Christian Democratic Party, CDU/CSU; one was a member of the Free Democratic Party, the professional staff member of the Free Democratic Party caucus; and two were directly elected members of the Reform Communist Party (Party of Democratic Socialism, PDS). I also spoke with a western German male member of the Green Party who moved to eastern Germany several years ago and was elected to the Bundestag there; a western female member of the SPD; a western male representative from the SPD who had a strong union background; a male and two female members of the CDU/CSU from western Germany; and an Eastern German male SPD representative. (The latter five were members of the Parliament Committee on Family, Seniors, Women, and Youth.) I had the opportunity to interview the former Speaker of the Bundestag from 1988 to 1998, Rita Suessmuth, a western German and CDU member who had previously served in the Kohl administration as minister for youth, family, and health from 1985 to 1986 and again (as minister for youth, family, women, and health) from 1986 to 1988. There were also a number of informal talks with men and women who were part of the last two previous governments. During the period before the 2005 election took place, I participated in the Seventh World Congress of the International Council for Central and East European Studies at the Humboldt University in Berlin and had the opportunity for extensive conversations about candidates and salient political issues with German social scientists from both the (former) East Germany and West Germany. In the fall of 2007, I again returned to Berlin and revisited the Bundestag to do a few selected interviews with women members from the former East Germany.

4. Marilyn Rueschemeyer and Hanna Schissler, "Women in the Two Germanys," *German Studies Review,* DAAD Special Issue (1990): 71–85.

5. Marilyn Rueschemeyer, "The Work Collective: Response and Adaptation in the Structure of Work in the German Democratic Republic," *Dialectical Anthropology* 7,

no. 2 (September 1982): 155–63; and Marilyn Rueschemeyer, "Integrating Work and Personal Life: An Analysis of Three Work Collectives in the GDR," *GDR Monitor* (1983): 27–47.

6. See Hildegard Nickel, "Sex Role Socialization in Relationships as a Function of the Division of Labor," in *The Quality of Life in the German Democratic Republic: Changes and Developments in a State Socialist Society,* ed. Marilyn Rueschemeyer and Christiane Lemke (Armonk, N.Y.: M. E. Sharpe, 1989), 48–73; Eva Kolinsky, "Women in Politics in Western Germany," in *Women in the Politics of Postcommunist Eastern Europe,* ed. Marilyn Rueschemeyer (Armonk, N.Y.: M. E. Sharpe, 1998), 64–85; and Marilyn Rueschemeyer, "Women in the Politics of Eastern Germany," in *Women in the Politics of Postcommunist Eastern Europe,* ed. Rueschemeyer, 89–115.

7. This did not, of course, guarantee integration into the job and many women in the GDR expressed fear of falling behind their colleagues. See Marilyn Rueschemeyer, *Professional Work and Marriage: An East-West Comparison* (London and New York: Macmillan for St. Antony's College, Oxford, and St. Martin's Press, 1981), 112–69.

8. Rueschemeyer, "Women in the Politics of Eastern Germany," 92.

9. See Sabine Schenk, "Employment Opportunities and Labour Market Exclusion: Towards a New Pattern of Gender Stratification?" in *Reinventing Gender: Women in Eastern Germany since Unification,* ed. Eva Kolinsky and Hildegard Maria Nickel (London: Frank Cass, 2003), 55. It is difficult to assess the meaning of the unemployment rate because many women—in the east and west, but especially in the west—do not apply for jobs.

10. Interview with Rita Suessmuth.

11. In Germany, each citizen has two votes. With the first, the voter selects from the candidates proposed by parties in a single electoral district. The candidate elected is the one who receives the most votes. With the second vote, the voter chooses among lists of candidates determined by the political parties of the *Land* (state). The distribution of seats is on the basis of the proportion of second votes a party receives, provided that this proportion is higher than 5 percent; the party's directly elected candidates are offset against this proportion. This electoral system, then, joins the direct election of candidates in constituencies with proportional representation; the 5 percent threshold prevents the proliferation of very small parties. Proportional representation tends to favor women's representation. See Richard Matland and Kathleen Montgomery, eds., *Women's Access to Political Power in Post-Communist Europe* (Oxford: Oxford University Press, 2003).

12. Joanne Bay Brzinski, "Women's Representation in Germany: A Comparison of East and West," in *Women's Access,* ed. Matland and Montgomery, 63–80.

13. The CDU had formulated a quota recommendation but hesitated with enforcement regulations.

14. In the Upper House or Senate (the Bundesrat), women represented approximately a quarter of the sixty-nine members. But because the members of the Bundesrat are representatives of the state governments and follow instructions of these governments, this study, as mentioned above, focused only on the lower house.

15. To form an official party caucus in the Parliament, the party needs to have at least 5 percent of the members of Parliament (in the 2002 election, this means at least thirty-one deputies). There were four such official parties in the 2002–5 Parliament: the Social Democratic Party, with 251 representatives; the Union Party (combined CDU/CSU), with 248 representatives, the Alliance 90 / Green Party, with fifty-five (in the coalition

government with the Social Democratic Party); and the FDP, with forty-seven representatives. Directly elected members without a party caucus (under 5 percent) may not have all the facilities at their disposal as other members; there was a protest when the two women from the Reformed Communist Party received neither at table nor a telephone in the parliament. Members of the Bundestag without a caucus are not entitled to committee membership, but they can be nonvoting members of a Parliament committee.

16. The population of eastern Germany is about 20 percent of the total population of the Federal Republic of Germany.

17. Marilyn Rueschemeyer, "Social Democrats after the End of Communist Rule: Eastern Germany and the Czech Republic," *Sociological Analysis* 1, no. 3 (September 1998): 41–59.

18. These included the Committee on Foreign Affairs; the Committee on Internal Affairs; the Finance Committee; the Budget Committee; the Defense Committee; the Committee for Family Affairs, Senior Citizens, Women, and Youth; the Committee on Transport, Building, and Housing; the Health and Security Committee; the Committee on Affairs of the European Union; and the Committee on Culture and Media.

19. For an interesting comment on Merkel during this period, see Lynn Kamenitsa and Brigitte Geissel, "WPAs and Political Representation in Germany," in *State Feminism and Political Representation,* ed. Joni Lovenduski (Cambridge: Cambridge University Press, 2005), 106–29.

20. Company-based bargaining reduces the power of the labor unions. The number of employees covered by collective bargaining agreements has fallen in both eastern and western Germany but even more so in the east than in the west.

21. In Germany, health care is paid for by 250 public and private health insurance corporations, mostly funded by company and employee contributions.

22. Bundesagentur fuer Arbeit,2007.

23. See Eila Tuominen and Sini Laitinen-Kuikka, "Pension Policy in the European Union: Responses to the Changing Division of Labor in Family Life," *Gender Issues* 22, no. 3 (Summer 2005): 46–78.

24. Gender mainstreaming was anchored in European Union law as part of the Treaty of Amsterdam, 1999. The (then) fifteen member states as well as the future accession countries were to commit themselves to equal opportunity policies based on these principles. A road map has been set out by the European Commission for 2006–10 with six priority areas: achieving equal economic independence for women and men; enhancing the reconciliation of work, private, and family life; promoting equal participation of men and women in decisionmaking; eradicating gender-based violence and trafficking; eliminating gender stereotypes in society; and promoting gender equality outside the EU (http://cc.europea.eu/employment_social/emplweb/news/news_en.cfm?id=136). Also see Mary E. Daly, "Gender Mainstreaming in Theory and Practice," *Social Politics: International Studies in Gender, State and Society* 12, no. 3 (Fall 2005): 433–50.

25. Interview with Christine Lucyga.

26. Interview with Anton Schaaf, a member of the SPD and a member of the Parliament Committee on Family, Seniors, Women, and Youth.

27. Interviews with Representative Cornelia Pieper and Daniela Zehentner, a lawyer and member of Pieper's professional staff.

28. Interview with Christel Riemann-Hanewinckel.

29. Interview with Margrit Spielmann.

30. The Green Party, with a 50 percent quota for its electoral lists, is supposed to have a woman as its first candidate.

31. Interview with Gesine Loetzsch. See also Olga Avdeyeva, "Enlarging the Club: When Do Candidate States Enforce Gender Equality Laws?" *Newsletter of the European Politics and Society Section of the American Political Science Association,* Spring–Summer 2007, 10–11; and Katya M. Guenther, "Understanding Policy Diffusion across Feminist Movements: The Case of Gender Mainstreaming in Eastern Germany," *Politics & Gender* 4, no. 4 (2008): 587–613.

32. During my return visit in 2007, these demands continued, with assistants reminding the parliamentarians to end our conversation, hectic searches for papers, keys, etc., requests to continue our talks in the bathroom or on the way to their next meeting (vivid reminders of the lives of many professionals in the United States).

33. In addition to this development in Hamburg, in April 2008, Germany's Green Party approved the first-ever coalition agreement with the CDU at the state level. For some background on becoming members of state parliaments in eastern Germany, see Louise K. Davidson-Schmich, *Becoming Politicians: Eastern German State Legislators in the Decade Following Democratization* (Notre Dame, Ind.: University of Notre Dame Press, 2006). Bettina van Hoven-Iganski has done interesting dissertation research on women in "postsocialist" rural society in Mecklenburg-Westpommerania. See Bettina van Hoven-Iganski, "Rural Women's Perception and Experience of Local Democracy," in *Made in the GDR: The Changing Geographies of Women in the Post-Socialist Rural Society in Mecklenburg-Westpommerania,* Netherlands Geographical Studies 267 (Utrecht: Koninklijk Nederlands Aardrijkskundig Genootschap, 2000), 169–95.

34. The new Left Party presents a somewhat different environment.

35. The challenge of the New Left Party to the earlier reforms that were initiated after the 2002 elections have had an impact on both the CDU and the SPD, and members of both political parties are engaged in intense discussions about these issues. Kurt Beck, then the leader of the SPD, had been especially committed to change. To take only one example, I attended the Forum of the Historical Commission in October 2007, where he spoke and, together with academic speakers, engaged a broader audience in discussing the possible modifications of the earlier reforms. In the following months, proposals for changing some of these became more important. One outstanding example concerned changing unemployment insurance for older workers over forty-five years of age from twelve to fifteen months and for those over fifty from eighteen to twenty-four months before beginning the Hartz IV funding discussed earlier in the chapter. A similar fight about softening the impact of earlier reductions in pension benefits continued into 2008.

Chapter 7

The Return of the King: Women in the Bulgarian Parliament

Kristen Ghodsee

On June 17, 2001, Bulgaria became the first nation in more than 150 years to democratically elect a former monarch to become its political leader.[1] In that same year, women won more than 26 percent of the seats in the National Assembly,[2] and Bulgaria became the former socialist country with the highest percentage of women parliamentarians in Central and Eastern Europe. This high percentage of women in Bulgaria's National Assembly was due almost exclusively to the electoral success of the National Move-

The author thanks the National Council of Eurasian and East European Research, the International Research and Exchanges Board, and Bowdoin College for their generous support of this research. She is also grateful to the editors for their expert comments. A special thanks are offered to the Woodrow Wilson International Center for Scholars, the Institute for Advanced Study, and Bowdon College for institutionally supporting her while she worked on this chapter. She also thanks Anelia Atanassova at the Local Government Initiative for her assistance in organizing many of the interviews, and the members of Parliament who took time out of their very busy schedules to discuss their experiences. Finally, the author expresses her deepest appreciation to Genevieve Creedon for her assistance with the preparation of this chapter.

ment of Simeon the Second (NMSS), the political movement led by Bulgaria's once-exiled king, Simeon Saxecoburgotski, who intentionally included women on his electoral lists even though he did not run on a pro-women or profeminist platform.

When Saxecoburgotski's government started its mandate, more than 40 percent of its members of parliament (MPs) were women. This high percentage of women in parliament in Bulgaria is even more astonishing when compared with the gender representation in local politics, where women generally have tended to do better than at the national level.[3] In the 2003 municipal elections, only 18 percent of 264 Municipal Council chairs and 21 percent of the 5,300 Municipal Council members were women.[4] This means that there was higher representation of women at the national level than at the local level, a relatively rare outcome in most democracies.

In this chapter, I examine the effects that the increased number of women in the Thirty-Ninth National Assembly had on Bulgarian politics. In particular, I discuss whether or not women in politics believe that Bulgarian women are more likely to vote for female candidates or for parties with a higher percentage of women on their electoral lists. I also examine whether the higher number of women in the legislature has had an effect on the proposition of or the floor debates surrounding what I loosely define as women's issues. These issues include maternity leaves, pension reforms, divorce, protection of children, trafficking in persons, antidiscrimination, sexual assault, sexual harassment, and domestic violence.

It is important to note, however, that my definition of "women's" issues did not always overlap with what my interviewees considered "women's" issues. With the exception of domestic violence and sexual harassment, which were considered women's issues imported by feminists from the United States and Western Europe, my informants preferred to consider the rest as "social issues" not directly linked to any kind of feminist agenda.

I also examine whether or not women with differing political views ever cross party lines to vote together as a bloc on issues of concern to women. Finally, I end the chapter with a discussion of how women politicians fared in the 2005 parliamentary elections, when the Bulgarian political landscape was radically altered once again with the election of seven different parties into the Fortieth National Assembly.

Following the work of Susan Gal and Gail Kligman[5] and Vlasta Jalušić and Milica Antić,[6] I found that women holding elected office in the Thirty-Ninth Bulgarian National Assembly did not organize themselves along gender lines and resisted being pigeonholed into dealing with "women's issues." Political convictions divided women just as powerfully as they divided men, and women on opposite sides of the political spectrum did not always form alliances based on their shared sex. On the other hand, however, I propose that Simeon II did want to increase women's participation in his government, even if this meant including many politically inexperienced women on his lists. The large number of "filler" women in his parliament that made up more than a quarter of all MPs, combined with active women's organizations and lobbyists in some ways did result in larger attention to women's issues. Thus, although it may not have been the intention of the former king to raise awareness of women's issues, the inclusion of so many women on his electoral lists and ultimately in parliament, did, on the surface, seem to increase the amount of legislation proposed around these issues. This increase, however, may be less to do with an actual commitment to women's issues and more to do with individual self promotion by women looking to distinguish themselves politically.

The research for this chapter was based on fieldwork in Bulgaria in 2001, 2003, 2004, and 2005, and on formal interviews with eleven of the sixty-six women in parliament in the summer of 2004. I interviewed two women from the Bulgarian Socialist Party, three women who came into parliament as part of the Union of Democratic Forces, and six women who became MPs with the NMSS. I also spoke with the directors and employees of four organizations that were involved in advocacy efforts to increase the political participation of women or lobbying parliament on women's issues: the Women's Alliance for Development, the Bulgaria Gender Research Foundation, the Local Government Initiative, and the National Association of Municipalities in the Republic of Bulgaria. Finally, I examined the Bulgarian press for articles and reader forums on the issue of women's political representation.

A Brief History of Women in the Bulgarian Parliament

Bulgarian women were politically enfranchised when the country became a people's republic after World War II. The equality of men and women as workers and comrades was one of the core ideological goals of the Bulgarian Communists. They encouraged women's political participation by instituting a quota system that guaranteed women a certain number of seats in the National Assembly. Although the percentage of women varied from assembly to assembly, after the mid-1970s, women's participation in parliament regularly hovered around 20 percent (see table 7.1).[7]

Under the Communist regime, however, the National Assembly had very little power and served mostly as a rubber-stamping mechanism for decisions made by Bulgaria's male political elite. In fact, at the very top levels of the Communist government, women were rarely represented despite the state's commitment to the legal equality of the sexes. The few women with influential positions often obtained them through family connections as daughters, wives, or sisters—the most famous of these being Todor Zhivkov's much-loved daughter, Lyudmila Zhivkova.[8] The rest of the women in the upper echelons of the Communist hierarchy were usually members of the *nomenklatura,* or they were brought to Sofia from the villages because of their fervent support for Communism as examples of socialist egalitarianism. With very few exceptions, most of them had little or no real power.

After the unexpected resignation of Zhivkov in 1989, the Bulgarian Communist Party renamed itself the Bulgarian Socialist Party (BSP) and won the first democratic elections in 1990. But Bulgarian politics during the 1990s were characterized by both political and economic chaos. This period witnessed the ravages of banking collapses, hyperinflation, the rise of organized crime, and a dramatic decline in the standard of living of ordinary Bulgarians. There was a rapid succession of governments. None of these governments completed its entire four-year mandate as power shifted back and forth between socialist and "democratic" (right-wing) control of

Table 7.1. Women in the Bulgarian Parliament, 1976–2005

| | Women Members | | |
Period	Number of Members of Parliament	Number of Women Members of Parliament	of Parliament as Percentage of Total Members
1976–81	400	78	19.5
1981–86	400	87	21.7
1986–90	400	84	21.0
1990–91	400	34	8.5
1991–94	240	34	14.1
1995–97	240	31	12.9
1997–2001	240	27	11.2
2001–5	240	61	26.0

Source: Krassimira Daskalova and Pavlina Filipova, "Citizenship and Women's Political Participation in Bulgaria," *Social Rights Bulgaria,* March 2, 2004 (http://www.socialrights.org/spip/article494.html).

parliament. During this period of electoral flip-flopping, the country briefly had a female prime minister, Reneta Indjova, in 1994. Other than this one high-profile and temporary appointment of a female politician, women's participation in parliament was relatively low compared with the Communist era.[9]

This low level of women's representation occurred in spite of the fact that the electoral system set up under Bulgaria's new Constitution was one that should have been favorable to women candidates. After 1991, MPs were elected in multimember constituencies using a system of proportional representation, whereby citizens vote for party lists rather than individual candidates. Parties that do not receive more than 4 percent of the vote are disqualified and not allocated any seats. The percentage of the vote that a party gets in a specific voting district determines how many people from the proposed list become MPs, starting from the top of the list and working down toward the bottom. Politicians in the first two or three slots of their parties' lists have a much better chance of being elected to parliament than those at the bottom of the lists, who only become MPs if the party wins a large majority of votes in a voting district. Thus, positions on the lists are very strategic and are specific to each voting district, depending on whether or not it is a party's stronghold.

In general, women have a higher chance of being elected when they occupy a fixed place on a party list than they do when they run as individuals.[10] Additionally, Bulgaria employs a closed-list system, whereby the placement of the names on the list is fixed, so that parties cannot pick and choose who they want to become MPs but must pick them in numerical order from the top of the list down. These changes, however, also included the removal of the Communist-era system of quotas, which had once guaranteed women participation in parliament. Most Bulgarians continued to view quotas as an "undemocratic" legacy of Communism, and only the BSP retained a party-level quota system that guarantees that women make up about one-third of all party lists. But even the BSP's quotas are largely ineffective. The party routinely puts the 30 percent of its female candidates on the very bottom of its electoral lists in constituencies where it is not likely to get many votes.

In 1996 the BSP was in charge of the country when the entire economy collapsed. The massive demonstrations that followed the collapse left the government only two choices: to clear the streets with blood or to resign and hold new elections. The BSP chose the latter, and a Union of Democratic Forces (UDF) government was swept into power. Under Prime Minister Ivan Kostov, the UDF government was the first Bulgarian administration to fulfill its entire four-year mandate, albeit after several cabinet reshuffles due to corruption. Its close cooperation with the International Monetary Fund and the implementation of a currency board brought back both political and economic stability to the country in the late 1990s but caused great economic hardships for most Bulgarians. Kostov appointed a woman, Nadezhda Milailova, to be his minister of foreign affairs. There were two other women cabinet-level appointments, and there were many women appointed at the deputy ministerial level. But once again, very few women held elected positions in parliament. From 1997 to 2001, only 11.7 percent of the MPs were women (table 7.2).

Despite the many successes of the UDF government, corruption scandals and growing poverty throughout Bulgaria as stabilization and structural adjustment policies were implemented meant that a massive protest vote against the UDF was looming in the next parliamentary elections. By all accounts, at the beginning of 2001, it looked as if the BSP was again poised to take power in Bulgaria as the pendulum swung once more to the left of the now-established national two-party system. But the unexpected entry of Bulgaria's former king into the political arena in April 2001 dramatically changed the two-party landscape in Bulgaria and women's representation in parliament.

Table 7.2. Women in the Bulgarian National Assembly by party, group, or coalition, 1997–2001 and 2001–2005

Party or Coalition[a]	1997–2001		2001–5	
	Total Seats	Percent Women	Total Seats	Percent Women
Bulgarian Socialist Party	58	10.3	48	10.4
Union of Democratic Forces	137	11.7	51	17.6
Movement for Rights and Freedom	19	5.3	21	9.5
Bulgarian Business Bloc	15	—	—	—
Euroleft	14	14.4	—	—
National Movement Simeon II	—	—	120	40.0

Note: — = none.
[a]Many of the political parties formed coalitions with smaller parties not listed here.
Sources: Web site of the Bulgarian National Assembly (www.parliament.bg); Tatiana Kostandinova "Women's Legislative Representation in Post-Communist Bulgaria," in *Women's Access to Political Power in Post-Communist Europe,* ed. Richard E. Matland and Kathleen A. Montgomery (Oxford: Oxford University Press, 2003).

Simeon Saxecoburgotski and the Creation of the NMSS

Simeon II is the grandson of Tsar Ferdinand Saxe Coburg von Gotha, a German prince who was Bulgaria's second king after its liberation from the Ottoman Empire.[11] Simeon's father was Boris III, a much loved monarch in Bulgaria who is best remembered internationally for his role in saving Bulgaria's Jewish population from the death camps despite his political alliance with the Nazis in World War II. Although he was never officially crowned, Simeon succeeded his father after Boris III's suspicious death in 1943.[12] Because Simeon II was only six years old at the time, a regency was formed, and for a brief time after the war, Bulgaria was a Communist monarchy.[13] But as the Communists consolidated power in the country, they staged a referendum and the monarchy was officially abolished in 1946.

Simeon II fled Bulgaria and eventually settled in Spain, where he lived as an exiled monarch for more than four decades until his reentry onto the Bulgarian political scene. When Communism collapsed in 1989, the possibility of Simeon's return loomed large in the minds of the country's politicians. Although Bulgaria's new Constitution unequivocally declared the nation a republic, a special provision was included in the document to prevent Saxecoburgotski's return to power through democratic means. This provision required that anyone who wanted to run for the office of president had to have been a resident of the country for at least five years before the election.[14] This measure was passed specifically to prevent the presidential candidacy of Simeon II in 1991.[15] When Saxecoburgotski declared his intention to run for the presidency ten years later in 2001, he challenged the provision, but the Bulgarian Supreme Court upheld it. Saxecoburgotski was not allowed to run.

The prime minister of Bulgaria at the time, Ivan Kostov, probably hoped that Simeon II would lay his political ambitions to rest after being barred from the presidency. But much to Kostov's dismay, Saxecoburgotski instead formed a political "movement" called the National Movement of Simeon II in April 2001. Because of the rules governing the registration of political parties, and the ruling party's desire to keep him out of the election, Simeon was unable to register his own party officially until after the elections had already taken place.[16] His "movement" was instead registered through two little-known (but already registered) political parties: the Oborishte National Revival Party and the Bulgarian Women's Party. With the elections scheduled for June 2001, Simeon and his political allies had less than two months to fill the NMSS's lists with the names of would-be MPs in all Bulgaria's voting districts.[17]

Filling the NMSS's lists in such a short period of time was a challenging task. Before 2001, Bulgaria had a two-party system, and most people with professional experience in government were already aligned with either the socialists or the democratic forces. Although Simeon managed to convince a few BSP and UDF politicians and bureaucrats to join his movement, for the most part he had to look elsewhere to find people to run on an NMSS ticket. But time was running out.

Through a wide network of personal connections, Saxecoburgotski, his family, and his associates began calling their friends, their families, and their associates. At first, they focused on well-known and respected Bulgarian professionals who had not previously been involved in politics directly: businesspeople, lawyers, academics, doctors, journalists, and the like. Young Bulgarian professionals who had emigrated to the United States and Western Europe during the 1990s were also asked to be on the lists. But many in these populations had preexisting political allegiances, and so the NMSS began to widen the net, to include seemingly almost anyone who would agree to run, and many of those were women.

Politically inclined Bulgarians may have been reluctant to join the NMSS because it had no political platform. Saxecoburgotski's campaign slogan consisted of two simple words: "Trust me." He never clearly stated his stance on any of the issues. It was also unclear who would become the prime minister should the NMSS win the election, or who would be appointed to the cabinet. The entire campaign was based on the enigma of the former king, the disgust that most Bulgarians felt toward the two established political parties, and the widespread perception that the other parties were irredeemably corrupt.

The haphazard process through which Simeon II put together his political lists was a constant theme that I heard in my interviews with those in the other parliamentary groups. In one telling example, a university student had been working in a local political office of the UDF. One day, she apparently received a call from someone working with the NMSS and was asked if she would like to run for the National Assembly. She agreed and was subsequently asked if she knew of anyone else who might be interested in being on Saxecoburgotski's lists. She then proceeded to approach five of her professors at the university. Three of them said "no" and two of them said "yes." After the 2001 election, the university student and her two professors were MPs as part of the NMSS.

An MP from the parliamentary group Democrats for a Strong Bulgaria (a splinter group from the UDF), told me, "All of the MPs from the king's party have a story about how they were laying on the couch and watching TV when suddenly they got the call [from the NMSS]. Some of them were retired or unemployed with nothing better to do. Why not become a member of parliament?"[18] Indeed, when I asked about the backgrounds of the women in the NMSS, it turned out that very few of them had any previous political experience, and most had no intention of getting involved in politics until they were invited by Saxecoburgotski.

The same MP explained that at the beginning of the Thirty-Ninth National Assembly, the lack of parliamentary experience by the NMSS delegates hindered legislative debate, because few understood the proper procedures. "They are learning," she said, "but parliament is not supposed to be a school."[19] Also in reference to the inexperience of the NMSS MPs, an MP from the Socialist Party confided, "The only difference between the [NMSS] men and women is that the men always speak in committee even if they don't know what they are talking about, and the women never speak at all."[20]

The haste of the process also made it difficult to ascertain the intentionality of having more than a third of the NMSS's lists populated with women. There were many explanations for the increased number of women. The official position of the NMSS was that Saxecoburgotski deliberately placed women on his lists because he believed that women were capable and deserved their fair share of political power. In a May 2004 article on women in Bulgarian politics in the national newspaper *Sega* (Now), a pro-NMSS journalist argued that "the Tsar"[21] promised to put women in office and had kept his promises.[22] The prime minister's supporters also referenced the appointment of a woman, Lydia Shuleva, to be his deputy prime minister and minister of economy, one of the most powerful positions in the government. They explained away the general lack of political experience of many NMSS MPs by saying that the prime minister wanted to bring new faces into parliament to counter the corruption and favoritism that were rampant in previous National Assemblies. A reader's forum comment on the article mentioned above echoed the sentiment that women in politics were less corrupt, and therefore argued that the king had done well to choose women for his government. The reader wrote: "Bulgarian politicians—men and women—don't do anything. But I think that women are less corrupt or at least less susceptible to corruption. And because, in politics, we are always faced with the choice between evil and more evil, women politicians are the lesser evil."[23]

Certainly from their placement on the electoral lists, it could be interpreted that Saxecoburgotski deliberately wanted to increase the percentage of women in parliament. Slightly more than 48 percent of the NMSS candidates in the first position on their party list were women in the 2001 elections. Of the total NMSS candidates that were number two on their lists, 38.7 percent were women, and 54.8 percent of number three spots were filled by women.[24]

MPs in the opposition, however, did not agree with the NMSS's spin on the reasons for its inclusion of women in its movement. Several of the women MPs I interviewed partially agreed that Saxecoburgotski had intentionally sought out women as candidates, but said that he was unable to find enough who were politically qualified. They thought that he filled the rest of the lists with inexperienced women because he just needed names. An opposition MP from the BSP claimed that Saxecoburgotski would have preferred male politicians but that not enough men were interested in running on his ticket. Yet another believed that he deliberately chose inexperienced women because they were willing to follow his lead without knowing what his political platform was, and they would be more docile once elected. This MP felt that Saxecoburgotski wanted discipline in his party and believed that Bulgarian women would give him less trouble than Bulgarian men. Whatever the actual reasons, the NMSS government did bring into office the largest percentage of women since the end of Communism, and the evidence, including their placement on the electoral lists, suggests that this result was at least partially intentional. But it was the "quality" of those women whom he chose that frustrated many women MPs in the opposition and women's advocates.

The Educational and Professional
Backgrounds of Women MPs

The educational level for all the members of the Thirty-Ninth National Assembly was impressive, with 98 percent of the MPs having a university degree or higher. Of the women in the 2001–5 Parliament, 23 percent were lawyers and 18 percent engineers.[25] Several were medical doctors and university professors, but there were also many women who had entered politics from nontraditional backgrounds, particularly with the NMSS. Of the women I interviewed in the opposition parties, three were attorneys, one was an economist, and one was an English and Russian philologist. Within the NMSS, I interviewed one banker, one economics professor, one Bulgarian philologist, one lawyer, one secretary, and one journalist with a previous career as a fashion model (table 7.3).

The other important difference between the opposition and the NMSS's MPs was the amount of political experience they had before the Thirty-Ninth National Assembly. All the women in the UDF and BSP had served in previous parliaments, whereas only one of the NMSS MPs I interviewed had been active in politics before 2001. Indeed, the five youngest female new MPs belonged to the NMSS. The youngest, Ralitza Againe, was only twenty-five years old in 2001 when she became an MP on Saxecoburgotski's lists. The NMSS MP Siyka Dimovska was twenty-six. Adrianna Brancheva, Nina Chilova, and Silvia Neicheva were all born in 1972 and were either twenty-nine or thirty in 2001 when they entered the National Assembly. Although they all had university degrees, they had very little professional, let alone political, experience.

The most notorious member of Saxecoburgotski's government was Julianna Doncheva, a former model who was given as the favorite example of the lack of political experience of the NMSS MPs. MP Doncheva was a very beautiful woman in her late thirties and became a style darling of the Bulgarian media. In just one example, she appeared on the cover of the Bulgarian fashion and lifestyle magazine *Maximum* in April 2002 with the tagline "Beautiful and Political: Julianna Doncheva." The magazine fea-

Table 7.3. Personal background of the members of the Bulgarian Parliament interviewed for this study, 2001–2005

Party Affiliation	Age (years)	Education	Professional Background	Marital Status
NMSS	36	University	Jurist	Married
NMSS	36	University	Academic (Bulgarian philology)	Married
NMSS	46	University	Academic (economics)	Married
NMSS	50	University	Banking	Married
NMSS	63	University	Secretary/teacher	Widowed
NMSS	36	University	Journalist/model	Married
BSP	41	University	Jurist	Single
BSP	52	University	Academic (economics)	Married
UDF	43	University	Academic (English/Russian philology)	Married
UDF/DSB	45	University	Jurist	Single
UDF/DSB	47	University	Jurist	Widowed

Note: NMSS = National Movement of Simeon the Second; BSP = Bulgarian Socialist Party; UDF = Union of Democratic Forces; DSB = Democrats for a Strong Bulgaria.
Sources: Web site of the Bulgarian National Assembly (www.parliament.bg) and personal interviews.

tured a fashion spread and an interview with the former model. The MP brought readers into her home, dispensed advice on clothing and interior design, and expounded upon whether or not it helped or hurt to be a "beautiful woman in a man's world."[26]

The two BSP MPs I interviewed both felt that the NMSS women had lowered Bulgarians' respect for women in politics. One said, "People should care about what politicians think and how they vote, not about what they wear. I want to be judged on how good a politician I am, not on how long my legs are or how big is my bust."[27] The other BSP MP, a political veteran of two previous parliaments, called the Thirty-Ninth National Assembly the "party parliament" and said that many of the women MPs were there for purely "social reasons,"[28] meaning that they liked to go to all the parliamentary parties, enjoy the special perks awarded to MPs, and generally use their positions as MPs to increase their social status in society. She said, "This may be the most incompetent parliament in Bulgaria's recent history, but it is certainly the most beautiful."[29] Whatever the controversies regarding how the NMSS women got into parliament, the fact was that they made up 40 percent of the NMSS's MPs and raised the percentage of women in Bulgaria's National Assembly higher than it had been in over three decades.

Women's Constituencies for Women in Politics

In my interviews with MPs and lobbyists, I wanted to know how the greatly increased number of women in the National Assembly had an impact on the culture of politics in Bulgaria. I was curious to find out whether the women politicians believed that Bulgarian women voted for female politicians on the basis of gender. There were two distinct perspectives on this issue. MPs with previous political experience—those from the BSP and the UDF, and one MP from the NMSS—were certain that women in Bulgaria did not consciously vote for female politicians. The reasons for this lack of a female constituency, however, varied. One UDF MP explained that women do not vote for women because female politicians in Bulgaria rarely serve as advocates for women's causes in public.[30] A NMSS MP agreed with this assessment. She had run for mayor in one of Bulgaria's major cities and had received more votes from men than women. Reflecting upon her loss, she suggested that she did not appeal to women because she did not "take up women's issues."[31] In her defense, she said that she did not believe that there were women's issues, only political issues. During her campaign, I knew from another MP that this NMSS MP had made a very antifeminist speech to a group of visiting Albanian female politicians and Bulgarian women's nongovernmental organization (NGOs). Not only did she not "take up" women's issues, she publicly claimed that there were no "women's" issues.

A BSP MP argued that Bulgarians do not want female politicians because it would remind them too much of Communist times.[32] One example she gave is that the BSP (the "heir" of the Bulgarian Communist Party) still maintains a gender quota—30 percent of all BSP candidates should be women. The gender quota is not something the party openly campaigns upon, and despite the quota, the BSP had a smaller percentage of women as MPs than either the NMSS or the UDF.[33] In the 2001 elections, only two women candidates were on the top positions on the BSP lists, and only five of the 48 BSP seats were held by women. This BSP MP felt that too many women on the lists and in parliament might hurt the BSP rather than help it if Bulgarians associated women in power with Communism. Finally, she suggested that women simply might not want female politicians. She said, "Women are 52 percent of the electorate; if they voted along gendered lines, we would have a whole government full of women. But women consistently vote for men."[34]

Another BSP MP claimed that Bulgarian women did not consciously vote for women, but that Bulgarian men would vote for a male candidate to unseat an incumbent female politician simply because of her gender. Thus, she felt that being a woman was a bit of a political liability.[35] A UDF MP told me that Bulgarian women would only vote for what she called "masculine" women—women who are pragmatic and aggressive.[36] Another UDF MP said: "It has become a kind of fashion for parties to put one or two women on the top of their lists; it is a flirt with voters, not conscious politics."[37] This MP also stressed that the female electorate in Bulgaria is very educated and politically knowledgeable. Major issues divide the political parties in Bulgaria, and women are smart enough to vote for their political convictions rather than for the gender of the party candidates. She also argued that it was more difficult to get to the top of the list in a traditional party because there are fewer well-known female politicians than male ones. Parties naturally want to put the most popular politicians at the top of their lists. The gender of the candidates is less important than whether or not voters know who they are.

On the other side of the debate were all but one of the female NMSS MPs that I interviewed. From their perspective, Bulgarian women do consciously vote for women politicians. One MP felt that there was a popular perception that women politicians were less corrupt, less self-interested, and more results oriented than male politicians, who are far more concerned with their own ego maintenance than with the lives of their constituents. "The prominent women in previous parliaments have distinguished themselves as being more practical and focused on consensus building."[38] Rather than jockeying for the limelight, this MP argued that women in parliament were just as happy to work behind the scenes to achieve desired results. She felt that voters were slowly beginning to recognize this, and that Bulgarians would be more likely to vote for women in the future.

Another NMSS MP pointed out that public opinion had already accepted that a quarter of the parliamentarians were women. She thought this was important because Bulgaria had not had so many women in the National Assembly since Communism, and public acceptance of women in power was a crucial step for increasing women's political participation in the future.[39] Furthermore, when a group of MPs splintered off from the NMSS to form their own parliamentary group (the New Time), the founders publicly stressed that more than 40 percent of their members were women. She felt that this public attention to the presence of women in a new parliamentary group was also a victory for women, because only a few years earlier Bulgarians would not have cared about this at all. She also stressed the youth of Bulgarian democracy and pointed out that many women's NGOs were still actively organizing women's voter education. In years to come, she felt that political allegiances would become increasingly issue based as the Bulgarian electorate matured. Her opinion was that female politicians were better representatives of social issues, and that Bulgarian women were starting to realize that.

Women in Parliament and Support for Women's Issues

Increasing the number of women in parliament can increase the legislative attention paid to women's issues, or to what my informants would consider "social issues." There were two other questions that I asked in all my interviews. First, did the MPs in the Thirty-Ninth National Assembly feel that having more women in parliament affected the legislative agenda and/or the floor debates regarding women's issues? Second, did women politicians ever cross party lines to vote together on issues of particular concern to women?

I started by looking at the composition of parliamentary committees that would deal with bills on social issues, and I compared the gender composition of these committees with that of the more "serious" economic, legal, and national security committees. The composition of these committees is extremely important because all the major work on proposed bills is first done in committee before it goes to the full parliament. Of the twenty-two parliamentary committees that existed in September 2004, I chose to look at the gender composition of eight of them: four committees dealing with social issues—Labor and Social Policy; Health Care; Education and Science; and Children, Youth, and Sports Affairs; and the four most prominent committees—Economic Policy; Budget and Finance; Foreign Policy, Defense, and Security; and Legal Affairs. Table 7.4 shows the results of these comparisons.

Because 27.5 percent of the members of the National Assembly were women, they would make up roughly the same share of all the committees if they were distributed proportionally among them.[40] In fact, what I found was that women MPs were overrepresented on the Education and Science and the Children, Youth, and Sports Affairs committees. Women MPs were underrepresented on the Health Care and the Economic Policy committees, but they were proportionately represented on all other committees, including the important Budget and Finance and Foreign Policy committees. Women MPs were certainly not being "ghettoized" into only serving on "social issue" committees, but they were slightly better represented on those committees, indicating that at least some female MPs gravitated toward or were steered to these committees by their party leadership.

The women I interviewed also believed that women of all political parties cared more about women's or "social" issues than men. As one senior MP said, "I'm not talking about feminism here, but there is more attention

Table 7.4. Gender composition of the Bulgarian Parliamentary committees, 2004

Committee	Total Number of Members	Total Number of Women Members	Percent Women Members
Labor and Social Policy	22	7	31.8
Education and Science	23	10	43.5
Health Care	25	4	16.0
Children, Youth, and Sports Affairs	19	9	47.4
Economic Policy	26	6	23.1
Budget and Finance	26	9	34.6
Foreign Policy, Defense, and Security	28	9	32.1
Legal Affairs	24	7	29.2

Source: Web site of the Bulgarian National Assembly (www.parliament.bg), September 15, 2004.

to social issues when there are more women in parliament. We are more compassionate."[41] This matched a popular perception of women in politics among the Bulgarian public. According to a February 2003 national representative survey, 57.2 percent of those surveyed agreed that women in politics are more responsive to the problems of ordinary people.[42] The MPs, however, were very careful to distinguish "social issues" from "women's issues." On several occasions, they emphasized that there were no purely women's issues, "only budget issues."[43] The category of "gender issues" was even less appealing to women MPs than "women's issues," and most actively distanced themselves from anything having to do with the imported Anglo-American word and concept of "gender," which refers to the socially constructed categories of "men" and "women" versus the more familiar biological definitions of male and female. Pavlina Filipova, the director of a women's NGO in Sofia complained: "In the last parliament there were only 10 percent women, but most of them were gender aware. In this parliament there are 27 percent women and almost none of them are gender aware."

Bulgarian politicians, like Bulgarian women, are very suspicious of Western "feminist" ideas and do not generally believe that women's issues can be separated from men's issues.[44] They recognize that both men and women have been negatively affected by the transition from Communism, and that the lives of Bulgarian men and women are intricately intertwined. From this perspective, there are no "women's issues" that do not also affect men in some way, especially if those issues require a part of Bulgaria's scarce fiscal resources. For example, maternity leaves and child allowances were two fiercely contested political issues because of the costs associated with them, even though they directly affected women. Women MPs consistently corrected me when I referred to them as women's issues. The expense to both state and private employers associated with the Bulgarian tradition of extended maternity leaves could not be ignored in the political debates surrounding them, and women of different political parties had very different views on whether longer maternity leaves helped or hurt women in the workforce. The BSP MPs believed that the state had a responsibility to pay for or force employers to pay for the costs of extended maternity leaves and argued that Bulgaria's severely low fertility rates warranted urgent state action.

Deputies holding the more free market political views of the UDF and the NMSS, however, resisted calls for maternity leaves. They argued that the state budget was too tight to pay for extended maternity leaves and that forcing employers to do so would constitute undue state influence in the market, which would force employers to discriminate against women of childbearing age in hiring decisions. On both sides of the political spectrum, however, there was an agreement that generous maternity leave policies would benefit primarily Bulgaria's Roma population, which already had the highest birthrates. The political complications of supporting expensive maternity leaves even tempered the BSP's ability to successfully advocate for them.

One of the most powerful MPs in the BSP is an outspoken and experienced leader of her party. With regard to "women's issues," she stated:

> I never met a man who thought that paid maternity leaves and child allowances were a bad thing. But Bulgaria cannot afford them. We have to fight the battles we can win. For instance, trying to increase pensions for retirees in Bulgaria. At the moment they are very low, and the older generation is one of our core constituencies. Although this is not specifically a women's issue, it does have great importance for women, because women in Bulgaria outlive men by several years and an increase in pensions will help many older women. But increasing pensions also costs money, and we may have to do so at the expense of child allowances. We are helping women in both cases, but different women, and some men, of course. These are the hard choices politicians have to make.[45]

Indeed, strategically, the issue of pension increases for Bulgaria's rapidly aging population is a core concern of the BSP, whose constituency is disproportionately made up of those over fifty-five years of age. Even younger Bulgarians are concerned with the pension issue because the sons and daughters of pensioners are forced to supplement their parents' living expenses out of their own already-paltry wages. But the issue of increasing pensions breaks down along party lines; the left argues that it is absolutely necessary, and the right argues that it is too expensive and not a productive use of limited budget resources. Whether this is a "women's issue" is also hotly contested. Although women pensioners do outnumber men, and women's organizations admit that widows and older divorcees are among the poorest individuals in the country, pension increases are rarely considered "women's issues" by women's NGOs and their international feminist donors.[46]

As a women's issue, reproductive rights have not yet come to the fore, because they have not yet been challenged in Bulgaria. Women have free access to abortion, and birth control is easily available to all who want it. The only issues considered purely "women's issues" were domestic violence and sexual harassment because both were "imported" from the West,[47]

and neither had direct budgetary implications. As described above, the traditional parties had strict political stances on most issues from which
deputies were not allowed to deviate: The BSP is in favor of longer maternity leaves, but the UDF is against them; the BSP is in favor of child allowances, but the UDF against them; and so on. The apparent exception to
this was the NMSS, which had no clear political position on many issues.
One opposition MP claimed that "the NMSS women have more freedom to
pursue women's issues because they have a very loose party platform."[48]
Thus, even though almost all the women I interviewed said they cared more
about social issues, they did not necessarily "care" about them in the same
way. Instead, the way they cared about social issues was often strictly determined by their party's political platform.

Because of these ideological divisions, I found that Bulgarian women
MPs rarely worked together if their parties disagreed. One opposition MP
claimed that there were no natural allegiances among women. She said,
"Men and women of the same political party have more in common with
each other than women in opposing parties do."[49] An NMSS MP, however,
stated that female politicians of different political parties were much more
"civilized" with each other than were men in different parties.[50] This same
MP claimed that the large presence of women in the National Assembly actually made the debates less hostile and more collegial—she thought that
female MPs diffused intraparliamentary conflicts. Her explanation for
women's camaraderie was that all the female MPs shared the same challenges of being a woman in Bulgarian national politics. In fact, all but one
MP confided that women in parliament faced more difficulties than men.[51]
Most of the MPs interviewed complained about the long hours, the challenges of combining work and family life, the need for supportive husbands
or families, and the hardships of distinguishing oneself as a competent
leader to both one's own party and the electorate. One UDF MP said,
"Women have to work twice as hard as men to become politicians. For
women, it is always a fight."[52]

But even these shared experiences as women were not enough to create
a real women's lobby in the National Assembly. Bulgarian women in parliament were first and foremost allied with their parties. To further explore
this question of whether women in the National Assembly pay more attention to social issues, and to find out if female MPs cross party lines to vote
together on proposed laws that might be beneficial for women, I asked all
my informants about specific pieces of proposed legislation and the debates
surrounding them. My theory was that if the higher percentage of women

in the Bulgarian parliament was having the effect of implementing a more "feminist" agenda, then female MPs would cross party lines to vote together on bills that dealt specifically with women's issues.

There were various examples of "women's" legislation that demonstrated that women did not band together to vote as a bloc. The first example was a piece of proposed legislation from the Thirty-Eighth National Assembly when the UDF had been in power and the BSP in the opposition. The BSP had proposed a law that would have required political quotas for women in all elected offices. There were four cosponsors of the legislation from the ruling UDF, but when it came time to vote, the four UDF cosponsors left the hall and did not cast votes. Their party was against quotas in principle, and the women (even though they were sponsors of the legislation) would not vote against their own party platform. The legislation failed by seven votes.

Examples from the Thirty-Ninth National Assembly show similar divisions between women of different political parties. In one example, the UDF had proposed legislation that would have reduced the tax burden on certain populations of women and increased divorcees' access to child support. The NMSS and its female MPs rejected the bill. The UDF MPs said that it was voted down because the NMSS would not vote for a law proposed by the opposition. An NMSS MP claimed that it was a "tax cut" in disguise. In another case, a UDF MP had proposed a law establishing a national hotline for child victims of sexual assault. This proposal required 850,000 leva from the national budget,[53] and this MP strongly lobbied all the other women in parliament to back the law. Again, the legislation did not pass. The UDF MP blamed partisan politics. NMSS MPs claimed that the hotline was too expensive and of dubious value. Finally, the UDF had proposed a law on "equal opportunities" that would legally enshrine the equality of men and women in Bulgaria, and guarantee equal opportunities for men and women in the economy and polity. Women in the NMSS majority once again rejected this legislation, claiming that they did not vote for it because they believed that men and women were already equal in Bulgaria and that it was thus unnecessary to legislate on the issue. Another NMSS MP told me that it was also a very poorly written law, "a mixture of different European Directives and gender nonsense."

Conversely, social legislation proposed by the NMSS had much more success because it has an almost absolute majority in parliament. It proposed a more general "antidiscrimination" law that prohibited employers from discriminating on the basis of sex, ethnicity, religion, age, disability,

and the like. Beyond the low government salaries of the nine antidiscrimination commissioners, the law cost taxpayers very little, and the punitive
fines that it could levy on employers and educational institutions found
guilty of discrimination could actually make money for the national budget.
This law was passed with a majority of women in parliament voting in favor. MPs of all parties also stood united behind a relatively budget neutral
amendment to the Law on the Protection of the Child.

In fact, there seemed to be a strong correlation between the budgetary
impact of a proposed law and the divisions between women in different parties—the more money a law required the less likely women of different parties were to stand behind it. Alternatively, if the legislation had little or no
budgetary impact, women could and did cross party lines to support it, but
only if men from their parties did the same. I conducted my interviews during the time when parliament was voting on the first reading of a proposed
law on domestic violence.[54] The draft law had been written by a Bulgarian
women's NGO in Sofia, and the initiative was being spearheaded by an MP
from the NMSS. When I interviewed her, she explained that she had worked
very closely with the Bulgarian Gender Research Foundation to write the
law, and that the legislation was an excellent example of how the high percentage of women in parliament was translating into more attention for
women's issues.[55] The law as proposed in the first reading imposed fines on
men who beat their wives and children—instead of being revenue neutral,
the law also could generate revenue for the state. Every woman in parliament supported the first reading. The MP's efforts on the domestic violence
legislation have made a name for her within the NMSS, and she has risen
from political obscurity to national attention. Her success with the legislation has given an example to other NMSS MPs on how to distinguish themselves within the king's party if they desire to do so. This is an important
point to which I will return below.

Outside parliament, lobbyists also have mixed feelings about the extent
to which female politicians care more about social issues. The director of
the Bulgarian Gender Research Foundation, Genoveva Tisheva, argued
that female politicians do pay more attention to women's issues and that
the higher percentage of women in parliament was beginning to translate
into greater support for what Western feminists would consider "women's
causes," even if those MPs may not view them as being unique to women.
The foundation's close work with the NMSS on the domestic violence law
was heralded as a great success for Bulgarian women, and Tisheva believed
that there would be increasing attention paid to women's issues in the fu-

ture: "Building a women's lobby takes time. We have already come so far since the early 1990s. We are taking steps in the right direction." As a lawyer herself, Tisheva felt that her work on the domestic violence law set a good precedent for government-NGO cooperation in the future.

However, Pavlina Filipova, the director of the other major women's NGO in Sofia, the Women's Alliance for Development, felt that the women in parliament were openly hostile to and not interested in promoting a feminist agenda in terms of openly advocating for women's rights. Filipova's organization had helped to draft the failed Law on Equal Opportunities proposed by the UDF. She felt that female politicians could not be counted on to take up Bulgarian women's issues, because in many cases they did not believe that the issues were real. She said that it was important for women politicians to run for office on a feminist or at least openly prowomen platform, and that the mere presence of women in parliament did not automatically translate into more attention to gender issues, especially if they merely used women's issues to promote their political careers without following through with support for legislation. Her organization had coordinated several well-funded national campaigns over previous years to increase women's participation in politics, both as voters and potential candidates. She was very frustrated with many of the women in parliament who wanted nothing to do with advocating for women's rights. She said: "We helped to get those women into parliament, and now they will not listen to us at all. Sometimes they are even worse than the men."

Despite the hostility, Filipova admitted that some female MPs were willing to work with her organization, and that several important pieces of legislation for which they had lobbied had been passed: the antidiscrimination law and the law against the trafficking in persons. She also claimed that the high number of women in parliament did set an important precedent. Her organization planned to continue to advocate for women's rights and work to increase the number of women in politics. She was also committed to continuing her organization's efforts to lobby the National Assembly for more social legislation that would improve the material conditions of women's lives. She told me that Kina Andreeva of the UDF has always provided a friendly ear to the Women's Alliance for Development during her time in parliament. Andreeva apparently was a strident advocate for women's issues (see her personal testimony in chapter 13 of this volume).

It was in this interaction between female MPs and NGOs that I found the greatest possibilities for women in parliament pursuing women's issues (however loosely defined), albeit more by coincidence rather than by design, particularly for the MPs of the NMSS. As mentioned above, many of the women who became MPs for the NMSS were not politicians and had no legal background before joining the king's movement. They were for the most part, however, professionally trained women with prior careers (excluding, of course, the university students). They were journalists, medical doctors, professors, and researchers, as well as many other types of white-collar professionals. Although lacking in political experience, they were generally educated and capable women. Like the NMSS MP who proposed the domestic violence legislation, they were new to national politics and at a great disadvantage compared with women MPs in the traditional political parties who had served in previous parliaments or had held high-level appointed positions within the government. As MPs, these women were expected to give up their jobs, leave their families, move to Sofia, and show up to the National Assembly three times a week when parliament was in session. They were expected to go to committee meetings, be present for floor debates and votes, and generally contribute to the workings of the Bulgarian legislative process. Given all this activity, it should come as no surprise that at least a handful of the more than fifty relatively intelligent women in the NMSS actually took a liking to politics and decided that they wanted to pursue a political career beyond 2005, when the next parliamentary elections would be held.

But a place high enough on the NMSS lists to guarantee reelection was not a given for MPs (whether male or female) because the king would have far more time to put his lists together for the 2005 election, and it was not likely that the NMSS would enjoy the same electoral success. If an MP wanted to continue her career in politics, the best avenue was to generate parliamentary activity and positive publicity for the NMSS. One way to do this was by proposing or advocating for draft legislation on a certain issue for which the MP could become the party "expert." Because Bulgarian women are expected to care more about social issues, one of the best ways for a rookie female politician to call attention to herself both within her party and within parliament was to sponsor some fairly benign legislation on a social issue, preferably a bill with comparatively little budgetary impact —legislation on domestic violence, antidiscrimination, protection of children, and the like. It would be even better if this legislation helped to harmonize Bulgaria's laws with the existing laws in the European Union, because the EU had many legislative requirements with which Bulgaria needed to comply in the run-up to its accession. This strategy was very successfully employed by Jenny Zhivkova, a fashion designer and the granddaughter of Bulgaria's Communist ruler. She solidified her otherwise purely hereditary political credentials within the BSP by becoming a tireless parliamentary advocate for "youth issues."

But because so few of the NMSS deputies were jurists (lawyers, judges, etc.), those women who wanted to propose legislation often went "shopping" for draft legislation at different NGOs and associations in Sofia. This appears to be the way the NMSS MP took charge of the domestic violence bill and UDF MPs got behind the law on equal opportunities. Essentially, then, the women in the National Assembly could meet with different lobbyists to look for suitable draft legislation that they could then take to their party leadership and propose to the assembly. If there are women's associations preparing draft bills on "women's issues," and these bills are relevant and sensitive to the Bulgarian political context, then female politicians looking for new legislation will have an incentive to gravitate toward "women's" issues.

Of course, too radical a "feminist" agenda would be political suicide in Bulgaria, and so the legislation needs to be prepared by women's organizations that are realistic about how much "best practices" can be imported from feminist legislation in the West. Furthermore, even though the legislation is proposed, it will not necessarily become law. Nevertheless, because women in politics in Bulgaria believe that they care more about social issues, it makes sense that they use those issues to further their own political careers. Just proposing a law is enough to generate media attention to an issue, and this attention is good not only for the proposing politician but also for raising awareness of the issue itself. Thus, it is through this ironic manifestation of enlightened self-interest that more "gender empowerment" may result from having many women in parliament, even if those women are openly antifeminist. But this phenomenon needs to be studied more carefully in the future before firm conclusions can be drawn.

Conclusions

The increased number of women in Bulgaria's Thirty-Ninth National Assembly was not the result of a sudden surge in popular support for women politicians. Nor did it result from a reinstitution of electoral quotas. The dramatic increase in women's presence as MPs was rather the result of a historical anomaly. The unexpected return of Bulgaria's ex-king, the speed with which he registered his party, and the overwhelming electoral support he received were primarily responsible for the high percentage of women in Bulgaria's parliament. Although women made up more than a quarter of all MPs, I found no evidence that their presence had intentionally translated into more support for women's/social issues or precipitated the formation of a woman's lobby within parliament. It was clear that women are just as divided by political ideology as men, and that the increased number of women in parliament did not lead to the legislative implementation of a "feminist" agenda, however broadly defined.

However, there were some indications that the increase in the number of women in parliament, particularly of those without previous political experience, could translate into increased awareness of women's issues if they worked together with local NGOs. One way this could happen is if there are active women's organizations lobbying parliament with relevant legislative proposals. Of course, these legislative proposals would have to address the real needs of Bulgarian women with locally appropriate and politically acceptable solutions rather than just importing feminist agendas and laws from the United States and Western Europe. The ability of local women's organizations to become valuable allies of women MPs will depend on their sensitivity to the political realities that women politicians face in a society that is still rather hostile to anything considered overtly feminist.

After I had conducted all the interviews for this study in the summer of 2004, there were new parliamentary elections in July 2005. These new elections once again dramatically changed the political landscape in Bulgaria. Seven parties or coalitions earned more than 4 percent of the vote and entered parliament. These included three new parties: the Democrats for a Strong Bulgaria, led by Bulgaria's former prime minister, Ivan Kostov; the Bulgarian People's Union, led by Sofia's charismatic but controversial mayor, Stefan Sofianski; and "Attack," a right-wing, anti-Turkish, anti-Roma party that surprisingly became the fourth-strongest party in parliament. The NMSS lost its dominance to the BSP, but the BSP did not win enough seats to form a government. After months of political jockeying and strategic stalemates, a coalition government was formed between the BSP, the NMSS, and the Turkish Movement for Rights and Freedoms (MRF) with the BSP's Sergei Stanishev as prime minister.

The key issues in the election were the economy, Bulgaria's relationship with the International Monetary Fund, Bulgaria's planned accession to the European Union, and a growing Bulgarian nationalism that had been festering in the country since the fall of Communism. The BSP promised to raise pensions and public-sector wages against the dictates of the International Monetary Fund, whereas the NMSS and the other center-right parties claimed that raising pensions and wages would cause inflation and create economic instability. All the parties were pro–European Union accession except for the right-wing Attack, which argued that Bulgaria had already given up too much of its sovereignty to the EU and had received nothing in return. Because of its promises to raise people's living standards, all the early polls predicted that the BSP would win the election. But the BSP's leaders admitted before the election that they would form a coalition with the ethnic Turkish party, the MRF, a very unpopular move among many ethnic Bulgarians. Attack—with its openly anti-Turkish and anti-Roma rhetoric, combined with its outspoken position against the European Union—managed to capture a significant portion of the vote that might otherwise have gone to the BSP. Many working-class Bulgarians abandoned the BSP on election day and made Attack the fourth-largest party in parliament.

Despite the high percentage of women on the electoral lists of several parties, exit polls showed that women did not seem to vote for parties with more women on their lists.[56] Of all the votes the NMSS received, 55.8 percent came from women.[57] The New Time (which failed to pass the 4 percent threshold) received 54.3 percent of its votes from women. However, for the BSP, which had fewer women on its lists than the NMSS and the New Time, women still made up 55.5 percent of its electorate. On the other side of the coin, the two parties with the fewest women on their lists, the MRF and Attack, also had the fewest number of women voters; respectively, 47 percent for the MRF and 42.3 percent for Attack.

However, it is impossible to gauge what effect the women on the lists had on voters, and there are many confounding factors that cannot be controlled for with the available data. Overall, I do not think that women voted along gendered lines as much as they were concerned about the political platforms of the parties themselves. This explains the high percentage of women who voted for the BSP despite the fact that there were fewer women on its lists. Moreover, the BSP took 31.17 percent of the total vote and the NMSS won 19.91 percent. If women were truly voting along gendered lines, then the NMSS should have performed much better than it did.

The most significant gender difference in voting patterns was indeed for the party Attack. This new party emerged onto the scene rather late in the game, and it started gaining popularity only in the last month before the elections. Its basic platform was that Bulgaria should be for the ethnic Bulgarians. Quite surprisingly, 293,139 people voted for it—8.2 percent of the electorate. A total of 57.7 percent of these votes came from men, and, interestingly, 38.8 percent from people with a university education. And 99.2 percent of the votes for Attack came from ethnic Bulgarians (for the other ethnic-based party, the MRF, 80 percent of votes came from ethic Turks). In Attack's twenty seats, they have only one woman; and in MRF's thirty-four seats, they have only three women. These two parties have by far the lowest proportions of women MPs.

Despite this, the percentage of women in parliament did not fall as severely as some had expected. Women made up about 21.3 percent of the MPs in the Fortieth National Assembly, a drop from the 26 percent they had held in the Thirty-Ninth National Assembly,[58] but still well above the post-socialist norm that had been established between 1990 and 2001. Once again, the large representation of women in parliament was overwhelmingly due to the composition of the NMSS, which, even though it had lost more than fifty seats in this election, had slightly increased the percentage of women representing it in parliament. In November 2005, 41.5 percent of the NMSS MPs were women, compared with only 19.5 percent of the BSP MPs (table 7.5).

Finally, the doubts that had surrounded Saxecoburgotski's motives for including so many women on his lists for the 2001 elections were tempered by 2005. The prime minister had plenty of time and opportunity to arrange the electoral lists to his liking, but he continued to place women in his party on the top of his electoral lists, despite the fact that most pollsters had predicted that the NMSS would lose the election. Thirty-seven percent of the candidates in the top five positions on the former king's lists were women, far more than any other party (table 7.6).

Table 7.5. Women in the fortieth Bulgarian National Assembly by party, group, or coalition, 2005

Party, Group, or Coalition	Total Number of Seats	Percent Women
Bulgarian Socialist Party	82	19.5
National Movement of Simeon the Second	53	41.5
Movement for Rights and Freedom	34	2.9
"Attack"	17	5.9
Union of Democratic Forces	20	17.6
Democrats for a Strong Bulgaria	17	23.5
Bulgarian People's Union	13	7.7
Independent	4	0.0
Total	240	21.3

Source: Web site of the Bulgarian National Assembly (www.parliament.bg), November 14, 2005.

Table 7.6. Women candidates in the top five places on their parties' lists in the 2005 Bulgarian Parliamentary elections

Position on the Party List	BSP	NMSS	UDF	MRF	DSB	BPU	New Time
1	6.5	25.8	9.7	12.9	19.4	12.9	22.6
2	22.6	41.9	12.9	3.2	19.4	12.9	39.7
3	32.3	35.5	12.9	22.6	22.6	16.1	32.3
4	25.8	38.7	12.9	16.1	48.4	16.1	29.0
5	16.1	45.2	19.4	16.1	19.4	25.8	25.8
Number in top five places	32	58	21	22	40	25	46
Percentage of women in top five places	20.6	37.4	13.5	14.2	25.8	16.1	29.7

Note: BSP = Bulgarian Socialist Party; NMSS = National Movement of Simeon the Second; UDF = Union of Democratic Forces; MRF = Movement for Rights and Freedoms; DSB = Democrats for a Strong Bulgaria; BPU = Bulgarian People's Union.
Source: Gender Project for Bulgaria, *Bulletin 1* (http://www.gender-bg.org/_bg/news_bg.html).

Many of these women are now serving their second term as NMSS MPs, and it could be argued that Saxecoburgotski trained a new crop of women politicians with the experience and know-how necessary for running the Bulgarian government. In fact, women in the Fortieth National Assembly were particularly active, and filled high-level ministerial positions within the cabinet of the NMSS-BSP-MRF coalition government. By 2008, of the twenty-one cabinet positions, Bulgarian women held seven key posts in the government. These included that of deputy prime minister, and the ministers of justice, European affairs, emergency situations, labor and social policy, as well as the directors of the State Agency for Tourism and the State Agency for Youth and Sport. Furthermore, deputies in the BSP, such as Tantanya Doncheva and Emilia Maslarova, were serving their third or fourth consecutive term in parliament, placing them among the senior parliamentarians. Doncheva even ran for mayor of Sofia, one of the most influential political positions in the country. Although she lost to an upstart populist, Boiko Borrisov, she ran a successful campaign and garnered enough votes to force a runoff.

In the 2007 elections for the European Parliament, Bulgarian women had a strong showing, and approximately 45 percent of the members Bulgaria sent to Brussels were women. Women candidates did not fair so well in the municipal elections in late 2007, however, because Borissov's new political party, Citizens for European Development of Bulgaria (CEDB), won those elections in a landslide and had relatively fewer women on his lists.

In it widely predicted that the CEDB will win the parliamentary elections scheduled to be held in 2009, and unless a conscious effort is made to increase the representation of women in the CEDB, then the Forty-First National Assembly may see a further drop in the participation of women as MPs from its peak in the Thirty-Ninth National Assembly.

What is clear, however, is that there is now an active cadre of female politicians in almost all political parties, a handful of whom are senior MPs. These women were able to support legislation that promoted specific women's issues, such as having the National Health Insurance help pay for in vitro fertility treatments for women that were having difficulty conceiving children. The continued presence of women in parliament, together with the increasing lobbying efforts of women's NGOs, could eventually form the basis for a "women's lobby" in parliament that could further the cause of legislation more sensitive and favorable to women's social issues. For now, however, the major issues that faced parliament after the 2005 elections were tackling the problems of corruption and organized crime and managing Bulgaria's faltering economy and low standard of living. With Bulgaria's accession to the European Union on January 1, 2007, a whole new phase of the country's post-Communist history began. As Bulgaria moves into the twenty-first century, it is hoped that the gains made by women politicians through their affiliation with the former tsar of Bulgaria and his political party in 2001 will endure.

Notes

1. Louis Napoleon was the last case in postrevolutionary France.

2. Bulgaria has a unicameral legislature called the Narodno Sobranie (National Assembly).

3. Irene Tinker, "Quotas for Women in Elected Legislatures: Do They Really Empower Women?" *Women's Studies International Forum* 27, nos. 5–6 (2004): 531–46.

4. Personal communication with the National Association of Municipalities in the Republic of Bulgaria in August 2004.

5. Susan Gal and Gail Kligman, *The Politics of Gender after Socialism* (Princeton, N.J.: Princeton University Press, 2000).

6. Vlasta Jalušić and Milica Antić, *Prospects for Gender Equality Policies in Central and Eastern Europe,* Social Consequences of Economic Transformation in East Central Europe Project Paper 79 (Vienna: Institute for Human Sciences, 2000), http://www.iwm.at/publ-spp/soco79pp.pdf.

7. Dobrinka Kostova, "Similar or Different? Women in Postcommunist Bulgaria," in *Women in the Politics of Postcommunist Eastern Europe,* ed. Marilyn Rueschemeyer (Armonk, N.Y.: M. E. Sharpe, 1998).

8. Todor Zhivkov was Bulgaria's Communist leader for more than thirty-five years.

9. Krassimira Daskalova and Pavlina Filipova, "Citizenship and Women's Political Participation in Bulgaria," published online by Social Rights Bulgaria on March 2, 2004 (http://www.socialrights.org/spip/article494.html); Tatiana Kostandinova, "Women's Legislative Representation in Post-Communist Bulgaria," in *Women's Access to Political Power in Post-Communist Europe,* ed. Richard E. Matland and Kathleen A. Montgomery (Oxford: Oxford University Press, 2003), 304–20.

10. Tinker, "Quotas for Women"; Matland and Montgomery, *Women's Access.*

11. R. J. Crampton, *A Concise History of Bulgaria* (Cambridge: Cambridge University Press, 1997).

12. Many people believe that Hitler poisoned Boris III for his refusal to turn Bulgaria's Jewish population over to the Germans.

13. M. Lalkov, *A History of Bulgaria: An Outline* (Sofia: St. Kliment Ohridski University Press, 1998).

14. Constitution of the Republic of Bulgaria, Promulgated in State Gazette 56/13, July 1991, amended in *State Gazette 85/26,* September 2003, available at www.parliament.bg.

15. Crampton, *Concise History of Bulgaria.*

16. This was apparently due to technical irregularities in his registration documents.

17. Each voting district consists of 10,000 voters.

18. Interview with UDF MP #1.

19. Interview with UDF MP #1.

20. Interview with BSP MP #1.

21. The journalist refers to Simeon Saxecoburgotski as "Tsarya"—literally, "the King."

22. Nevena Petrova, "Bulgarskata Politika Ima Problem, Zhenite sa Malko" (Bulgarian Politics Has a Problem, Women Are Few), *Sega,* May 18, 2004, htttp://www.segabg.com/18052004/p0050003.asp.

23. An online comment made by "Hammer" on May 18, 2004, on the *Sega* Web site, http://www.segabg.com/18052004/p0050003.asp.

24. Kostandinova, *Women's Legislative Representation,* 313.

25. Data adapted from the official Web site of the Bulgarian parliament at www.parliament.bg.

26. Lydia Spirieva, "Julianna Doncheva: Nezhna e Vlasta (Tender is the Power)," *Macksimum,* no. 33 (April 2002): 24–28. For the record, based on my own interview with her, I found MP Doncheva to be both professional and intelligent.

27. Interview with BSP MP #1.

28. Interview with BSP MP #2.

29. Interview with BSP MP #2.

30. Interview with UDF MP #1.

31. Interview with NMSS MP #1.

32. Interview with BSP MP #1.

33. The party achieves this result by putting most of the women on the bottom of their lists.

34. Interview with BSP MP #1.

35. Interview with BSP MP #2.

36. Interview with UDF MP #2.

37. Interview with UDF MP #3.

38. Interview with NMSS MP #3.

39. Interview with NMSS MP #4.

40. The chairperson of each committee is from the ruling parliamentary group, with one deputy chairperson from each other parliamentary group. The representation of different parliamentary groups in the committees must be proportionate to the representation of each group in the National Assembly.

41. Interview with BSP MP #1.

42. National Center for the Survey of Public Opinion, "Public Opinion about Women in Politics," from the Web site of the Women's Alliance for Development at www.womenbg.org.

43. Interview with BSP MP #1.

44. Kristen Ghodsee, "Feminism-by-Design: Emerging Capitalisms, Cultural Feminism and Women's Nongovernmental Organizations in Post-Socialist Eastern Europe," *Signs: Journal of Women in Culture and Society* 29, no. 3 (Spring 2004): 727–53.

45. Interview with BSP MP #1.

46. For more on the politics of women's organization in Bulgaria, see Ghodsee, "Feminism-by-Design."

47. Although domestic violence certainly existed under Communism, it was considered a private matter between families, and not something the state should be involved in. The concept of sexual harassment also did not really exist in Bulgaria until after 1989, despite the widespread practice of it.

48. Interview with UDF MP #2.

49. Interview with UDF MP #1.

50. Interview with NMSS MP #2.

51. This MP felt that both men and women faced difficulties in the world of politics: "They may be different kinds of difficulties, but they are still difficulties." Interview with NMSS MP #5.

52. Interview with UDF MP #3.

53. The Bulgarian currency is the lev; "leva" is the plural of lev.

54. Bulgarian bills are voted upon in two readings. A bill becomes law if it receives the required votes at the second reading.

55. Interview with NMSS MP #3.

56. Central Electoral Commission, *Biuletin za rezultatite ot izborite, proizvedeni na 25 Juni 2005 godina* (Sofia: Tsentralna Izbiratelna Komisiia za izbor na narodni predstaviteli, 2005).

57. All exit poll data come from tables published in the newspapers *24 Chasa, Trud,* and *Monitor* on July 27, 2005.

58. Although the NMSS entered Parliament in 2001 with 120 seats, a handful of MPs from the NMSS became independent members of parliament or joined together to form a new parliamentary group called the New Time, which ran in the 2005 parliamentary elections but did not receive more than the necessary 4 percent of the vote to enter Parliament.

Part II

Perspectives of Women Parliamentarians

Chapter 8

Russian Women Parliamentarians: In Their Own Voices

Compiled and Translated by Carol Nechemias

The excerpts from the twenty-five interviews with current and former State Duma women deputies bring to life the complexity and diverse character of these women politicians. Emphasis has been placed on covering views and perspectives not discussed in chapter 2, on women parliamentarians in Russia, or on amplifying issues that were raised there. Brief commentaries follow excerpts where there is a need to clarify references to events or people for nonspecialist readers or to note connections with the longer chapter on women in the Russian State Duma.

How did you become involved in national politics? What did you do before running for the State Duma?

A Rodina (Motherland) deputy: I became interested in politics in 1991. At that time, the Congress of People's Deputies was televised practically continuously, and many people spoke on national problems, like Buburin and Pavlov, and I became acquainted with their program, and I went to Baburin and began to take up social activism after work . . . in 1993. . . . We quickly went to the White House, and stayed there until the end, we were the last to leave the White House, when it was already burning, many had been killed; all this took place in front of our eyes, and after that situation to leave politics was impossible because I had seen how these people conducted themselves. . . .

Commentary: This deputy refers to Sergei Baburin and Nikolai Pavlov, two leading parliamentary figures who opposed President Boris Yeltsin and figured prominently in the showdown with Yeltsin in the fall of 1993. That confrontation between the president and parliament led to pitched battles in Moscow and the president's employment of military force to dissolve parliament. The building that housed parliament at that time was known as the White House.

A deputy who served in several small liberal, promarket parties: I was a businessperson and . . . I understood that the future for Russian did not lie in NEP but in a real market model, and our bureaucratic officials were not ready for that; our political elite also was not ready. At that moment I made the decision, that, on the one hand, I had experience teaching in higher education—that is, a Soviet type of person—and on the other hand, I was a person who had gone through the school of the market, and such people were needed in politics, so I made the decision to enter the Duma.

Commentary: NEP—the New Economic Policy—was the economic policy promulgated by the Bolshevik regime from 1921 to 1928. NEP restored private trade and permitted the establishment of small private industries and cooperatives, while large-scale industry remained under state administration. During perestroika, there was intense interest in NEP as a possible model for economic reform.

An independent deputy: I was a university professor specializing in economics and finance. . . . Boldyrev invited me to run on the party list for Yabloko. . . . I was an active person, I was in the Communist Party. . . . I was a member of the Komsomol committee at my institute. . . . I was socially active by temperament, and Boldyrev invited me as a specialist on budgetary matters. . . . It was a continuation of my professional interests. . . . I thought it better to prepare decisions myself [than simply do applied economic research].

Commentary: Boldyrev was one of the major figures in Yabloko, a party that promoted itself as the "democratic opposition" to the government. Led by

Grigorii Yavlinskii, the party has stood for a more socially oriented econ-omy and a pro-Western stance.

A United Russia deputy: I finished . . . agricultural institute, was active in Komsomol, and combined teaching at the institute with Komsomol work and graduate studies. . . . I defended my dissertation in agriculture. . . . In 1991 I became a member of and then deputy chair of our republic's com-mittee on youth affairs. . . . That was the beginning of my political career. In 1999 I was elected to our republic legislature and became vice speaker. In that same year it was suggested that I run for the State Duma. . . . I had never thought about a career. . . . I simply liked working with people; by na-ture I am a social activist—since childhood—I wanted to do something use-ful, . . . the opportunity to contribute to the country.

A Liberal Democratic deputy: I worked in the sphere of culture, then I worked a bit as an administrator for my husband, but in 1995 he recom-mended that I help the party. He knew about our party from its beginning. . . . He is a successful entrepreneur. . . . He wanted our party to do well in our region and recommended me to a deputy. . . . I worked as an assistant to a State Duma deputy . . . and also learned about coordinating party work in our district.

A United Russia deputy: I did not have any political experience, I only knew business, not any politics before my entry into the State Duma. . . . It all be-gan . . . with an old friend, a comrade, who had become a member of the co-ordinating council. He knew me as a successful entrepreneur, and therefore a conversation took place, and then specialists from the Union of Right Forces arrived. . . . Any party wants its candidate to be well known in his region, and I was well known. . . . I conducted the campaign with my own money. . . .

Commentary: As noted in chapter 2, on women in the Russian State Duma, this deputy is unusual in that she comes from an entrepreneurial background and could finance her own election campaign. More common backgrounds involve social activity, as expressed by other deputies. Before joining United Russia, this deputy's entrance into the political arena stemmed from re-cruitment by the Union of Right Forces, a party oriented toward democracy and a Western-style market economy.

Are there special challenges or difficulties women parliamentarians face?

A United Russia deputy: The first problem: . . . We have equal rights with men, but . . . the results of any election . . . show that these rights are insufficient.

Up to this time, there is the opinion that if you are a woman, you are weaker, that if you are a woman, you are not suited for holding a post but simply for working. In Russia, in my view, a woman must work significantly more, must prove herself more. . . . I do not call this discrimination, because there is no difference in pay. I am speaking of women's place in society. . . . Our government . . . is taking steps toward democratizing our society. . . . Our society still lacks the consciousness that it is necessary to have women in politics, in our public life.

A United Russia deputy: It's a minus that I'm a woman, because the male contingent does not accept women higher than themselves. A Russian woman always was lower than a man. Men were the breadwinners, the heads of households; . . . that's history. . . . In our government, there are virtually no women, only in secondary roles. A horse that hauls a load—that's us, while the leaders are men. . . .

A Women of Russia deputy: Work in the Duma is hard for everybody, but women are faced with more scrutiny. If a man fails to make a good speech, nobody will think twice of it. If a woman fails, she will be reminded of it and discussed for a long time afterward. But this is not a peculiarity of Russia but a worldwide phenomenon.

A Women of Russia deputy: I never felt any gender-based discrimination in the Duma. As Zhirinovsky [head of the Liberal Democratic Party] put it, it's only on March 8 [International Women's Day] that you are women, and the rest of the year we are all deputies.

A Rodina (Motherland) deputy: In general, the work is hard, . . . more difficult than for men. I don't know, but if a woman has a family and small children, then it seems to me that in that situation, it would be better if the woman does not work.

A Liberal Democratic deputy: . . . I don't feel any differences. There is support, a warm welcome in our fraction. . . . They offer advice, even former deputies; it's possible to go to them for advice, whatever is needed, they help. . . . In the committee I joined, . . . if something is not clear—the committee has a very strong staff, competent. . . .

Are there special challenges or difficulties that women in general face? What do you see as the most important issues facing women? Are there special women's issues that are different from the issues faced by the rest of society?

A Communist Party deputy: Of course, there are specific problems. . . . The government does not stimulate the birthrate. . . . Mothers receive virtually no help. . . . Moreover, there is discrimination against women when it is a question of employment; they break the law, they demand that she sign a paper that she will not give birth, only then will they hire her.

A Rodina (Motherland) deputy: The main problem in Russia—it's demographic. Children's allowances are needed first of all, and benefits for mothers. Without question, we need to turn our attention to health issues. . . . What are women's problems? To give birth to a child? I do not think it's a woman's problem, because a child needs a father, a child needs to eat. The basic function of women—it is motherhood. Our women have lost that function. . . . But for women to give birth—it's men's problem.

A Liberal Democratic deputy: The state should care about both men and women the same, give attention to everyone. Women's problems—doctors are women, teachers are women. . . . The problem is low pay. What do these women need? Everyone has children, they need to clothe them; . . . it's expensive, there's the problem. This problem is the highest priority and can be resolved by raising people's pay so that they can live decently.

A Women of Russia deputy: As for problems facing women in Russia, they lie mainly in the sphere of employment and earnings. Women are concentrated in low-prestige and low-paid jobs. . . . It is difficult to overcome the prejudices of employers who are reluctant to promote women to positions of responsibility. The way out . . . lies first of all in the sphere of law enforcement. In spite of the fact that the Russian Constitution . . . prohibits gender discrimination, it is impossible in practice to prosecute an employer who, for example, advertises a job for "a good-looking girl age twenty to twenty-eight for secretarial work" or "managerial work for men up to forty-five years in age." An important step will be adoption by the Duma of a law guaranteeing equal rights and opportunities for men and women.

A Unified Russia deputy: I know that women's problems largely involve problems connected with the socioeconomic development of the country, . . . and we cannot resolve women's problems separately. . . . My position: Why should we separate women—when on the whole we are all poor?

A Unified Russia deputy: Of course, the position of women is tied to the economic growth of our country, but at the same time women's problems are more than that—but it's not purely a women's issue, it's a general problem for both men and for women. . . . When we speak about family problems, we talk about how there is a woman, a mother, in the family, but we are silent about the role of the father in raising children.

A Unified Russia deputy: I consider that to resolve . . . women's problems, it is necessary to decide a basic question, the problem of women's representation in power. Because it's my deep conviction that until there is a minimum of 30 percent women's representation in power, these issues will not be resolved.

A Liberal Democratic deputy: I think it is necessary to gradually solve all problems. Women—they are the strong sex, they are stronger than men, they sustain everything.

A Deputy who served in several small liberal, promarket parties: . . . [About] discrimination: For women, it's hard to make a career; in the largest commercial corporations, she might reach the level of the second or third person, but she will never be first.

A Unified Russia deputy: In legislation, we have many laws that protect women, mothers; I do not think that there are special problems in legislation in this area. . . There is a law on children's allowances—it's the size of the benefit. . . .

Commentary: As noted in chapter 2, on women deputies in the Russian State Duma, the cohort of women serving after the 2003 election generally do not perceive women's problems as separate from those of men or society as a whole. Women of Russia deputies are more outspoken about discrimination against women, but this faction enjoyed electoral success only in 1993 and has passed from the scene as a parliamentary force. As is evident in the deputies' comments, demographic issues are salient in Russian politics. President Vladimir Putin has addressed this issue in major public addresses, and in May 2006 he sought to reverse the population decline by more than doubling the monthly child support payments and offering substantial bonuses to women who have a second baby.

What is the extent of your contact with women nongovernmental organizations and groups outside your party?

An independent deputy: There was support from organizations in my district. There were women's groups, that is parents of invalid children, mothers with many children, but they were not the main ones. . . . We have veterans' organizations—two-thirds of pensioners are women, practically all veterans' groups are women's organizations. . . . Beyond that, it can be said that women's organizations are very weak.

A Unified Russia deputy [the name of the organization has been deleted to protect the deputy's anonymity]: I became a member of a woman's organization and I'm very proud of it. . . . It's a strong organization, . . . a remarkable organization that supported me in my electoral campaigns. . . . We maintain good relations, and I hope to be very useful to them in my work in the State Duma. . . .

A United Russia deputy: . . . I don't simply work with women's organizations, I help them. I have served since 1996 on the Russian government's Commission for the Improvement of the Status of Women, was involved for several years with the association of women's organizations in my republic, have headed that association since 2000. . . . We continually conduct women's forums. . . . The idea of these forums is to discuss with women's public organizations those painful problems. . . .

A United Russia deputy: We interact. . . . For example, one woman's organization, Mothers Against Narcotics, . . . in our district came to my reception [meeting with constituents] with concrete suggestions for me. . . .

A United Russia deputy: I headed the regional branch of the association named Business Women of Russia in our oblast [region]. It was created not long ago. . . .

A United Russia deputy: The session just started, little time has passed, but professional unions have turned to me with concrete suggestions, letters— nothing from women's organizations yet.

A United Russia deputy: Professional unions, of course, no ties with women's organizations. . . . I did not work with women, and I might say that women do not support me for some reason. Women's organizations do not support me.

Commentary: There is great variation among the women deputies with respect to ties with women's organizations. These range from nonexistent to close working relationships. In some cases, links developed after election to the State Duma and reflect lobbying efforts.

To what extent is there cooperation with other women in parliament to address women's issues?

A Women of Russia deputy: [Ekaterina] Lakhova [former Women of Russia leader and currently a United Russia deputy] heads the Committee on Women, Family, and Youth, which is traditionally the basis for uniting women.

A United Russia deputy: . . . There are few women in power; with us it's a harsh selection process, and there is the instinct for self survival among the women. . . . I am not speaking of myself, I am very loyal and try to support women, but it seems to me that it is our general problem, not only among the deputies here in the State Duma but also at other levels, that there is envy, the desire to survive, you must play by the rules, which were set up by men. If you do not play by those rules, there are other women, and you will be no more. . . . Nonetheless, I think it is necessary to teach all women to rise above their personal interests in order to solve more global issues and not fear putting forward those issues. . . .

An independent deputy: I thought that the committee on women in the last Duma worked well under the leadership of [Svetlana] Goriacheva, who set the program; . . . there was a good orientation. They did not get stuck on . . . women's rights, which don't concern women very much, women above all are worried about the situation of children—the committee studied children's issues. . . . They correctly structured their work in the previous Duma, didn't focus on nonsense like equal rights, equal opportunities. . . .

Commentary: Svetlana Goriacheva chaired the Committee on Women, Family, and Children in the third (1999–2003) session of the State Duma. In 2002, she was expelled from the Communist Party and was elected in 2003 as an independent candidate.

A United Russia deputy: Of course, an organization among women deputies exists and will probably exist. . . . Of the forty-four women deputies, ten remain from the previous session, perhaps fifteen. In the main, we are new, and we are getting used to one another and we will try. . . . On laws like the tax code, and the budget, . . . on wages, on these things, we can talk, we will try to support one another; . . . it is natural.

A United Russia deputy: I would like to be mistaken, but I think that in this Duma there will not be an interfactional association [among women]. . . . Women are more polarized . . . to socialize with the Communist Party, Motherland, and Liberal Democratic Party representatives. . . . It's an entirely different ideology, an entirely different stance, different political views, and for us women in politics, it would be hard to overcome these difficulties. . . .

A Communist Party deputy: I think not, because in this Duma there is so much of a schism based on political party, that they don't allow those poor women from Unified Russia to even think about this; . . . they call it discipline. . . .

A Liberal Democratic deputy: Right now, there is no association, but I have been thinking that Liubov Konstantinovna [Sliska] has already been here a long time, a knowledgeable woman; I am here for the first time, I do not know anyone, I am getting acquainted a bit, but I have the idea that it would be good for someone to organize us, to teach us, to share experience, and to do something, in order that we would deal with women's problems on the basis of a variety of directions.

Commentary: These views are consistent with the analysis in chapter 2, on women in the Russian State Duma. Cooperation among women across party lines has declined over time. The women refer to two possible leaders among United Russia deputies. These include Ekaterina Lakhova, a long-time activist on women's issues and former Women of Russia coleader, and Liubov Sliska, a member of Unified Russia's Supreme Council and first deputy speaker of the State Duma.

Do international influences affect your views regarding your work or women's issues? Have international organizations influenced the "woman question" in Russia?

A Women of Russia deputy: The influence of international organizations in general has been positive. All international initiatives aimed at promoting socioeconomic security and justice are welcome. Such documents as the [Russian] Family Code, the Law on the Rights of Children, and the National Plan of Action for Women were elaborated on the basis of UN documents and norms. The ratification of the EU Social Charter is of crucial importance. . . . Some of the World Bank activities are of interest, like gender research, since it is vital to replace feminist approaches with gender-based approaches.

A Liberal Democratic Party deputy: I've heard about that [international organizations, the European Union], but it's hard for me to say, because I have had no contact with them, have not worked with them.

An independent deputy: They [European organizations] have no influence, but they feed some women's organizations, which in their turn also have no influence. . . . They finance work on equal rights and equal opportunities, they give grants, and they are all like parrots, repeating reports on the status of women that do not touch and will not affect our women.

An independent deputy: Minimal influence, perhaps some, but minimal. The government adopts resolutions, the State Duma even passes some decision, even enumerates some sort of plan to fulfill an international recommendation, but these documents are embraced by state organs in a formal manner; . . . it doesn't go any further.

A Unified Russia deputy: . . . I dream that our party, as in Sweden, will adopt a decision—even without a law—to put together a party list . . . [reflecting great parity for women]. . . . As members of the commission [the Federation Council's Commission on Women], . . . we went to Sweden, where we met with leaders and studied the government and legislative activity.

A Women of Russia deputy: Our country is not so poor as it is perceived to be. Look at Finland—a country without any national resources. Why is it that they have found money to support mothers adequately and we can't?

A Communist Party deputy: Rather negatively, it seems to me, because they [the European Union; international organizations] try to build our organizations according to their models, but we have a totally different country, different problems. For example, their favorite theme involves violence, but for us it's not that, but how to live [feed ourselves], to find work.

A Communist Party deputy: I have a very negative attitude toward feminism; I consider that it is a sort of distortion, because feminists that I know, they do not raise concrete problems. . . . We were in England . . . and met with women who were part of the European Women's Union. . . . We became acquainted with their work, but in many ways they cannot understand us, their problems—for us, they are funny problems. . . . I visited an English prison for youth; if our soldiers lived in such conditions, mothers would prefer to give up their sons not for a year but for two or for five.

A deputy who served in several small liberal, promarket parties: On the general status of women—not any influence, but on the status of women active in civil society, serious help in the form of grants.

What committees or policy areas are you involved in?

A United Russia deputy: I have a definite task that I wish to fulfill in my work as a State Duma deputy—it is, above all . . . to actively participate in the reform of the health care system, because I am a doctor, I have extensive practical experience, including work as an organizer of health care, . . . and here I will be useful.

A Unified Russia deputy: I am on the culture committee . . . since our oblast is rich with museums, historical monuments. . . . I have met with the leadership of [name deleted] oblast. . . . They are delighted that I am on this committee, as the governor values culture. . . .

A Liberal Democratic deputy: I will be working on the Federation Committee and as I did the past two years in the previous Duma session, I will be working on budgetary issues, . . . and the main task I have as a deputy involves how our republic, . . . and my electoral district might receive more opportunities for development through interbudgetary relations, because if there is money, a correct distribution of taxes, the money will go toward goals connected with the development of social programs and investments.
. . . Besides that, we created charitable funds. . . . I am one of the initiators. . . . We conduct a variety of projects, summer programs for children, books for rural libraries, rural stadiums. . . .

A United Russia deputy: . . . What the women's movement has requested, it's what I am trying to work on in the Duma. . . . This is the question of pay for public-sector employees, because in the main teachers are women, and music schools, and libraries, the entire budgetary sphere, it's doctors. . . . In the main, it's women. . . . And I am deputy chair of the committee on culture in the State Duma, and we have delegated to a working group, along with other committees, which are involved with the budgetary sphere, of course, this is above all the matter of pay, now we are beginning to study all of this.

A Communist Party deputy: . . . I will introduce the proposal to return awards to mothers, correct pension laws so that women with many children also have beneficial pensions. Tomorrow, there will be a session of the pension fund committee and I will raise this issue. . . . And, of course, for youth, . . . restore the housing policy that . . . provides credit to young families— on these questions I will be working.

A deputy who served in several small liberal, promarket parties: I thought there was another way to defend equal opportunities for women—immerse yourself in those themes traditionally dominated by men. That is, I've always been interested in economic issues, national defense, the struggle with terrorism, when that arose, foreign policy. . . . Aside from Governor Matvienko, I'm the only [woman] politician who discusses traditionally male themes on equal terms with men.

Commentary: Among the eighty-nine constituent units of the Russian Federation, only one has a woman governor, Valentina Matvienko of Saint Petersburg, who served as deputy prime minister for social policy from 1998 to 2003 and thus was the highest-ranking woman in the Putin administration. During the 1990s, she served in the diplomatic corps, including stints as Russia's ambassador to Malta and later to Greece; she thus has credentials in the field of foreign policy as well as a background working on domestic issues.

Chapter 9

The Perspective of the Head of the Parliamentary Women's Group in Poland

Senator Dorota Kempka
Speaks with Agnieszka Majcher

This is an interview with Senator Dorota Kempka, candidate of the Election Committee of the Coalition of the Democratic Left Alliance and the Labor Union, Bydgoszcz Electoral District, and a member of the Sejm of the Republic of Poland during its tenth term and of the Senat of the Republic of Poland during its third, fourth, and fifth terms. The introduction and interview are by Agnieszka Majcher, who is at the Ministry of Labor and Social Affairs and is also affiliated with the Institute for Social Studies at Warsaw University.

Senator Dorota Kempka was born in 1935 in Piotrkowice to a working-class family. Her father, a former soldier of the Uprising of Wielkopolska, worked as a manager of the State Land Office after the war. In 1966, she graduated from the Faculty of Pedagogy of the University of Warsaw. Starting in 1953, she worked as a teacher. From 1960 to 1974, she was a full-time employee of the Polish Scouting and Guiding Association (known as ZHP). For nineteen years, she was the director of the Youth Center "Pałac Młodzieży" in

Bydgoszcz. From 1983 to 1989, she was a member of the National Council for Culture. She is an honorary director of the International Meetings of Young Musicians "Bydgoszcz Musical Impressions" and an honorary chairwoman of the Coalition for Women in Bydgoszcz. She is a member of the Polish Teachers' Union. As a member of the Sejm during its tenth term, Senator Kempka was a cofounder of the Parliamentary Association of Women (now the Parliamentary Group of Women). As a senator during the third term of the Senat, she was a deputy chairwoman of the Commission for Regulation and Senat Affairs. Since February 1996, she has been the chairwoman of the Parliamentary Group of Women. She was in charge of the Provincial Electoral Board of Aleksander Kwasniewski in 1995, of the Provincial Electoral Board during the parliamentary election in 1997, and of the Provincial Electoral Board during the local government election in 1998; she was also a member of the Honorary Committee of the presidential candidate Aleksander Kwasniewski for the 2000 election, as well as a member of the initiative group of the Committee of Włodzimierz Cimoszewicz for the 2005 presidential election.

As a senator in the Senat's fifth term, Kempka is the deputy chairperson of the Commission of Culture and Media, a member of the Commission for Local Self-Government and State Administration, a member of the Senat Club of the Democratic Left Alliance and the Labor Union "Lewica Razem." From 1960 to 1990, she was a member of the Polish United Workers' Party. She is a member of the Democratic Left Alliance. Her husband, Zbigniew, is a lawyer who runs his own company. Her daughter, Joanna Gęsikowska, a graduate of the University of Gdańsk, works at the Academy of Technology and Agriculture in Bydgoszcz.

How did you get into the world of politics? How did you become a member of the Sejm and then the Senat?
I was born to a family with strong traditions, both nationalistic and liberationist. My father and his siblings fought during the Uprising of Wielkopolska; so did my parents and the siblings of my mother. The Uprising of Wielkopolska [1918–19] brought them together, and they got married. In their professional work, they also engaged in activities on behalf of their community. My mother was involved in charity activities during the interwar period, while my father promoted education among farmers.

Afterward, there was the war and the postwar period. I joined the Polish Scouting and Guiding Association and—for a short time—the School Sports Association. As a university student, I was also under the strong influence of one of my professors, a great promoter of scouting methods, who passed on his experiences to us—the future teachers. Mainly because of this, when I worked as a teacher in a rural community, I concluded that there was a need to give something more to children—not only pure theoretical knowledge. At that time already, as a very young teacher, I engaged in various activities to change the ways of bringing up children and youth. I established very good relations with youth organizations and farmers' associations. I learned that thanks to mediation and communication skills, a lot could be changed in the rural environment. Therefore, the extracurricular activities of my children were organized in a completely different way. They did not have to get back to farm work after school—they met after the lessons, we organized trips to the forest, they learned how to build shelters. . . . I also helped them—which, I think, is very important—to find out more about the history and culture of Poland.

As a result of all these activities, my professional career quickly became associated with work for a social organization, and then with politics. Therefore, after 1956, I joined the Polish Scouting and Guiding Association. I became a district commissioner and then a regional commissioner. Later on, I started to work for the Youth Center Pałac Młodzieży in Bydgoszcz. The center was built by volunteers, and it was opened on the thirtieth anniversary of the establishment of the People's Republic of Poland. Everyone worked at the construction site of the Youth Center, including the youngest inhabitants of the city. I also cleaned bricks on the construction site, although I didn't imagine at the time that I would become a director of the center; afterward, I worked as a director for nineteen years. What I had learned earlier in my life was confirmed by my work for the center— exceptional initiatives, new ideas, including the idea of launching the International Center for Cultural Education in Bydgoszcz, as well as the initiation of the International Meetings of Young Musicians. I was a director of the event for nineteen years; now I am an honorary director. It was my dream to show young people from abroad that Poland was a country of great cultural traditions, and that the young people, who participated in the events organized at the Youth Center, were exceptional people. I thought we managed to achieve this objective every time. . . .

It was also confirmed by the participation of our members in international festivals, because the Bydgoszcz Musical Impressions were sort of a visa for the artistic groups, allowing them to participate in international festivals and to get to know other countries. Speaking of work and creative activities at the Youth Center, I would like to emphasize that the center was well known not only for its role in the cultural education it provided for children and youth. The departments of science and sports were also very well developed. I am talking about this because my professional and social work was associated very strongly with what I did for the small community, to promote Bydgoszcz and to bring the inhabitants of the city closer to each other, but also to promote Poland and Polish culture. Because of all this, when I got the proposal to become a candidate for the Sejm during the election in 1989, I had some objections. At the time, I believed that the most beautiful work I could do, which gave me the opportunity to influence the development of the youngest inhabitants of Bydgoszcz, was management of the Youth Center. I thought that Parliament was not for me. Anyhow, I decided to participate, and I became a member of the Sejm.

So, until 1989, you had been fully satisfied with social and cultural activity and you had no political ambitions. . . . But as I know, you were a member. . . .
. . . of the National Council for Culture. It could be added that thanks to the activity of the Youth Center and its role in educating children and youth in Poland and Europe, I was appointed a member of the National Council for Culture, and I was one of the few people who participated in the works of the National Council for Culture until the dismissal of Professor Suchodol-ski—that is, for two terms.

You were also a member of the party. . . . Was it a necessity or . . . .
I have to emphasize one fact: . . . I became a member of the Polish United Workers' Party in 1960. From the perspective of my party membership—I was a member until the moment of closing of the convention in 1990—I have to admit we undoubtedly made a lot of mistakes, but I had always underlined and explained to my coworkers that being a member of the party meant more obligations, more honesty and reliability in performance of one's duties. . . . I was always a member of the party. . . .

But you had no functions in the party? You were not actively involved in the activity of the party?. . .
I was a delegate during the Sixth Convention of the party, when Edward Gierek was elected, and I want to say that it was an exceptional choice. I identified myself with all the people there, all who participated in the party convention, because I believe that he was able to do the most important thing for our group—mobilize people to work well. . . .

Getting back to the beginnings of your "adventure" in Parliament, . . . due to your professional and social activity, you were very well known in Byd-

goszcz, which was decisive for selecting you as a candidate. What was the process behind the scenes of this election? Were there many other activists eager to participate?

There were really a lot of candidates, and, to be honest, I really did not feel like participating. I believed myself to be a good director. I felt I was in the right place, people wanted to work with me, but there were various circumstances. In January 1989, I became a godmother of the "Bydgoszcz" ship. Therefore, I undertook numerous activities to provide the best equipment for it and to make sure the sailors would feel emotionally tied to Bydgoszcz. When I got the proposal to become a candidate, I did not agree immediately. The truth is that the leaders of youth organizations, the tourist associations, and the League of Women would say to me: "Stand for it. You are very well known." I had already been in charge of the Youth Center for fifteen years. I had worked for the Polish Scouting and Guiding Association for equally long—everyone, from cub scouts to senior scouts, everyone knew me, in the entire province. The district commissioner said, "Listen, stand for it, I have no chance and you will win." Someone else, from the Sporting Association, said, "Stand for it, you have a chance." A friend from the League of Women said, "Stand for it; I will give it up on your behalf." Of course, I did not win during the first round; no one from the Polish United Workers' Party did. I won in the second round. But I would like to emphasize that it was mainly the decision of the inhabitants of Bydgoszcz; because of them I became a member of Parliament.

What was your debut like in Parliament, when the situation was so difficult? It was a new role for you. . . .

It was functioning in a completely different way! At that time, we only realized one thing, that we were supposed to make the law for the Third Republic of Poland, that various legal acts would be amended, but it was sad—and it was particularly significant for me—that we, members of the Polish United Workers' Party, were completely ignored by everyone else. I always laugh that here, in Parliament, I learned to walk proudly, holding my head up high. I am convinced that what I did during my youth and in my adult life was good from the perspective, which, to me, is most important—of education of children and youth.

At that time, an idea emerged to create an association of women in Parliament, regardless of party membership. A starting point for this lobby was a conference in Geneva and then the conference "Women in Modern Poland—Opportunities and Threats." I organized the entire conference with my friends. I also believed very strongly that women, regardless of their organizational membership, would be able to fight for women's rights. In the Sejm, we were successful, because at that time, there was no such party discipline as there is today. Ladies from all political groups were members of the Parliamentary Association of Women. Those activities were very important, and we made a fully conscious choice, electing Barbara Labuda as our chairwoman. During the conference in Geneva, together with other female members of Parliament, she proposed the establishment of an organization for women in Parliament. We did not manage to establish a commission for women's affairs in the Sejm. Therefore, the Parliamentary Association of Women was created. We passed several important declarations, including the basic one—to defend the rights of women despite political differences, to defend women's right to abortion, to make decisions concerning their families, to supervise the creation of law that would not be discriminating against women, and to help women get jobs, because they were the first ones to be dismissed and found it difficult to cope with the new reality, while they were overburdened with all kinds of duties. And that's how my first term of office was concluded.

Before we go further, please tell me, what do you regard to be your greatest success of that term?
The greatest success of the Sejm was that we created the Parliamentary Association of Women, that we managed to get women together despite political differences, and that we spoke with a single voice about affairs concerning women. My personal, unbelievable success was also due to the fact that I spoke a lot about the cultural education of children and youth, and I keep underlining that bringing up of children and young people and influencing their development, the development of their personality, is very important. They will be the ones to shape the fate of our country in the future. . . .

Do you think that the lobby of women was successful in "pushing their way through" in Parliament? Was this voice of women really heard?
Yes. After the conference in December 1990, letters were sent to Prime Minister Jan Krzysztof Bielecki concerning the appointment of the government representative for women and family affairs. A letter was also sent to President Lech Walesa to appoint a person at the Chancellery of the President to deal with women's affairs. We put emphasis on the word "women," while the decisionmakers at the time decided it would be a representative for family and women. The emphasis was changed; family was most important, and we—women—were only an addition to it. We spoke loudly of the right to

abortion and to make family decisions, but we did not manage to deal with everything. We did not force the Sejm to establish a commission for women's affairs. . . .

And then?
There was the Sejm election in 1991, and I want to say—and I am fully convinced of it—that I lost this election. On the other hand, I achieved something exceptional in politics. I strengthened my position, because I was fifth in the province of Bydgoszcz—I got ten thousand votes. I did not get a seat, while members of other political parties got seats despite the fact that they had fewer votes. Therefore, I have always underlined the fact that I have the support of the people in our province. Members of Parliament from other groups got four thousand votes each, and they got the seats, . . . but that's an advantage of the proportional voting system. Besides, I was still a director of the Youth Center. . . .

But in the meantime, you came to like your political activity. . . .
I think I both got to like it and my work was appreciated by my political organization. The Democratic Left Alliance proposed that I be their candidate for the Senat. I said "yes." I knew already that I would not manage the Youth Center, because, according to the legal provisions, I could retire. And thus, since 1993, I have participated in three Senat elections. I have always won and achieved the best result. I have always occupied the first position. I defeated many competitors from various political groups. Whether there was a shift to the left or to the right, I always got the seat. . . .

You ceased to participate in Sejm elections?
Yes. The Senat voting system is different—according to majority. The lists of candidates are prepared in alphabetical order. I was always sixth, seventh, or eighth, and the voters looked for my name. . . .

How did you assess the differences in the manner of functioning of the Sejm and the Senat?
The Sejm and the Senat are completely different, and I always emphasize that the law is made at the Sejm. The Sejm members play the most important role in the preparation of legal acts and drafts. The Senat also has the right to present such drafts, just like the president, but the truth is that an act passed by the Senat still has to be passed by the Sejm, and the entire legislative process concerning a draft act takes very long. Let's look, for example, at the act on the legal status of women and men. In 2002, it was passed by the Senat and presented to the Sejm, and in 2005 it was subject to voting.

Of course, it was rejected. Thus, the law is made in the Sejm, but the Senat, on the other hand, is very much needed, because numerous merit-based amendments, proposed by the Senat, are passed by the Sejm afterward.

What are the issues that you deal with at the Senat? What projects have you worked on?

Since I became a member of the Sejm, I have always worked for the commission for culture, because I believed that as a teacher, working for this commission I would have most influence on the acts that pertain to the functioning of artistic institutions and activities on behalf of children and youth with regard to cultural education. When I became a senator, I came back to the commission for culture, and I have been a member of this commission since 1993. During each term, the name of the commission is different, but we always deal with the same affairs; that is, legal acts that are associated with culture, the protection of monuments, and the promotion of national cultural heritage. A special field that I have dealt with and that I treat as my personal success is the promotion of the importance of the proper cultural education of children and youth in preparation for being active recipients of culture. . . .

As a Parliament member, whose representative are you in the first place? Whose interests are you concerned about? Those of the people from your region, women? . . .

In the first place, I am a rational senator. I am familiar with the problems of my community and my people, because they are the ones who deserve my attention in the first place. Therefore, one day a week, on Monday, regardless of what is going on in Warsaw, I travel to Bydgoszcz. At the same time, I do a lot to defend women's rights and to guarantee institutional solutions that would ensure the equal status of women. It has been the most important domain of my activity at the Senat since the moment when I became a chairwoman of the Parliamentary Group of Women—that is, since 1996.

What do you find particularly satisfying and particularly frustrating about parliamentary work?

It is very complicated. On one hand, women parliamentarians come here from specific political groups, and they are obliged to implement the programs of their parties; on the other hand, they are members of the Parliamentary Group of Women, which assumes that we are defending the rights of women despite any political differences, and we make sure that such provisions are present in the legal acts passed. It leads to a conflict of interest.

Not all political groups believe that women have the right to participate in political life or to make decisions concerning their families and their own roles, and it is a source of stress and misunderstandings. A specific example is the act on conscious parenthood. There are women in the Parliamentary Group of Women who feel responsible for the creation of a good law, who support the idea of the participation of women in political and social life, but when it comes to the act on conscious parenthood, their particular political group says "no." It says, "Women have no right to abortion." "The parliamentarian has no right to vote to pass the act on the equal status of women and men." On the contrary, they work for rejection of the act. This makes the political life of women difficult and stressful. Paradoxically, women who have worked in Parliament for several terms of office, who had once supported the act on the equal status of women and men, who used to be convinced that it met European standards and that it was needed, at present follow the policy of their parties and work for the rejection of the act.

How about everyday work as a parliamentarian—contacts with friends, family, and professional obligations? Is it also a source of frustration?
It is a very difficult situation, although I must say that in this term of office, there are women here who have become wives and mothers, who have small children, and I think that they are coping very well and they are able to reconcile parliamentary work with family affairs. Nevertheless, I don't know if everyone is able to do that, because parliamentary work is very difficult and it requires particular commitment—not eight hours a day, but from morning until night. . . .

And there is no hope of changing the work culture, for instance, by providing facilities for female parliamentarians who have small children?
There once was an idea to establish a room for moms who have small children. There was also an idea to create a kindergarten group and a small infirmary, but after an attack by the men, we withdrew such proposals. They were never realized, although some European parliaments have decided to provide substantial support for women with small children.

What were the arguments used by the men?
The men in Parliament are very traditional. They still believe that women should stay at home, that they should care about the professional careers of their husbands and make sure they get the best possible conditions. Therefore, every time, whenever they can, they try to ridicule and ignore all ideas of implementation of the principle of equal rights of women and men. I also

want to emphasize one thing—it is not an issue associated with those from the rightist groups. Such behaviors are also typical for some of my male colleagues from the Democratic Left Alliance. When we discussed the act on the equal status of women and men in the Senat, some of them made so many amendments that the only thing left was the title and the article specifying the date the act would come into force. It shows that the most difficult matter that the Parliamentary Group of Women deals with, engaging in numerous activities, is a change in awareness. I think that within the last fifteen years, a lot has been done, but not everything, and therefore those female parliamentarians who join the Polish Parliament during the subsequent terms of office will have a lot of work. . . .

Do you think that discrimination against women in the Polish Parliament, for instance, is present with regard to access to important functions and positions and in selection of members of key commissions?
I believe that we encounter discrimination in Parliament all the time. Look—among the members of the Sejm Presidium, there are no women. In the Senat, there is one—Jolanta Danielak, the Senate speaker. The number of women who have been chairpersons of parliamentary commissions is also low, and it is not because they are not qualified or prepared to perform such a function. In fact, there is the unspoken rule of granting managerial functions to men, and therefore, we keep emphasizing that the participation of women in the decisionmaking groups is insufficient. The situation is changing for the better, but unfortunately, too little has been done—for example, the principle of maintaining the proportion of both men and women at the level of at least 30 percent. The most difficult part is always the issue of parliamentary and self-government elections. At present, the Parliamentary Group of Women has sent a letter to all leaders of clubs to which the group members belong in which we ask them to accept the rule of a 30 percent share of men and women while preparing lists of election candidates, because women should stand for elections. We also show that women should be leaders and not just additions to these lists, somewhere near the end. We have not yet received a reply.

It is hard to tell what it will be like, but thanks to the hard work of the Parliamentary Group of Women, undoubtedly a lot has changed. Thanks to our postulates—that democracy without women is only half a democracy, that full democracy is one in which women participate—the number of women in the Polish Parliament has increased. More than 20 percent of Sejm members and 24 percent of Senat members are women, but it does not mean that all women in Parliament support the idea of the equal rights. This has been proven by statements of female parliamentarians from rightist parties who have criticized the act on equal status. All rightist groups have opposed this act, and thus it has been rejected, . . . after ten years of our work.

[*Editors' note:* The first version of the act on equal status of women and men was presented to the Sejm by the Parliamentary Group of Women in 1996, but it was not considered. In 1997, another draft was presented, and it was read for the first time. The next step was presentation in 1998, once again by the group, of another draft version, which was evaluated negatively by the government, and it was not considered by the Sejm. In December 2002, the Senat passed the resolution concerning presentation of a new draft of the act of equal status of women and men, prepared by the Senat. In 2004, the government expressed its approval for this legislation initiative. In 2005, the draft act was finally rejected.]

Let us get back for a moment to the issue of participation of women in the decisionmaking groups. Isn't it true that women are less eager to occupy such positions as well? That while they are active in various fields, and their professional careers are successfully developed, they do not care much about prestigious functions? That the number of interested women is just too low? . . .

It is not like that. A man who gets such proposal does not think for one minute whether he has the qualifications to lead a given commission, to manage a given area, . . . regardless of whether he is familiar with it or not. He gets a proposal, and he accepts the proposal. Women, on the other hand, are very critical about themselves. If they confirm their eagerness to manage a given team or area, to be a leader of the provincial self-government, they ask themselves whether they will be able to perform these duties successfully. I can only say one thing: Women really often wonder whether their knowledge and psychological and physical predispositions allow them to be team leaders. . . . One thing is for sure—and it has been emphasized by all research results—those women who have joined the Polish Parliament are much better prepared to be parliamentarians, . . . because earlier they worked for nongovernmental organizations or managed groups of people, or they have knowledge and experience. . . .

So, when they are offered managerial functions, women often hesitate and refuse?

Such proposals are, in fact, made very rarely. Usually, a man is selected for the post. In fact, at the Democratic Left Alliance, there are almost no women as party leaders, except for Krystyna Łybacka in Wielkopolska and Mał-gorzata Ostrowska in Pomorze. In our country, only one woman is a chair-person of a provincial government assembly, in Kujawskie Province, for the second time in a row. When the lists for the provincial self-government were established, I managed to make sure that for my party, women would be at the top of the lists in 30 percent of all districts. In the case of the elections to the European Parliament, women were also leaders on the lists in 30 per-cent of all districts. But it's not always like that, and I can't tell what it will be like during this term. . . .

Getting back to the problem of the low level of participation of women in political life, it also seems that women themselves show less interest in a political career. You are also a classical example of a woman occupying a high position, renowned in her community, who had to be convinced to stand for election and engage in politics. How do you think we should overcome this barrier of political initiation?

In the first place, the process of preparing young girls for adult life should be different. It should be shown in various ways, and much more often, that women, like men, have the right to participate actively in political life, to aim at becoming leaders within a party and then develop their careers within this party, because every woman has to be aware of one fact—in order to participate actively in political life, she has to be a party member. That's what the political scene is like. . . . Only a strong position in the party will allow women to make decisions regarding the place of women in politics. My male colleagues say women don't want to participate actively in the work of the party, and therefore it is difficult to convince them to become candidates for positions within the party structures, to put their names on the parliamentary and self-government election lists. I think there is yet an-other factor—that many women have such aspirations, and they know how to fight for their positions, especially among younger, better educated women —and in the next generations, this situation will be changing for the better. These will no longer be women who have been brought up in accordance with the rule that the man is the head of the family. . . . They will be self-confident, and they will do their best to show they are the right leaders of party structures.

Have you already "brought up" your "female successors"?

When I led the team for equal status, preparing the election program of the Democratic Left Alliance in 2001, a lot of young people worked with me; I have always believed my experience has to be passed on to younger people who will occupy various positions in the future. I also believe that many people have taken advantage of my experience and knowledge, introducing a new style of their own as well. My younger female colleagues who started with me occupy various positions in political and social life now. The best example is the volunteers of the Parliamentary Group of Women. All women who did their training as volunteers in the group acquired specific knowledge and are coping particularly well. They have not reached very high positions yet, but they have unique knowledge, which cannot be acquired from any university; they have met various people—people of science, activists from nongovernmental organizations. . . .

Let's get to the issue of gender mainstreaming. What is it, to what extent does it "work" in Parliament, and what conditions have to be met in order to achieve equal status for women and men and counteract discrimination against women?

I think we just have to convince women working for nongovernmental organizations, convince them more efficiently than we have, that in order to make decisions with regard to the changing situation in Poland, they have to join party structures and cooperate with various parties. They will be able to influence their local communities, but the situation will be more difficult with regard to the decisions made at the central level. Therefore, I believe that whatever is happening right now with regard to the Office of the Government Representative for the Equal Status of Women and Men is particularly important.

In your opinion, how can the increase in the number of women in Parliament be translated into an increase in the significance and understanding of the issue of equality and women's rights?

I would like to emphasize again that women who want to influence the making of Polish legislation have to become party members. In the democratic system, the parties prepare lists and select candidates for Parliament. All the meetings that I organized as a leader of the Parliamentary Group of Women for nongovernmental organizations were aimed at increasing the awareness of women that acting in nongovernmental organizations and on behalf of a civic society, they have to make friends with—if not be members of—specific political groups. There will be a chance for them to become members of the Polish Parliament or self-government, to influence Polish legislation. If not, the number of women in the rightist parliamentary groups will be higher—in fact, it will be thanks to our difficult and hard work—but they will follow the orders of their party leaders.

What is your personal interpretation of this relatively high number of women parliamentarians from rightist and extreme groups, such as the League of Polish Families or Self-Defense? What role do they play in these parties?

Have you noticed how women are presented within individual parties? For instance, the League of Polish Families—when are women from this political group presented? Never or almost never. If the leader of Self-Defense is shown, there are women who support him in the background. The Civic Platform—women are rarely shown here as well. . . .

Women from the Democratic Left Alliance and other leftist parties are in a better position—their parties use gender equality as one of their slogans. . . .

It is true, their situation is better, but at the same time they work hard to convince their colleagues to accept their arguments. All legal acts that promote equality and the role of women that have been passed by the Polish Parliament were not accepted out of fondness for the female colleagues at the Sejm and the Senat who prepared these acts, but because the men were convinced that such legal solutions were needed. It is sad that the Democratic Left Alliance is a leftist party that has become so liberal. . . . [*Editors' note:* "liberal" in the European sense, i.e., conservative or supportive of center-right positions.] But I know one thing: We did our best to force our male colleagues to accept acts that guarantee the equal rights of women and men and eliminate discrimination. The results vary, but without the hard work of the members of the Parliamentary Group of Women, there would not have been so many female parliamentarians. . . .

Looking at gender and equality issues from the perspective of several decades, have you noticed any progress in this regard? What will remain to be done by the younger or future generation of Polish women parliamentarians?

There has been progress. For example, there are the nongovernmental organizations that I cooperate with. In addition, I think these changes are taking place smoothly. Some time ago, when conferences were organized, women from the Rural Association of Housewives, the League of Polish Women, and other large nongovernmental organizations participated in them. . . . Those were usually very solemn, elderly women. Today, these organizations are represented by young women who are familiar with EU grants, who know how to write applications, and who know how to get resources and cooperate with international organizations. There is one more thing that I cannot understand, but perhaps it takes time, too: . . . In

Warsaw, there are numerous nongovernmental organizations—Mazowsze Province, in general, is home to most of them, anyway—there are lots of really small organizations established after 1989 that do not have nationwide structures. I call them the single-topic organizations—defense of women's rights, promotion of women, active women, women over forty. . . . It's not bad. However, I believe that these organizations have to learn to cooperate with each other, in order to establish a specific group that will allow them to fight for the equal status of women and men. The government information that we received recently concerning implementation of the act on public benefit organizations and voluntary work shows that the number of small and poor organizations among the nongovernmental organizations has increased. In 2001, they constituted 15 percent of all nongovernmental organizations; now they constitute more than 20 percent. It shows that if they don't learn to unite to take advantage of financial resources, they will not be able to survive.

Don't you think we are witnessing regression in some fields? The future female parliamentarians will still have to face, for instance, the issue of the defense of rights of women with regard to reproduction; it is as if we went back to the 1930s.
Of course! This problem will be present as it was in 1918, when women participated in the parliamentary elections for the first time, when they fought for workplaces, for their right to study and to participate in political life. Recently, I participated in a meeting organized by the Democratic Left Alliance, and one of our younger female colleagues started talking about the problems that we had pointed out during our very first conference organized within the Polish Parliament. The unemployment rate, participation in political life, and the right to participate in the decisionmaking processes; . . . she only failed to take one thing into account: that some things have been done in these fifteen years—that the provision on equal status of women and men became part of the Constitution, that more women joined Parliament. . . . It has been done, it would not have been there otherwise. . . .

Moreover, at present, everyone talks about discrimination, and not only gender related, in Poland. This topic used to be ignored. I remember 1995 and the Peking conference. One of the topics discussed was violence against women. At the time, there were no materials on the subject. At present, a lot is being said in Poland about family violence. Parliament is now preparing an act on counteracting family violence. The act will surely be passed. It shows that within the last fifteen years, the Parliamentary Group of Women has done a lot to publicize the problem, which had been restricted to the private space of our apartments. . . .

How do you perceive the role of the European Union in the promotion of equal rights for women and men and in promoting women?
I think that the European Union has played an enormous role in raising many issues and the preparation of many new solutions in Poland. The European Union knows that women have the right to make decisions concerning their lives. . . . Its member states are obliged to implement its directives, while, on the other hand, they are able to choose the means of implementation of the rule on equal opportunities. Therefore, I think it's great that the period of preparation to join the European Union was parallel to activity of the Parliamentary Group of Women, which won more support thanks to this fact. The directives will have to be implemented. . . . We believe that a central office for the equal status of women and men should exist, while our male parliamentarians consider it to be completely unnecessary—that it means a new office, new posts, and that women only want to rule—it is a misunderstanding! Therefore, it is a good thing that we are a member of the European Union and our women work at the Council of Europe, although it is a pity that some representatives of our country participating in the equality commissions have no idea what the principle of equality is. Once again, we are dealing with the political aspect here. It is a misunderstanding—a person who is a member of the commission for the equal status of women and men in the Sejm, who occupies the position of a deputy chairman of this commission, votes against the act for the equal status of women and men! Perhaps the position of the Civic Platform, which did not put any of its members on the commission, is more responsible? On the other hand, how could the Civic Platform, the European Platform, fail to take into account the fact that women have the right to decide? How can a female representative of this platform say that this act is unnecessary?

Ending the interview, and taking advantage of the fact that the campaign for the parliamentary election is about to start. . . . Are you going to be a candidate once again?
No, I will not. I believe that replacement by representatives of a younger generation is needed in some nongovernmental organizations, as well as in political parties and Parliament itself. Therefore, I assumed consciously that this term of office would be my last term of active work in Parliament, although it does not mean that I will withdraw from activity in my province

and from the structures of the Polish Scouting and Guiding Association, which has always been my field. My generation—and I am speaking specifically about myself—has lived through various times; it has specific experiences, specific attitudes towards leaders and authority. . . . The younger generation is completely different, and they should get the chance to try, by taking over leadership, to make sure that we live in a democratic country, free of discrimination due to gender, beliefs, interests. . . .

Therefore, last year I decided to leave the position of leader of the League of Polish Women. I was replaced by a representative of a younger generation—a smart, well-educated woman who is a doctor of economic sciences and a senator. I think such changes should take place in other organizations as well. I also believe that in my electoral district, people who have experience, but who are representatives of a younger generation, should become Senat candidates.

Chapter 10

A Specialist in Culture
in the Slovene Parliament
Majda Širca

I am a member of the largest parliamentary party, the Liberal Democracy of Slovenia (LDS), and this is my second term of office as a parliamentary deputy. In the past term (2000–2004), the party included four women among thirty-four official deputies. During the present term, there were only three women among twenty-three LDS deputies.

I began participating in politics relatively late. In 1998, I started working at the Ministry of Culture as a state secretary. Before my post as a state secretary, I had a successful career as a journalist and editor. I wrote film reviews, was involved in journalism, and created many television documentaries and shows.

I am convinced that the minister of culture invited me because I was very well known for being a realistic critic of Slovenian cultural policy. To mention a few examples, I warned the public about political ignorance in connection to culture, I analyzed the effects of weak political moves, and with the help of written reviews as well as televised ones, I tried to increase the value of creative production. It is very interesting, however, that my comments met a wide response, and in some cases, even influenced decision-making at the ministry. At one point, my comments almost led to the discharge of an inefficient minister of culture. People trusted me because I have always built my credibility on strong arguments, and I never strived for admiration. In this way, I helped to promote the belief in film art, because that was my field of work. Nevertheless, as a journalist, I could only influence decisionmaking indirectly, via media appearances and my writing. The ministry's invitation presented a great challenge for me. It was an opportunity to be involved in direct decisionmaking, namely, inside the government. Although it was a difficult decision, I accepted. Why? As an author and an editor of cultural shows, I achieved many goals. I asked myself: Is there anything more that I can do if I am not a part of direct decisionmaking process? If I only criticize, but do not have any "real" influence? The experience at the ministry was very useful because I could see the problems from different points of view. It was difficult for me to give up creative work, but I tried my best to understand politics as an art of managing public affairs.

After I entered politics, I came across certain problems: People would not accept me with the same enthusiasm as they had before. Although many positive things happened in the field of culture during my term of office, it was difficult for the public to fully appreciate them. A few examples of what happened may be helpful. At the beginning of my term, I encouraged the construction of a film studio that should have been built a long time ago. We increased the funds for film art, cultural heritage, libraries, and the like. Our work at the ministry was transparent, public, and open. I noticed that for a number of posts, which were decided by an official process, we named many professional, responsible people who were not politically oriented (museums, galleries, supervisory boards, etc.). There were several women appointed to these posts, and they did excellent work after being named to these positions and proved themselves deserving of the appointments they received. Regardless of many positive results, the public did not indicate any significant "recognition" of our work. If I achieved an increase of funds, those who received them stated that the increases were not high enough; if investments increased, there were complaints made by those who still had not received them, and so on. The position of "power" has two opposite sides: You never do well enough because there are always some people who remain dissatisfied, and there is no place for patience here. If you bear responsibility, you also bear guilt. This is how politics works.

In short, if I received awards as a journalist, I received ambivalent responses in politics, although my thinking was as liberal as before. Guilt, however, is part of politics. For women "being guilty" just because of being a part of authority, is a greater problem than for men. I think this is mostly because we are more sensitive. We do not understand authority as power or prestige but as the way to achieve good decisions. These decisions, however, are rarely noticed, let alone praised. In professional work, the situation is different. If you are good, you typically reap the fruits of your work. This rarely happens in politics. Maybe this is the reason why the position of women in politics is more difficult.

But why did I run as a candidate in the parliamentary elections? You will not believe me, but it was because of fear. This is because, for half a year, the right-wing parties had been gaining power, and it seemed to me that the future of Slovenia was uncertain. My party became active and made up a list of strong candidates. Women represented fewer than 30 percent of the candidates, and not all of them had the possibility of being elected. Elections are always the mirror of the party. If the party does not encourage women or include them in its work, then it is difficult for women to get integrated. Because of that, "the force" in the form of quotas is an essential measure for maintaining political correctness.

So I ended up in Parliament, where I am now for the second term. At the beginning, it was awful. The level of discussions was low. The theatrical performance of my colleagues seemed like "showing off" to me. Women, however, behaved differently. We worked in the background. We settled things before the final discussion, and when everything was done, we were quiet. We were ashamed of talking about the things that we had already done. Our male colleagues arrogated our work to themselves. We were discussing rationally, nonaggressively, without discrediting others.

But because we were not scandalous, convincing, and aggressive, the media did not notice us. It was our clothes and appearance that were noticed. This made us think. We changed our tactics, but not with the intention to become popular and likeable. We started speaking out and publicly expressing and defending our points of view—by providing arguments, of course.

I am certain that we are more tolerant and less prone to conflicts. It is difficult for us to pretend (i.e., by talking about things we did not know). We are fairly loyal. Probably we lack diplomacy (e.g., we do not care about our promotion). I believe that it is very difficult for the women in Parliament to "bluff," because we study each problem thoroughly before making any decisions. Therefore, we spend more energy and time, and we do not make a big deal out of our work; perhaps we do not know how to present our work by using public relations. Sometimes, we draw back too quickly when we sense that we do not enjoy enough support.

We can connect with parliamentary women from other parties when we believe that there is consensus among most of the women on a particular issue or case. This situation, however, is very rare. Cooperation with other parties proved successful in the case of modifying the Constitution with regard to a better representation of women in public as well as in political life. However, cooperation on issues on which liberal and conservative views are too different is very difficult. I think that we are in front of a wall that was created by different views of the world, and therefore alliances among women are not as successful as they should be. However, in cases where we represent the same views, we establish strong cooperation. It is not difficult for us to establish contact with other parties. We are not aggressive. We do not offend our political opponents, and we do not disqualify them either. I think that we have inherent sense of honesty.

In a very diplomatic way, we were able to have an impact on the amendment of the Constitution. With this amendment, we achieved measures being included in the regulations on elections that resulted in a stronger presence of women. We managed to persuade almost all the parties to sign the initiative for amending the Constitution. The obligatory quota (40 percent) was included in the EU Elections Act. The success was obvious: There were seven members elected to the European Parliament, three of whom were women. I am convinced that if we had not changed the act, there would not be three very interesting and professional female members of Parliament now representing Slovenia.

However, we still have to deal with the National Assembly Elections Act. This is about to happen, but I am afraid that the National Assembly Elections Act prepared by the new conservative government will not be optimal. The aim of the act is to determine the equality of sexes to at least 35 percent of the candidates of one sex on the list, starting with 25 percent in the first elections, in 2008. We should remind readers that the 2004 elections changed the state authorities, that my liberal party is in opposition, and that the ruling coalition consists of the parties from the right of the center—the Slovene Democratic Party, New Slovenia, the Democratic Party of Pensioners, and the Slovene People's Party. Therefore, the Local Elections Act, which anticipates a gradual meeting of the quota, is not ambitious enough, either. It is interesting that women from parties that are now in coalition and hold power did not insist on optimal quotas and that those parliamentary women from the opposition could not convince them or lobby successfully either. Party discipline was therefore their priority.

The amendment of the Constitution, the adoption of the Equal Opportunities Act, public discussion on women in politics—these are all great achievements for Slovenia. Why? First, because in the past such attempts failed. Second, because this question has always been related to feminism, in the derogatory sense of the word. And third, because the public has realized that Slovenia cannot only be led by men. The legislation on equal opportunities in Slovenia is well regulated—including the act and the resolution on equal opportunities. However, theory is one thing and practice another. I believe that the most important issue here is awareness—discussions, meetings, opinions, publications, and the like. I am glad to receive many letters from students, almost on a daily basis, who prepare different programs, dissertations, seminars, and the like on equal opportunities, and on hostile speech and intolerance, which means that the younger generations are well aware of the significance of these issues. I also think that it is important that the antifeminist view that has been present for a long time has finally disappeared—in the sense of simplified thinking and reflections on women's issues.

Of course, it is difficult to change such attitudes if civil society does not support them. Developments in civil society are of great help to us, particularly the women's lobbies. There are several women's groups in Slovenia that are active on various issues, and parliamentary women occasionally cooperate with these groups. Our cooperation is established especially when we discuss the issues that we share—for instance, domestic violence, social security, problems involving working hours, paternal leave, and media issues. The Coalition for Equal Opportunities is active in the political field and mostly deals with women's political goals in public as well as political life; it includes almost every woman who is active in politics and different parties as well as representatives of civil society.

History is also important. During socialism, women achieved a lot:

- Already, in the 1970s, the right to freely decide about the birth of a child and abortion was included in the Constitution.
- People in common-law marriages had the same rights as those in "formal" marriages.
- The number of kindergartens increased.
- Many women were employed. But they had to work double shifts, not only at home but also at work. Nowadays, the situation is better, but in

spite of this it is more difficult for women to decide to have a career. Some job posts, however, still pay women less in comparison with their male colleagues, although their education is higher.

Women in Parliament have more contacts with noninstitutional organizations of civil society than our male colleagues. That is also because we are more willing to listen to different opinions. We do not decide before we have studied everything.

We are more involved in questions regarding human rights and problems concerning minorities. We were very active and united when discussing the Artificial Insemination Act. In a referendum, however, this act was not accepted by the Slovenian public. It was the general opinion of the public that single women do not have the right to be artificially inseminated.

Although we did not succeed in the referendum, we had public discussions on this problem: Why are single women not allowed to have a child with semen from an unknown donor? We also organized a strong campaign, traveled around Slovenia, and discussed this topic with the people. Maybe we were ahead of our time.

On May 1, 2004, Slovenia became a member of the European Union. For its population of 2 million, living in the heart of Europe, this was a very important decision. Slovenia's accession to the EU opened its position to the rest of the world. Slovenia is a small and beautiful country. If we would remain isolated, we would also remain more introverted.

It was also Europe that helped to promote women in political and public life. Up to now, Brussels and Strasbourg looked down on Slovenia because it was mainly represented by men. At present, however, the European Parliament consists of more than 34 percent women.

To conclude, I would like to tell you about the first amendment to the first act of my first term of office in Parliament. Women demanded that Slovenian legislation would grammatically equally refer to the male and female genders. Our male colleagues supported us, with smiles on their faces. It was a symbolic but a very important step.

During my term of office, we amended legislation, imposing greater penalties on those partners (mainly men) who do not pay alimony for their children. Women are more involved in culture, education, family and social policy, local self-government, ecology, and health care (the antialcohol act, antitobacco act, etc.). But unfortunately, we are less active in finances. During both terms of office, I have been active in the Committee for Culture, Education, and Sport, the Commission for Petitions, Equal Opportunities, and Human Rights, the Committee for Family and Social Affairs, the Constitutional Committee, and the Committee for European Affairs. Because I study every issue thoroughly and because of many other obligations, I have withdrawn from some other working bodies in my present term of office. However, I try to cooperate in discussions on issues that I find important. Let me say that I have never "swarmed" into managing the working bodies, because I am not in favor of the competition that always emerges, especially at the beginning of the term (mostly with men). This is too much connected to prestige. However, I admit that such retreats are not the best solution, especially from the authoritative point of view. Although I do not decide to be in the front rows, I act as if I am positioned right in these rows. And tomorrow? On the one hand, I want to stay in my profession. But I am marked by politics, which more or less closes possibilities. But one thing is true: Short trips to politics may be an adventure. Results, however, are based on persistence.

Some of our dilemmas are not faced by the younger generation. Equality of the sexes is becoming more obvious and self-evident. Sometimes my male colleagues say that the election quotas are good because they will need them in the future—when they find themselves in the minority!

[*Editors' note:* On November 21, 2008, Majda Širca was elected minister of culture by the National Assembly of Slovenia.]

Chapter 11

Negotiating the Czech Parliament

An Interview with Anna Čurdová,
House of Deputies, Czech Parliament

Anna Čurdová was born in 1963 in Nový Bydzov, a small town near Hradec Králové in Eastern Bohemia. Her father was an engineer, and her mother was a teacher. She studied Russian and pedagogy at the University in Hradec Králové. She later studied social and environmental sciences and worked as a teacher in a secondary technical school until 2003. She was first elected to Parliament in 1996 as a deputy for the Social Democratic Party and has since been reelected three times. She is married and has two daughters, age fifteen and eleven years. She is active in the Social Democratic Party and Sokol.

What kinds of political or social activity did you engage in prior to running for Parliament, and why did you decide to run for Parliament? What factors were most important in your victory?
My previous political experience prior to running for Parliament was not extensive. In 1986, I stood as a candidate for office as a member of the local council in Odolená Voda. I was elected and stayed in office for three

years, until the Velvet Revolution in 1989. In 1995 I decided to run for Parliament to help people and do something useful. A friend of mine was active in politics, so I decided to try it as well. I ran for Parliament four times, in 1996, 1998, 2002, and 2006. I was first elected in 2002. The very good election results of my party, the Social Democratic Party, in my district were the most important factor that helped me to win.

What are the most important activities you engage in as a parliamentarian? How often do you speak in Parliament? Give interviews to the press? Meet with people from your district? Participate in party meetings?
I engage in legislative activities—proposing of bills and measures. Once a week, I spend a day in my district, where I meet magistrates and mayors, visit schools and social institutions, and have office hours for the public. During these days, we try to help solve any problems I can help with as a member of Parliament. I also write articles for the press and internet media, and have started my own Web page. I also organize conferences and seminars on various topics and cooperate with nongovernmental organizations.

I speak in every session of Parliament on various subjects. I give interviews to the press only when it deals with an issue on which I work. I meet with people from my district quite often. As I mentioned, I go to my district and talk to people during the so-called MP days. And I participate in party meetings, of course.

Which committees do you sit on? What position do you occupy on these and which committees, if any, did you wish to join but did not succeed in joining?
I am a member of the Committee on European Affairs and serve as its vice chairperson, the Committee on Social Affairs, and the Commission on Family Affairs and Equal Opportunities. I am also a member and the head of the Permanent Delegation to the Parliamentary Assembly of the Council of Europe. I was elected to all the committees I wanted to be on, but in some cases, only after a very long time and complicated negotiations.

How do you see your role? Do you see yourself as representing women's interests, the interests of your party, or the interests of those who elected you?
I see myself as representing the interests of women, of those who elected me and of my party as well. Gender issues are being discussed in the Czech Republic now, but society and women often do not associate themselves with them. They do not see the processes and the effects on society. Even women themselves often do not want to be treated in a different way. They

do not want anyone helping them. I am glad the Social Democratic Party in the Czech Republic is starting to work on gender issues and talk about them openly.

What are the most gratifying and difficult aspects of your work as a parliamentarian?
The most gratifying aspect of my work is the contact with people and the fact that, at least sometimes, I can really help them. The most difficult or frustrating aspect is the way the media shape public opinion. For example, sometimes you try to do something good, but the information people get is quite the opposite.

How are women parliamentarians treated by their male colleagues? Are there special challenges or difficulties that women parliamentarians face that are not faced by their male colleagues?
I do not have any problems in cooperating with my male colleagues. But what is a bit of a problem is cooperation among women parliamentarians. It is much more difficult to make the women work together; they seem to fight for individual positions and not cooperate as a team.

Men are used to working as members of a team, and they are much better at cooperation than women. Gender issues are viewed by men as controversial. They cannot see all the connections to the economy and other spheres of life. Women who work on gender issues are seen as feminists. Being labeled feminists reduces our political power and discourages our voters.

What do you see as the most important issues facing women? Are there special women's issues that are different from the issues faced by the rest of society? What conditions are helpful for parliamentarians to really accomplish their goals with respect to the advancement of women in the Czech Republic?
The most important issue facing women is the reconciliation of family and work. This includes the problem of women's employment—their return to work after maternity leave and also the employment of women who are over fifty. Pension reform is another important issue for women. Nobody analyzed the effects it might have on women. And there are many more economic issues, where the effects of given measures on women are being ignored.

Of course there are special women's issues, but politicians cannot and do not want to see them as such. This topic (conditions that would foster action with respect to the advancement of women) is still on the edge of interest here. The media are starting to concentrate on it a little bit more, but the politicians, including women, are reacting very slowly.

To what extent is there cooperation with other women in Parliament to address these issues? On what kinds of issues do women from different parties cooperate? Can you give any specific examples?
We form ad hoc coalitions to support a common bill. In general, a women's lobby in Parliament does not exist, and it cannot exist because of the political situation. Women represent the interests of their political parties. Right-wing women parliamentarians refuse to fight for women's issues; they do not see gender issues as important. But there are a few examples when all the women in Parliament have cooperated, such as the legislation on child abduction and compensatory child support.

What is the extent of your contact with women's nongovernmental organizations and groups outside your parties?
I come into contact with various nongovernmental organizations quite often, and their cooperation is very good. But their influence is very limited. It is only a few elite groups in Prague and Brno that have some kind of influence.

What is the main reason there are not more women in Parliament, and what needs to change to increase the percentage of women?
It is the strategy of political parties and the men in them who are afraid of losing their influence. It is the political parties that must change, but not only that. It is the people who must clearly express their demand for more women in politics and make the parties listen.

What role does the EU play with regard to issues affecting women in the Czech Republic?
The EU is quite influential, but the public does not realize it.

What are your future political plans?
I do not have any specific future political plans. The situation is complicated now, so I will try to do the best with what the future brings.

Chapter 12

My Entry into Politics during the Time of German Reunification: Where Do East German Female Politicians Stand in Europe Today?

Constanze Krehl

Regine Hildebrandt, a famous East German politician who unfortunately died in 2001, spoke aptly when she said: "Actually, I was never really interested in politics. This changed with the fall of the Berlin Wall. I have realized one basic necessity: If something is ever going to change, other people will have to get involved."

After my studies in computer science in 1980, I worked in various computer centers until 1984. Unusually for East German women who had been integrated in the workforce since 1949, I decided in 1984 to become a housewife and take care of my two children. My political interest was limited to a careful observing of the media and to discussions in private surroundings. There, I was able to speak of my admiration for Willy Brandt, who was the first Social Democratic chancellor in the Federal Republic of Germany between 1969 and 1974. He won the Nobel Peace Prize in 1971 for his so-called new Eastern policy. He stood for cooperation and reconciliation between the European West and East. The conservative opposition accused him of betraying East Germany and accepting Germany's separation into two separate states.

However, things changed in 1989—for me as well as for Regine Hildebrandt. Now I was able to express my support for Social Democratic policies in public. I was involved in building up the East German Social Democratic Party in Eisenhüttenstadt, a small city near the Polish-German border in 1990. I am still active as a politician, and it was my choice to take political responsibility.

In March 1990, I was elected to the Volkskammer, the last parliamentary assembly of the German Democratic Republic. After reunification, I was a member of the Bundestag until my first introduction to the European Parliament. Due to the fact that I moved to Saxony, I was sent to the European Parliament as a so-called observer in 1991.

Observers are national parliamentarians who will run for election in the future but whose countries are not yet members of the European Union. Germany was a member; however, there had been no East German representatives. Even with the status of an observer and as a woman, I decided deliberately to be a member of the Budget Committee—a decision that might be atypical if you can choose committees like Employment and Social Affairs. I work in this committee to this day, now as a substitute member. The Budget Committee is a body of special importance because the budget of the European Union cannot become law without the approval of the European Parliament.

The European Parliament has more limited powers than most national parliaments. It cannot initiate legislation. The power to propose legislation is reserved to the executive, the European Commission. However, Parliament is not only consulted in the preparation of legislation; legislative proposals in most policy areas must be approved by both the Council, the direct representation of the member countries' executives, and by Parliament. In most policy areas, Parliament can veto and amend legislation. This power gives its consultative role in the preparation of laws considerable weight. Once legislation is adopted, it must be implemented within two years by the member states unless longer transition periods are provided in the legislation. In sum, the European Parliament has great influence on European legislation, which in turn is binding on the member states once adopted.

The willingness of women to work outside the house was widespread in the former German Democratic Republic (East Germany), and it gave that society its distinctive character. On the one hand, it meant that women were and had to be highly independent; on the other hand, women were enabled to pursue their careers because of, for instance, child care facilities. Even today, the use of such facilities is much higher in the eastern part of Germany —certainly due to the fact that many facilities had been built during East German times and survived the changes during the 1990s. In addition, young women in the eastern part were raised with the idea of putting their children in day care facilities.

The political engagement of women from the eastern part increased during the transformation process in Germany in 1989–90. Thus, it is not unusual that women began to fill positions in party structures. The party I belong to has had a quota for women since 1988. This quota was in response to the demands of the feminist movement. In spite of the achievements of feminism in the 1970s and 1980s, feminism is nowadays often less highly regarded, especially among young women. Young women often do not see themselves as facing discrimination. Many think that everything is OK. While the quota assures that at least 40 percent of all positions within the party have to be filled by women, the quota system is still discussed, and it is controversial. Critics argue that unqualified women are preferred to qualified men because of the quota. But the quota is the only possibility to ensure an adequate level of female representation. The proper functioning of democracy and social progress can only be guaranteed if there is equal participation of women in political and social decisionmaking structures.

Pressures for greater representation of women and in particular the introduction of different quota systems since the 1980s have led to a dramatic increase in the number of female members of the Bundestag. This is evident from figures 12.1 and 12.2.

Nevertheless, the practical implementation of quotas and other measures to increase the role of women in politics can be difficult sometimes. As former chairwoman of the Social Democratic Party in Saxony, I am still working on improving the percentage of women within the party. Right now we have about 23 percent female members in Saxony. In the Saxonian Parliament, the Social Democrats have four female representatives, about 31 percent of the total (figure 12.3).

In the European Parliament, it seems that generally women are more strongly represented than in the national parliaments. Their proportion varies in the different party groups, as is evident from figure 12.4. The German members of the Christian Democratic group have a somewhat higher percentage of women than that group as a whole, while the proportion of women among the German Social Democrats is the same as their representation in the Socialist group as whole. Having said this, I have to admit that the rep-

Figure 12.1. The growth in the number of female parliamentarians in the German Bundestag, 1949–2002

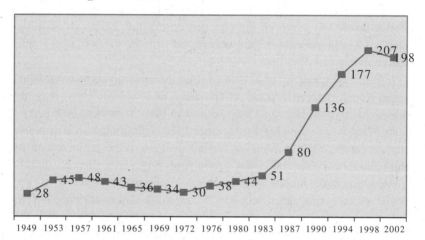

Source: Bundestag Web site (www.bundestag.de).

Figure 12.2. Number of women in the German Bundestag by party, 2005

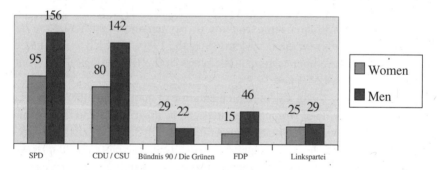

Note: SPD = German Social Democratic Party; CDU = Christian Democratic Union of Germany; CSU = Christian-Social Union of Bavaria (Germany); FDP = Free Democratic Party.
Source: Bundestag Web site (www.bundestag.de).

resentation of women from the eastern part of Germany in the European Parliament needs to be improved. Only four women out of thirty-one German female parliamentarians represent 6.9 million eastern German women on the European political decisionmaking level. Conversely, fourteen men from the eastern part of Germany represent 6.6 million eastern German men. These figures show clearly that we are still far from an equal representation.

Figure 12.3. Quotas for the numbers of women and men in the Parliament of the German state of Saxony, 2006

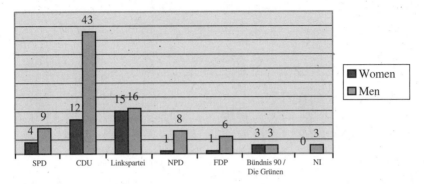

Note: SPD = German Social Democratic Party; CDU = Christian Democratic Union of Germany; NPD = National Democratic Party; FDP = Free Democratic Party; NI = nonattached.
Source: Sächsischer Landtag Web site (www.landtag.sachsen.de).

Figure 12.4. Number of women in the European Parliament by party, 2005

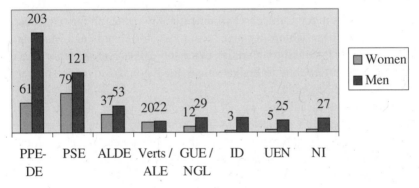

Note: PPE-DE = Group of the European People's Party (Christian Democrats) and European Democrats; PSE = Group of the Party of European Socialists; ALDE = Group of the European Liberal, Democrat, and Reform Party; Verts / ALE = Group of the Greens / European Free Alliance; GUE / NGL = Confederal Group of the European United Left / Nordic Green Left; ID = Independence / Democracy Group; UEN = Union for Europe of the Nations Group; NI = nonattached.
Source: European Parliament Web site (www.europarl.europa.eu).

Let me also say something about the latest development affecting the composition of the European Parliament, the enlargement in May 2004. Figure 12.5 shows the proportion of women by country and the size of the country delegations. In nearly all these delegations to the European Parliament, the percentage of women is higher than in their respective national

Figure 12.5. Women members of Parliament in the nations admitted to the European Union in 2004

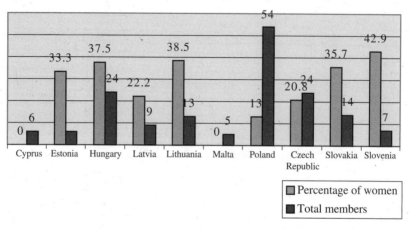

Source: European Parliament Web site (www.europarl.europa.eu).

parliaments. At the same time, the representation of women from the new member states in the European Parliament is lower than in the old fifteen-member European Union. It ranges from zero for Cyprus and Malta and 13 percent for Poland through ratios in the low 20 percent range for Latvia and the Czech Republic to higher values for Estonia, Slovakia, Hungary, Lithuania, and Slovenia.

For me, this means that we, as European politicians, need to support women and women's organizations in a number of the new member states to improve their situation. The truth is that, unfortunately, it will still take years to have an equal involvement of women and men at all levels of political and social life—on all levels of responsibility. Therefore, we have to work and encourage women to get more involved in major political initiatives, become more active in administration and governments, and help to enforce an equal participation of citizens in the political process. It is important to recall the inequalities that still exist between women and men. To achieve the goal of balance on all political and social levels, it is necessary to achieve a general awareness and permanent commitments to these objectives. Additionally, we have to focus on the many issues of "gender policy." Successful policies will in turn activate the political participation of women. That is why it was important that the former president of the European Parliament, Pat Cox, declared in the plenary on March 8, 2004,

"The bureau has taken the decision to set up a High-Level Group on Gender Equality. It will initiate gender mainstreaming throughout the activities and policies of Parliament and promote women's representation in Parliament's governing bodies and in all posts of responsibilities in Committees, Delegations, Administrations, etc." The High-Level Group on Gender Equality was set up to follow up on Parliament's Resolution of March 13, 2003, on gender mainstreaming in the European Parliament. The High-Level Group held its first meeting on November 23, 2004. It agreed that the European Parliament has a responsibility to act as a positive role model for equal opportunities, as regards both its political work and its own staff policy. Its priority areas include:

1. Monitoring gender mainstreaming across Parliament's legislative activities, in both its process and policies, and ensuring that the gender dimension is taken on board in areas such as committee work, the budget, and staff policy.
2. Integrating gender mainstreaming into the work of all committees (e.g., appointing a member in each committee to monitor the gender impact of the committee's legislative and political work, as well as awareness raising, monitoring, and follow-up activities).
3. Improving European Parliament communication and information policy and promoting gender-neutral language in parliamentary documents.
4. Promoting equal opportunities in internal staff policy, in particular pursuing gender balance as regards management posts and promoting workable measures to facilitate an appropriate work/life balance for all staff.

The group reports to the bureau and coordinates its work with other European Parliament bodies, in particular the Women's Rights and Gender Equality Committee and the Conference of Committee Chairs. In my opinion, this is a major political step for more chances and for advanced participation possibilities for female politicians.

In fact, women's issues are on the daily agenda at the European level. Some recent examples give an idea of what these are. First, a Socialist-initiated report, adopted by the European Parliament, proposed that each of its committees and delegations should designate a member to apply a gender mainstreaming approach to its work. Second, the European Parliament has established a Committee on Women's Rights and Equal Opportunities, which deals exclusively with matters related to women issues. And third, measures by the European Union have brought about a greater equality of rights between women and men. The European Parliament has wholeheart-edly supported legislative measures designed to combat discrimination in the field of employment, which cover equal pay for work of equal value, part-time work, maternity rights, parental leave, and the like. Expanding equal protection into areas outside the labor market and industrial relations has been a concern of European legislative work on gender as well as of measures prohibiting discrimination on the basis of race and ethnic back-ground. This includes equal access to goods and services such as education, housing, and public and private insurance systems.

The European Parliament nowadays reacts very quickly to emerging problems. A good example is the "Red Card to Forced Prostitution" cam-paign. This campaign, which is broadly supported throughout all political groups, fought human trafficking in relation to the soccer World Cup in Ger-many in 2006. Thousands of poor women risked being lured to Germany by false promises of work, only to be forced into prostitution. The campaign aimed to sensitize fans from around the world to the problem. Earlier, Par-liament adopted a resolution against human trafficking of women in gen-eral. Today, a hundred thousand women in the European Union are victims of this serious violation of human rights every day. In my opinion, it is very important that all European countries work together to eliminate this cruel treatment of women.

Chapter 13

Women in Politics in Bulgaria

Kina Andreeva

Bulgarian history is full of examples of brave and smart women who have played significant roles at different historical moments. If during the Ottoman oppression Bulgarian women had to disguise themselves in men's clothes in order to participate in the struggle against the conqueror, today, three centuries later, women in Bulgaria do not have to wear men's clothes in order to become part of the political, state, and economic elite. This fact, unfortunately, does not mean that joining that elite is an easy thing to achieve.

The role of women in patriarchal Bulgarian society leading up to the socialist revolution in 1944 was restricted to that of a good wife and mother. The false equality between men and women proclaimed during the Communist regime was manifested by women working as welders and crane or combine operators. Immediately after the fall of the Communist regime, the political scene was totally occupied by men. Now, sixteen years later, things are different, but not as different as we would like. Margaret Thatcher once said that there is only one requirement a woman seeking a high-ranking position in politics should meet: to be better than the competing men. Unfortunately, sometimes even that is not enough.

I was born in Sofia, the capital city of Bulgaria, to a doctor and a teacher. I have always lived in Sofia. My parents were not members of the Bulgarian Communist Party, and my father's family was repressed, their property nationalized.

I graduated from Sofia University with master's degrees in Russian language and literature and English language and literature. My professional life began in 1985 when I assumed the position of lecturer in Russian language at the Higher Institute of Civil Engineering and Architecture. In 1990, I started teaching English to the students of architecture and civil engineering as well, and in 1994 I was elected head of the Department of Foreign Languages. I remained in this position until the summer of 2001, when I was elected as a member of Parliament (MP), and I served in this position until June 2005.

Since September 2005, I have worked as a chief expert adviser on the State Administration Affairs Committee of the National Assembly. I have completed a thesis in the history of political transitions, and the defense of my graduation paper is forthcoming. I was also elected a member of the Managing Board of the National Civic Forum Bulgarka—a nongovernmental organization that works to strengthen democracy in Bulgaria, through the inclusion of women's issues. It is very artificial to separate one's life into political and professional realms, but in the academic field men and women are evaluated for their academic and pedagogical achievements, and academia is one field in which women in Bulgaria have reached very good positions. I cannot say the same about the political arena.

I started my political career in 1994 when I joined the Union of Democratic Forces (UDF), the democratic center-right organization established after the end of Communism. This party performed all the significant political, economic, and social reforms during the two periods when it governed the country, from 1991 to 1992 and 1997 to 2001. My decision to join the UDF was not an easy one, because in my post-totalitarian consciousness, the word "party" itself had negative connotations. I had never been a party member, and I never thought that I would become one. I thought democratic changes would happen easily, overnight, because the society was ready for them, and that it was enough just to go to demonstrations and vote for the UDF. It turned out that that was not the case. In 1994, the UDF suffered a devastating election loss at the hands of the Communist Party, which won an absolute majority of the vote only five years after the crimes they committed during the fifty years of the Communist regime gained publicity. That is when I decided that I could not just support the UDF; I had to work for the party as a member. The branch of the UDF I joined was one of the biggest organizations in Sofia, with more than five hundred members. A year later, I was on the ticket of local councillors for the local elections; I was listed in thirteenth place on the party list, even though there were only eleven mandates for the whole constituency. I did not despair over my low placement on the list; I worked hard during the campaign and contributed a lot to the successful final results.

In 1996, I was elected chair of the UDF in my region. My election to the post was a compromise; there were two male political leaders in the region, each having a significant group of supporters, and the party was practically divided into two antagonistic forces. The situation was very serious: Neither of the groups wanted to accept the other's leader. The divisions grew deeper, and the opposing groups found fewer and fewer common positions. The party leaders consequently decided that they needed someone for this position who was neutral in the eyes of both groups, and who could accommodate the differences and decrease the hostility and stresses in the structure. Who could be more appropriate than a woman? And so I became leader of the local organization. I had to bring these two groups together, settle all the conflicts, make this structure work, and play a significant role in the region. I stayed in this position for five years, until 2001, when I resigned after my election to Parliament in the Thirty-Ninth National Assembly. During this period, we won all the elections in our constituency—even in 2001, when my party sustained a devastating loss in the country as a whole.

During this period, I was reelected as party chair three times. There were other candidates in two of the elections, but I won in the face of strong competition. In 1999, when I was reelected for the third time, I was the only candidate. By then I was recognized and respected by the party members in the region as a leader. Of course, it cost me a lot of personal efforts and time. Very often my family suffered, and my husband and two daughters were deprived of my care and attention. But they have always supported me and have never complained.

In 2000, I was elected deputy chair of the Sofia party structure by the Regional Party Council, consisting of more than a hundred representatives from the twenty-four districts of Sofia. In 2001, I was nominated to run as an MP. The Sofia Council arranged the party ticket for the parliamentary elections by secret ballot, and I placed second on the list. Thus, in 2001 I became an MP from one of the constituencies in Sofia. I was deputy chair of the Committee on Culture and a member of the Committee on European Integration and the Committee on Children, Youth, and Sports Affairs. My work in the Thirty-Ninth National Assembly was not limited to issues connected with the work of these three committees. I was a strong advocate of the Bill on Equal Opportunities for Men and Women. Unfortunately, it did not become a law because of the strong opposition it met from the ruling majority.

Although it is difficult to realize your political ideas in opposition, I managed to pass in the plenary sittings some very important texts (which had been rejected by the majority in the relevant committees) in legislation concerning intellectual property rights, licenses of architects and designers, child protection, preservation of green areas in cities and towns, and urban development. I prepared these texts in collaboration with different professional organizations like Music Author, the Chamber of Architects, the Building Chamber, as well as with nongovernmental organizations like the Gender Project, Citizens for a Green Sofia, and Safe Children. Close cooperation with different professional and civil organizations also helped me to prevent two bills from passing: the Bill on the Monuments of Culture and Museums, and the Bill on Cultural Patronage. These had been submitted to the National Assembly by the government or by representatives of the majority; they were not in favor of Bulgaria's cultural heritage and contemporary culture but were developed to serve the interests of some of the former Secret Service officers, who became "capitalists" after the end of Communism and were eager to profiteer on our cultural and historical treasures by using them for money laundering. All this was obviously achieved with the help of the representatives of other political groups in Parliament. I looked for the support from women as well as from men, depending on the specific issue.

I was among the 9 out of 240 parliamentarians who addressed more than 100 questions at the time of parliamentary control to the prime minister and to the ministers. Most of our questions resulted in concrete measures by the relevant authorities to solve various personal, social, or institutional problems. This is the "bright," or successful, part of my political career.

During the twelve years I have been in public life, I have also sustained many blows, sometimes undeserved. I was often underestimated or offended, but politics does not differ from life, and here good and bad, failures and successes take turns. And, certainly, this is a field in which men forget to be gentlemen, even within their own parties, where all the members are supposed to be, if not friends, at least people who share the same values and ideas.

I would like to specially mention one very important moment of my political carrier. It happened in 2003, immediately after the local elections. The leader of the UDF ran for mayor of the capital. She could not make it to the second round, and although she had promised to hand in her resignation in case she lost, she refused to do it and announced her support for the candidate who had left the UDF between the first and second rounds of the 2001 presidential elections, which were very important for this political party. She was totally discredited among our electorate. So she left supporters of the right no other choice but to "vote for the Communist or vote for the crook." The electorate on the right did not forgive this, and more and more citizens and party members realized that there was no political force on the right that could possibly represent them. I think that there is no worse verdict for a political party than its supporters declaring that they no longer have political representation. Thus, under the pressure of the citizens, a new center-right party was formed in 2004, headed by the former prime minister, Ivan Kostov. Along with twenty-seven other parliamentarians of our group, I became one of the founders of the new right-wing party Democrats for a Strong Bulgaria.

As I write about these events, I am aware that this was the most difficult choice in my political life, but I made this decision, and I am sure that it was the right thing to do. I was a candidate for Parliament in Sofia as a representative of Democrats for a Strong Bulgaria. This time the tickets were arranged by all party members and supporters. New favorites and heroes came with the establishment of the new party and we, the so-called old faces, were pushed to the background. So I was placed seventh. My active work in Parliament turned out to be insufficient for getting a better position on my party ticket. The party won 7 percent of the vote, and I could not become an MP for a second mandate. Now I work as chair of the Party Committee on Culture, and I am responsible for the party's policy in the fields of culture, and national cultural and historical heritage. Of course, I do not think that this is the end of my political career. I gained such an experience during all these years that I think I still have something to contribute, both to my party and to my supporters in civil society. I am going to run in the 2009 elections to become a member of the European Parliament.

It is not because of self-importance that I have paid so much attention to my own political career but because I am an illustration of all the difficulties that women in politics must face in Bulgaria—and, I suppose, not only here. My observations of the political parties have allowed me to recognize two interesting tendencies. The first is that when a party is in crisis, men are not very eager to run for high-ranking party positions. After the election loss in 2001, our party leader resigned; a new leader had to be elected in order to overcome all the confusion among the party members and to motivate them once again to start fighting for voters' approval. At the National Conference called to elect the new leader, there were only two candidates, and both were women. Almost the same thing happened in Sofia when the party structure, torn apart by conflicts and contradictions, elected a female leader. Women in politics should not allow themselves to be considered a rescue team. Their presence in politics should be the result of a rationalized party policy and cognized public necessity. There is much work to be done in this respect.

The second tendency shows that although there are quite a lot of examples of women with successful political and state careers in Bulgaria, female politicians are still considered most appropriate for low-ranking and not very representative positions, where hard work and immense efforts are needed; top political and state positions remain closed to them. I could say that the reason for this trend lies not only in men but also in women. The Thirty-Ninth National Assembly had the highest female representation (63 out of 240) in the history of Bulgarian parliamentarian democracy. Observers then said that the negative tendency had been broken and the movement for equal participation of men and women in decisionmaking had gained a lot of new supporters. This large female presence was due to the newly formed (only one month before the elections of 2001) movement that included many women (86) on its ticket—34 percent of all candidates, 60 of whom were in the first slots. But this large female presence could not contribute to improving the overall image of female politicians, because there is something more important than the physical presence of women in politics, and that is their attitude toward various problems. Unfortunately, in our case, most of the women from the majority behaved more like top models than politicians who were sympathetic to people's problems, devoted to solving them, and ready to tackle even the most complicated ones. Day after day, they appeared in Parliament in fashionable suits, each costing much more than the average salary in the country. The media very often wrote about the prices of their accessories—jewelry, boutique clothes, designer's bags and shoes, and the like—and never about something they had done as MPs.

One could imagine that such a female presence would at least advocate and support the legislation concerning women's issues. Not so. I will give only one example: When our political group submitted a Bill on Equal Opportunities for Men and Women, the plenary session of Parliament rejected it with the votes of women from the majority. They did nothing to convince their colleagues that this law was necessary. This example illustrates why I think the equal presence of women in politics should not be guaranteed by equality in quantity, but rather in quality. Men and women are far more critical of female politicians than of male ones. In a society like ours, which has strongly established cultural stereotypes that do not favor female politicians, their mass presence may bring more liabilities than assets if they are perceived only as the more beautiful part of the political scene.

Another interesting phenomenon is one I call "the phenomenon of public hypocrisy." A recently conducted opinion poll on women's role in politics found that 57 percent of those polled said that women in politics are more responsive than men to people's concerns, and 61 percent think that they are more diplomatic and flexible. Only 18 percent believe that women in politics do not work as hard as men. Of those surveyed, 34 percent assume that women in politics are good wives and mothers, and 46 percent are convinced that women with successful professional careers are good in politics as well. To the question, "Would you personally vote for a female candidate competing with a male one?" 72 percent said yes for an MP election; 67 percent said yes for a mayoral race; 73 percent said yes for a local councillor; and 53 percent said they would vote for a woman over a man for president. Why, then, is there such a big discrepancy between public attitudes and reality? I can offer only one explanation: Most people find it prestigious to publicly support women; they are ashamed to confess in public their genuine views and to say frankly that the woman's place is at home. But even this is a step forward. The next step is to make the views reported in opinion polls inner convictions. This can be done when women who are in politics are responsible, effective, sensitive, and devoted to solving the problems of society.

In conclusion, it is a great challenge to fight to get public opinion on your side, to make male politicians consider women as equals, and to assume the positions we deserve, not because of vanity or any other selfish motivations, but because for Bulgaria to develop successfully in the coming years, Bulgarian women have to become more vital players in the political arena.

Chapter 14

Women in Power: Concluding Thoughts

Marilyn Rueschemeyer and Sharon L. Wolchik

This volume has brought together research on the experiences of women members of the national parliaments of Russia, Poland, the Czech Republic, Bulgaria, and Slovenia, as well as of eastern German deputies in the parliament of united Germany. In addition, women parliamentarians from these countries have offered their own observations.

The current role of women in these parliaments has to be seen against three backdrops: the historical developments during the last years of Communism and the period of political transition, the changing problems women faced in their societies, and the changing role of women in politics. In all three respects, the countries studied differed significantly from each other.

With this background in mind, our research on women parliamentarians focused on a number of common issues. We were concerned with the experience these women had with politics on the local and regional levels before entering the national parliaments. What other qualities and experiences were important for being considered viable candidates? Which parties were they most comfortable with, and why? And what role did these parties play in including women among the candidates in national elections? Did the women see themselves as representatives of women's issues? How did this relate to their choice of a party and their commitments to its goals? What was the extent of cooperation on certain issues among women across different parties? What was the role of women's organizations? How did their orientations and reactions change after entering parliament? What positions did they take on the central problems their countries faced, above all the reorientation of the economy and the transformation of state-society relations? Did international organizations or nongovernmental organizations (NGOs) reinforce initiatives they attempted to introduce? What difficulties did they encounter in their parliamentary work? When and how did these difficulties change over time? Did they participate on an equal level with male parliamentarians? How were they able to mediate between the demands in their personal lives and the demands of parliament?

The Background: The Experience of Women
before and after 1989–1990

The countries selected for our project differed during the period of Communism, and these differences were an important background for our research on the post-Communist period. They included differences in economic development, levels of general education, public participation in both official and nonofficial organizations and groups, the changing role of the state, the development of private initiatives during the last years of Communism and the early transformation period—and, related to all these, the position of women.

The preceding chapters first briefly reviewed developments with respect to women's roles during the Communist period—their ability to enter educational institutions; the role of the state in providing child care; the possibility of extensive periods of leave for giving birth to children, with guarantees of return to the workplace; and the quality of women's participation in professional organizations, work collectives, unions, and official parliaments. Our accounts then turned to the participation of women in the years immediately preceding the transformation in their society, their role in women's groups and in civic and political organizations, and whether or not these activities resulted in increased political participation—or a strong political voice—in the first years of the post-Communist transition. We briefly reviewed employment issues and changes in the organization of health care, child care, pensions, and the like, as well as post-Communist political developments—new and renewed parties, changes in the population in their support for newly developing parties, and the issue of quotas during the early transition years.

During the late Communist period, but especially afterward, when new, more conservative, political parties were being formed, many voiced severe criticisms about the role of women in Communism. Communist policies, it was argued, took women out of their "natural" place in the household and integrated them into the workplace, introduced quotas that resulted in "unprepared" women participating in political life (which in any case was controlled by the upper echelons of the Communist Party), and raised other issues, such as abortion, that remain salient in some of these countries.

However, many women in the Central and Eastern European countries during the Communist period made their way into professional life, were well trained in their occupations, used state-supported child care, developed relationships with colleagues, and negotiated their personal life in a variety of ways. Again, there were significant differences among the countries before and during the years of Communism—in economic development and educational opportunities available to the population as well as in the strength of traditional patterns of behavior shaping the role of women. Indeed, many Western observers thought the changes in the roles of women in Communist societies were incomplete, and certainly not sufficiently transformative by the standards of Western feminists.

Within some of the societies, small groups of women gathered—sometimes with visitors from the West—to express their continuing frustrations with the difficulties they encountered in their professional and personal lives. In the 1980s, connections with these colleagues increased considerably, and a number of women began to identify with issues that had previously been somewhat less salient for them.

At the same time, during the early transition years, many women in the East were critical of some of the advice and strategies of feminist visitors from the West; indeed, it was not always possible to work together. They were critical because, in many ways, they felt more advanced than women in the West, with greater supports from the state that allowed them to pursue a profession and a satisfactory, if often hectic, personal life. They were upset because, in the course of the post-Communist transition, a number of these social supports were dropped. They were worried by high unemployment. And they were appalled by certain social initiatives, such as the restrictions on abortion.

How was it that a number of women became politically active (albeit on a wide variety of levels)? Although many distrusted political parties, there were those who wanted to become engaged in shaping their society and, after a while, believed that joining a political party was the most sensible way to do so. Most had been involved in a variety of ways in their communities and in their professional associations, in unions, and in special interest groups both before and after the end of Communism. If we think of some of the factors that encouraged women to become part of the "new" political system, we recognize in this volume the importance of political parties in choosing candidates, the electoral system, the existence of quotas, and the cooperation with women's associations and other organized social groups. Even though in most post-Communist countries parties and party identifications are relatively weak, the experiences of the women we interviewed confirm the central importance of parties in processes of democratization as well as in democratic politics. At the same time, some unexpected developments in a particular country can lead to an increase in the political participation of women or hinder it.

Getting into Parliament

In post-Communist parliaments, the percentage of women members has increased since the early transformative years in four of the six countries in this study. Even if women had been active in civil society or in party-oppositional groups, their political power was not maintained in the early post-Communist period. Russia was the exception in our study. Women of Russia—a women's party, an unusual phenomenon in the countries discussed in this volume—was formed in 1993 to advance the interests of women, and it was supported by grassroots organizations and women's groups. During the first Duma, from 1993 to 1995, women in all the parties represented received 13.5 percent of the vote, and more than a third of the women elected were from Women of Russia. However, Women of Russia did not enter the Duma again, in part because two other parties increased the number of nominated women, and from 2003 to 2007, the Duma had the lowest percentage of women deputies among the countries included in this project.

Although the role of political parties is very important in choosing candidates, it is helpful to keep in mind that many of these parties were newly formed. They did not have established constituencies to offer support, and there was even a shortage of readily available candidates for parliamentary elections. Communist or reformed Communist parties in a number of countries did retain their organizations and constituencies. In a few of the countries, alternative organizations, such as Solidarity in Poland, increased their political power before the end of Communism. As Marilyn Rueschemeyer explains in chapter 6, in the former German Democratic Republic (GDR; East Germany), organizations such as environmental groups as well as large numbers of people attracted to the Christian Democratic "bloc" party retained the loyalty of their followers. But the newly formed eastern German Social Democratic Party had no such organized constituency to count on. This meant that new parties in the former GDR, as well as most of the other countries discussed in this volume, often reached out to those people who had been active in helping them create their organizations on a local or regional level or who had been involved in their communities, perhaps in the state administration, in professional associations, and in unions. Women with a university education and special expertise often had a greater chance of being selected; these included experts in law and economics, those with a strong background in business, and environmentalists. This did not mean that women were always sought after; in fact, the opposite was typically the case in a number of the countries in this study.

In those countries where leftist or center-left parties gained power, there was greater support for women candidates. The parties of the left tended to feel more comfortable with the participation of women in politics and were generally less reluctant than rightist or conservative parties to introduce quotas after the early transition years. In Bulgaria, the Bulgarian Socialist Party retained its quota and put 30 percent of women candidates on its party lists, but they ended up at the bottom. In the Czech Republic, the Social Democratic Party has a 25 percent quota. In Germany, the existence of quotas since the 1980s in the Social Democratic Party in the West and the West German Green Party was extended to the eastern parties. The now-united Social Democratic Party has a 40 percent quota, and both the Reformed Communist Party (and now the Left Party) and the Alliance 90 / Green Party have a 50 percent quota goal.[1] The Christian Democratic Party and the Free Democratic Party have increased the number of women candidates, though at a lower level. Quotas have been introduced in various post-Communist countries over the years due to pressure from international organizations,[2] especially the European Union, which legitimated internal efforts. The quotas that were introduced also had an effect on a number of more conservative parties. In chapter 3, Renata Siemieńska notes that in Poland even right-wing parties, such as the League of Polish Families, were influenced by these changes and put a number of women on their party lists for the Sejm. In chapter 2, Linda Cook and Carol Nechemias note that the Russian government has signed a number of agreements with international organizations, committing it to gender equality. The 2001 Law on Political Parties obligates parties to provide equal opportunities on lists of candidates for deputies and other elective offices, but quotas for gender representation have not been legislated.

The role of women's organizations was important in a few of these countries. For a number of the female members of parliament in Slovenia, their decision to enter politics (interestingly, for some, after suggestions by husbands or partners) was supported either by work colleagues, the women's party group, or other members of "civil society" groups; therefore, women in organized groups had and have some impact on their activities. In chapter 4, Milica Antić details the formation of a parliamentary commission to deal with women's policies and a governmental office for women's policies, both formed in the early 1990s. In the Slovene parliament, members' networking with women's organizations was more prevalent among those from left-wing parties, but still at a low level. However, in a nationwide network established in 2001, two thousand well-known women from different political backgrounds, together with some influential males, set the goal of "equal representation" in parliament and worked closely with some women members of parliament and prominent male leaders. A 40 percent quota for the European parliamentary elections was introduced, and the amendment was enacted in 2004, the year Slovenia joined the European Union. In 2006, a 35 percent gender quota for national elections was introduced.

In Poland, as Siemieńska explains, fifty organizations joined the Pre-Electoral Coalition of Women, a nonpartisan arrangement between women's organizations and groups that were politically somewhere between the center and left. They were supported by the Women's Parliamentary Group (the existence of which is unusual in post-Communist parliaments), and both contributed to the success of women in the 2001 elections. The participating women came from all parties, but it was the Democratic Alliance–Labor Union and the Freedom Union that supported the introduction of a gender quota.

Over the years, strong differences developed among the parties in Poland, which affected their participation in the Women's Parliamentary Group. But women parliamentarians in both Slovenia and Poland played an important role in bringing issues of gender to the wider public.

With respect to increasing the number of women elected to parliament, we will mention Bulgaria as one unusual example of change. Women's representation increased dramatically in the elections due to the unexpected development by the political movement led by its once-exiled king. Women were intentionally included in relatively large numbers on his electoral lists, though the platform of the movement was neither particularly prowoman nor profeminist. In chapter 7, Kristen Ghodsee notes that their inclusion resulted in a higher representation of women at the national level than at the local, which is a rather unusual outcome.

A Women's Agenda?

One question pursued in all our work was whether women parliamentarians thought of themselves as representatives struggling for women's rights. For instance, in Russia, the first two Dumas had women deputies from Women of Russia and the Communist Party of the Russian Federation who saw themselves as representing the interests of women, especially with respect to discrimination in employment. But in the fourth Duma, women deputies from United Russia took the position that Russia faced no specific women's issues but rather socioeconomic problems. In Bulgaria, with the exception of domestic violence and sexual harassment (considered pure women's issues, imported by feminists from Western Europe and the United States), the parliamentarians did not link social issues to a feminist agenda. However, the king's appointment of so many women on his electoral lists increased the number of women parliamentarians (as mentioned above), and that situation, together with active women's organizations and lobbyists, in some ways did result in more attention to women's issues—quite apart from any intention to see this happen.

Many of the parliamentarians believed that women cared more about social issues than men. However, this belief was rarely coupled with a focus on issues of particular importance for women as women's issues per se. In the Czech Republic, for example, as Sharon Wolchik explains in chapter 5, there was little popular support for seeing women's issues apart from those of society as a whole; women parliamentarians saw themselves as advocates for all citizens. In Germany, women parliamentarians from the former

GDR expressed concern about the major difficulties in the east after unification: unemployment, increased labor market "flexibility," and maintaining social supports, such as assistance after childbirth in order to continue one's occupation or profession. As in other countries, women's issues often coincided with political, economic, and social problems. In Slovenia, women members of parliament paid attention to gender-sensitive issues (e.g., the change in the Constitution for equal representation) and saw themselves as having different priorities than their male colleagues. They most frequently discussed issues pertaining to labor, family, and social matters, followed by health care issues and culture.

Links with women's groups also varyied among parliamentarians. In Germany, there were several strong women's associations, organized within political parties. Women parliamentarians in the Bundestag had contact with women's groups if they were active in the community or state where they were elected and continue to keep in contact with them. Several believed that women's groups had lost influence over the years; women came into leadership positions, and they had disagreements that sometimes reflected their different eastern-western backgrounds and sometimes party differences. In Russia, links with women's groups were generally weak, though Cook and Nechemias mention that three women deputies from regions with unusually strong, united, politically active women's organizations spoke of personal membership in the groups and worked closely with them. Russia's parties showed little interest in developing women's organizations in their ranks, aside from the Yabloko Party, which was not represented in the present Duma from 2003 to 2007. In the Czech Republic, Wolchik observes that one barrier to greater advocacy by women in parliament was their limited contact with NGOs working on women's issues. But it is in the interaction between female members of parliament and NGOs that Ghodsee found the greatest possibilities for parliamentarians pursuing "women's issues." She believes that legislative proposals need to address the real needs of Bulgarian women "with locally appropriate and politically acceptable solutions" rather than importing feminist agendas from the United States and Western Europe. In chapter 9, Dorota Kempka, who has been chairwoman of Poland's Parliamentary Group of Women for several years, stresses the importance of cooperation between women's organizations and parliamentarians and emphasizes that it was important for women active in NGOs to "make friends" with specific political groups—if not themselves become members of them.[3] Her statement was an attempt to challenge the assumption frequently expressed in some NGOs that one cannot rely on politicians to accomplish goals that advance the position of women.

Of course, some women's NGOs use lobbying techniques. And Maxine Forest notes, for those NGOs in governmental advisory councils, "lobbying does not exclude a corporatist relationship to the State."[4] In fact, a number of groups in Central and Eastern Europe still see the state as a source of financial aid—and as an institution providing legitimacy for the NGOs' agenda.

The Gender Mainstreaming Project of the European Union has been mentioned as helpful by parliamentarians in all the countries considered in this volume. This project has been used to legitimate quotas and the increase in social policies benefiting women, including maternity rights, parental leave, and other initiatives that enable women and men to enter the workforce while maintaining their families. Although a number of international organizations, such as the United Nations, address the interests of women, most of the women parliamentarians interviewed made reference to the impact of the European Union on the policy discussions that were taking place in their own country. But in some cases, women have not received the support they hoped for from the EU. This lack of support may be a result of a parliament that is divided on a particular issue, or it may be considered illegitimate for the EU to step in.

One vivid example of this situation vis-à-vis the EU is the liberalization of Poland's abortion law, in which the Polish Women's Parliamentary Group has been actively involved. After struggles in parliament, a more restrictive law was passed in the early 1990s, liberalized in 1996, and reversed again in 1997; it is still in effect. The Democratic Left Alliance–Labor Union coalition government was unwilling to challenge the restrictive abortion law because of fears of conflict with the Catholic Church, which would diminish the support needed to assure the electorate that the Church's cultural, religious, and economic situation would not be endangered by Poland's entry into the EU. Efforts by women's groups to have the EU help ease the current abortion regulations have until now been unsuccessful.

Poland and the Czech Republic were among those countries opting for existing equality provisions, and some analysts believe only limited changes have been introduced to meet EU requirements, mostly concerning labor markets and social benefits. As Constanze Krehl notes in chapter 12, once legislation is adopted by a member state, it must be implemented within two years unless there is provision for a longer transition period.

Women members of parliament are often reluctant to cooperate with women in different parties. Many women come into parliament already strongly identified with a particular party, and this identification seems only to increase over time as their different political opinions become more salient. That is one reason that the Women's Parliamentary Group in Poland has fewer members from the center and right-wing parties. Siemieńska writes that in the 2001–5 parliament, fifty-five of ninety-three female deputies in the Sejm belonged to the Women's Parliamentary Group. Where political parties demand adherence to their decisions on political issues and engage in intense discussion with those they believe are more sympathetic to another agenda, deputies in the end feel reluctant to vote against their own parties. Some women members of parliament also noted that if the majority of the members in their parties are for a certain policy, it is undemocratic to undermine it. Some votes in parliaments are less controlled than others and left to individual "conscience"—for example, abortion and stem cell research. Despite differences in perspective in eastern and western Germany on a number of issues, women parliamentarians have worked successfully together to prevent more rigid restrictions on abortion.

Nonbudgetary issues may also allow cooperation among members of different parties. Despite the lack of unity among Bulgarian women parliamentarians from different parties on a number of issues, where Ghodsee expected more consensus, she notes that social legislation proposed by the National Movement of Simeon the Second, which had a nearly absolute majority, generally had more success. However, an antidiscrimination law that prohibited employers from discriminating on the basis of sex, ethnicity, and the like—which posed little cost to taxpayers and might have led to actual increases in funding for the national budget if the employers had not complied—was passed with a majority of women voting in favor. Members of parliament also united behind a "relatively budget neutral" amendment to the Law on the Protection of the Child. If the legislation had little or no budgetary impact, women crossed party lines to support it, but only if the men in their parties did as well.

Of course, when the percentage of women in parliament is low, as in Slovenia, there are not many women representatives in the same party, making it difficult to effectively strategize. Antić notes that women parliamentarians have until now not formed a parliamentary group, at least officially, and only half of them support women's networking in parliament. At the same time, potential as well as new EU member states are influenced by the EU's requirement to seriously consider the policies that are proposed.

In Russia, the major initiative in family policy came from the executive.

In response to the country's declining population and low birthrate, President Vladimir Putin reinstated preexisting benefits (extended maternity leaves, pregnancy and maternity allowances) along with new legislation in 2006 that provides a woman giving birth to a second child with a payment to be used for housing or education or as a contribution to her pension. There have been initiatives by a number of countries to address these same issues, including the provision of adequate pensions. And of course, even if there is a common recognition among the parties of the problems to be addressed, there are likely to be strong differences in the solutions that are—or are not—advocated, and even in the implementation of social policies, as was the case when the German Christian Democratic Party sought to make the use of federal funding for all-day child care contingent on "flexible" cooperation by the states.

Once Elected: Women in Power

We now turn to the reactions of women parliamentarians when they first entered parliament. For many, their exhilaration was tempered by feelings of being overwhelmed by the greater previous experience of their colleagues. This was especially intense for the women from the former GDR in the Bundestag in comparison with western German parliamentarians and for nearly all the Bulgarian women who were part of the National Movement of Simeon the Second and represented a third of the women elected. They attended party meetings and special sessions with the leadership of their party if they differed in assessing an issue; they also participated in intense parliamentary sessions dealing with the many difficult problems to be addressed and the negotiations to resolve these issues. They had to be knowledgeable about the complex issues that were being discussed and voted on, which was an enormous challenge, even with dedicated assistants. During the 2002–5 German parliament, eastern German women and men from different political parties met regularly with each other to share assessments. They saw themselves as somewhat intimidated by the western parliamentarians, "obviously" without as much power, more cooperative than parliamentarians from the west, sharing a number of ideals, and having to deal with very serious issues in the former GDR such as unemployment and the reduction of social supports. Antić notes that in Slovenia, women's difficulties in introducing important changes in the 2004 parliament were in part due to the fact that they were newcomers. In the 2002 parliament, however, a number of important bills were passed:

the Employment Act, the Parenthood and Family Earning Act, the Marriage and Family Relations Act, and the Equal Opportunities Act (again, some were related to the impact of European directives).

The committees on which women sit and their positions in these committees give us some indication of the power they have to affect parliamentary decisions. In Poland, participation in a parliamentary committee depends on the outcome of postelection negotiations between parliamentary clubs. In the 2005 Sejm, six women became chairs of permanent committees (out of twenty-eight) and thirteen were appointed deputy chairs. Almost all these women had earlier experience in parliamentary work. In Slovenia in the current term, there are four women chairs (out of twenty-four) and six women deputy chairs. In the German Bundestag before the sudden election of 2005, eastern women were represented on nearly all twenty-one committees, though the eight women committee heads were all western German parliamentarians. After the 2005 election, there were again eight committees (out of twenty-two) headed by women parliamentarians; now one of the heads was an eastern German.

Similarly, women are underrepresented in government ministries, though there is considerable variation. In Slovenia, the Ministry for Labor, Family, and Social Affairs was led by a woman, and in 2008, Majda Širca (chapter 10) was elected minister of culture. In Poland, four out of nineteen ministers are women. In the German Bundestag, in addition to Chancellor Angela Merkel, women head five of the fifteen federal ministries.

Women in all the countries in this study tended to have less power than their male colleagues and more problems convincing not only the public but also party leaders of their competency. On parliamentary committees, members with more experience became chairs. Women have greater chances receiving a deputy chair, an appointment with more limited power.

During all our interviews, a number of remarks were made about the differences between men and women in parliament. Although a few women felt there were no particular differences and mentioned that they had received a warm welcome and support from their party, others perceived men as much more aggressive and less cooperative, more willing to speak "without a stop," less understanding of authority as "the way to achieve good decisions" rather than authority as "power or prestige," less willing than women to listen to others (which is why "women have more contacts with noninstitutional organizations in civil society"), less concerned about social issues and less compassionate than women, more reluctant to be active when the party is in difficulty, and likely to forget to be a "gentleman," even within their own party. Some deputies also noted that women parliamentarians often have difficulty working together.

Somewhat rarer, but still heard, were comments by women that they always have to "prove themselves," that the ambitions of men do not really allow them to accept the idea of women occupying the highest positions and offices, and that most of their male colleagues still believe that women belong at home. As recounted by Carol Nechemias in chapter 8, one deputy in the Russian Duma offered a rather dramatic opinion: "A Russian woman always was lower than a man. Men were the breadwinners, the heads of households; . . . that's history. . . . In our government, there are virtually no women, only in secondary roles. A horse that hauls a load—that's us, while the leaders are men."

Political Work and Personal Life

Women spoke about the difficulties of negotiating their personal lives while in parliament, even with the support of husbands and children. Given the time demands of parliamentary work and weekends that frequently involve participation in events in their constituencies, a number expressed great concern about their daughters and sons being deprived of attention. It seems that fewer women parliamentarians are married than their male colleagues. Women also have fewer children than their male colleagues. In Poland, to take one example, 70 percent of the women and 91 percent of the men are married; 27 percent of the women and 15 percent of the men have no children. The tensions about their personal lives are exacerbated by the pressures of parliamentary demands and the difficulties of adequately keeping up with all the information they need for their work. That some of the parliamentarians are often "on the edge" is an understatement.

Still, one should not underestimate the changes that are taking place. Women from the former GDR noted that parliamentarians from the east and west were talking to each other more, and that parliamentarians from the west were listening. The education and growing confidence of professional women in the GDR who took their own work and personal lives for granted, as well as their expectations of sources of support such as child care, added an important dimension to the discussions of these issues. Interestingly, women in several of the countries mentioned that at the beginning of their political involvement they did not believe in the need for quotas, and they assumed that with their professional qualifications and experience they could enter and advance in political life. But the longer they remained in politics, the more convinced they became that without quotas they would not have achieved their goals.

A number of women were quite nervous and insecure at the beginning of their political careers, especially when entering parliament. And many did not think of themselves as representatives of women or of representing policies that would benefit women. But the years of experience in parliamentary negotiation resulted in a stronger concern for "gender empowerment," even if the women were not feminists in the Western sense.

The attitudes of male parliamentarians were also slowly changing, and not only among the young; the longer women remained in parliament and the more experience they gained, the more respect they received from many of their male colleagues and the greater their access to power. A few of the men noted the women's "civilizing influence." In addition, political elites were affected by powerful international organizations advocating the inclusion of women in the political process. These observations are supported by studies, for instance in Poland, indicating that, generally, attitudes toward women are changing and that younger people, especially better-educated women, disagreed with the statements that men are more suited to politics and that the best place for a woman is in her home.

Conclusion

As the chapters in this book illustrate, the representation of women in most Central and Eastern European parliaments is increasing. This seems largely due to the underlying changes in these societies, partly induced by the Communist policies that had improved women's access to education and employment outside the household. A greater representation of women in political office is also advanced by quotas that bring more women into national and international parliaments, such as the parliament of the European Union.

Correspondingly, women parliamentarians are also beginning to acquire more political power. That Merkel, a physicist from the former GDR, became chancellor of Germany is the most remarkable instance of this process. But that women in several countries are now members of the national cabinet or are slowly on their way to becoming committee chairs is broader evidence of this change.

Do women parliamentarians pursue political goals that can be called a women's agenda? This is a complex question. At first sight, the answer seems to be no. The goals of these women politicians are roughly the same as the goals of men in their party caucuses. But on a closer look, some distinctions suggest themselves. Women's issues in Central and Eastern Europe derive from two major sources: from the social problems created by the economic and social transition these countries are experiencing, and from the clash of views on the appropriate roles for women in society. Many of the social problems are shared by men and women, though some are specific to women. The divergent views on the roles of women do not place women on one side and men on the other but divide the right from the left, roughly speaking. Not surprisingly, left-of-center parties are more concerned with mitigating social problems, favor nontraditional roles for women, and give women a greater chance to win parliamentary seats. On many issues, then, these women see no difference between a women's agenda and the policies of their party. On many issues, they see themselves separated from and opposed by women parliamentarians from the more conservative parties.

Yet this picture is still too simple. On several issues, we found that women did get together even across the major divides of the party systems. In Poland, there is even a parliamentary group that meets regularly across party lines, though it has more members from the left side of the political spectrum than from the right.

A diffuse support for such cross-party links among women parliamentarians seems to derive from their life and work experiences as women— from their initial difficulties in parliamentary work, from their attempt to meet family as well as political obligations, and from their sense that women act differently than men, both in politics and generally. At the same time, gender relations are being transformed.

All these changes take time. The transformation is a process. Success in political life is a process. The researchers and the parliamentarians involved in this study felt the excitement of women transforming themselves into players struggling with the salient issues of their societies. The parliamentarians believed in the importance of their efforts, and the longer they were in office, the more confident they became in their ability to engage with strength in the negotiations and power plays inherent in their work.

As we noted in chapter 1, our analyses reflect the fact that the societies where these women leaders live and work have experienced nearly two decades of transformation since the end of Communist rule. With the exception of Russia—where it is difficult to predict whether the trend toward authoritarianism under the leadership of Putin, first as president and now as prime minister, will be reversed—all these countries have succeeded in meeting many of the main goals commonly articulated soon after the fall of Communism. Thus, with the exception of Russia, they are all functioning democracies with market economies. And they all have also been admitted to the European Union and other European and transatlantic organizations. Political life in these countries, and the perspectives of their citizens and political leaders, continue to reflect the fact that they shared a common Communist past, which is now receding as they become increasingly integrated into the rest of Europe. This integration is an important guarantee of future democratic development as citizens and leaders struggle with the impact of the global economic crisis.

This volume has provided an analysis of how the exceptional women who have risen to positions of political leadership in these post-Communist societies see their roles and act as legislators. Just as we cannot predict whether Russia's leaders will move away from authoritarianism to enable women, as well as men, legislators to have more of an impact on political life, we cannot predict how women's leadership roles will change in the other countries treated here as integration proceeds. We hope, nonetheless, that by providing a snapshot of how women in these countries see their roles and act as leaders early in this process, we have both contributed insights into a previously neglected aspect of politics in these countries and established a baseline for future studies of women leaders in this region.

Notes

1. For some interesting observations on the transformations in the Reformed Communist Party, see Astrid Hedin, *The Politics of Social Networks,* Lund Political Study 118 (Lund: Department of Political Science, Lund University, 2001), 227–31.

2. Sheri Kunovich and Pamela Paxton refer to the importance of the international women's movement for the support of women in politics. Though not negating its effects, it is crucial to recognize and articulate differences among the countries. See Sheri Kunovich and Pamela Paxton, "Pathways to Power: The Role of Political Parties in Women's National Political Representation," *American Journal of Sociology* 111, no. 2 (September 2005): 502–52; the citation here is on 516.

3. Mikko Lagerspetz and Marek Skovajsa note that in Poland, private and corporate foundation stakeholders tend to adopt an antistate position, whereas public foundation representatives stress a close working relationship with the state, supporting a social democratic vision. See Mikko Lagerspetz and Marek Skovajsa, "Non-Profit Foundations in Four Countries of Central and Eastern Europe," *Polish Sociological Review* 2, no. 154 (2006): 187–208; the quotation here is on 199.

4. Maxine Forest, "Emerging Gender Interest Groups in the New Member States: The Case of the Czech Republic," *Perspectives on European Politics and Society* 7, no. 2 (2006): 170–84; the quotation here is on 178.

Selected Bibliography

Although there is a vast literature now on gender and women's issues and women in politics in the post-Communist era generally, there is very little on women political leaders per se. This bibliography includes works published in English that deal with gender issues in Communist and post-Communist European countries more generally as well as treatments of social policy and the impact of EU accession on policies toward women. Although many of them do not deal directly with women leaders (those much more limited works are generally cited in the individual chapters of this book), they may provide useful background information for readers interested in other aspects of women's situation and political behavior.

Anderson, Leah Seppanen. "European Union Gender Regulations in the East: The Czech and Polish Accession Process." *East European Politics and Societies* 20, no.1 (2006): 101–25.

Andreenovka, Anna V. "Women's Representation in the Parliaments of Russia and Ukraine." *Sociological Research* 31, no. 2 (March–April 2002): 5–25.

Antić, Milica G., and Sonja Lokar. "The Balkans: From Total Rejection to Gradual Acceptance of Gender Quotas." In *Women, Quotas and Politics,* ed. Drude Dahlerup. London: Routledge (2006): 138–67.

Antić, Milica G., and Ksenija H. Vidmar. "The Construction of Women's Identity in Socialism: The Case of Slovenia." In *Women's Movements, Networks and Debates in Post-Communist Countries in the 19th and 20th Centuries,* ed. Edith Saurer, Margareth Lazinger, and Elisabeth Frysak. Cologne: Bohlau Verlag (2006): 291–307.

Appel, Hilary. *A New Capitalist Order: Privatization and Ideology in Russia and Eastern Europe.* Pittsburgh: University of Pittsburgh Press, 2004.

Atkinson, Dorothy, Alexander Dallin, and Gail Warshofsky Lapidus, eds. *Women in Russia.* Stanford, Calif.: Stanford University Press, 1977.

Attwood, Lynne. *The New Soviet Man and Woman: Sex-Role Socialization in the USSR.* Bloomington: Indiana University Press, 1990.

Avdeyeva, Olga. "Enlarging the Club: When Do Candidate States Enforce Gender Equality Laws?" *Newsletter of the European Politics and Society Section of the American Political Science Association,* Spring–Summer 2007, 10–11.

Bagic, Aida. "Women's Organizing in Post-Yugoslav Countries: Talking about Donors." In *Global Feminism,* ed. Myra Marx Ferree and Aili Mari Tripp. New York: New York University Press (2006): 141–65.

Bahovec, Eva D., ed. *Gender and Governance: The Civic and Political Participation and Representation of Women in Central and Eastern Europe.* Ljubljana: Faculty of Arts and Society for Cultural Studies, 2005.

Ballington, Julie, and Azza Karam. *Women in Parliament: Beyond the Numbers.* Stockholm: International Idea, 2005.

Beckwith, Karen, and Kimberly Cowell-Meyers. "Sheer Numbers: Critical Representation Thresholds and Women's Political Representation." *Perspectives on Politics* (American Political Science Association) 5, no. 3 (September 2007): 553–65.

Berkman, Michael B., and Robert E. O'Connor. "Do Women Legislators Matter? Female Legislators and State Abortion Policy." In *Understanding the New Politics of Abortion,* ed. M. Goggin. Newbury Park, Calif.: Sage, 1994.

Bratton, Kathleen A., and Leonard P. Ray. "Descriptive Representation, Policy Outcomes, and Municipal Day-Care Coverage in Norway." *American Journal of Political Science* 46, no. 2 (April 2002): 428–37.

Brzinski, Joanne Bay. "Women's Representation in Germany: A Comparison of East and West." In *Women's Access to Political Power in Post-Communist Europe,* ed. Richard E. Matland and Kathleen A. Montgomery. Oxford: Oxford University Press (2003): 63–80.

Buckley, Mary. "Adaptation of the Soviet Women's Committee Deputies' Voices from 'Women of Russia.'" In *Post-Soviet Women: From the Baltic to Central Asia,* ed. Mary Buckley. Cambridge: Cambridge University Press (1997): 157–95.

———. *Women and Ideology in the Soviet Union.* Ann Arbor: University of Michigan Press, 1989.

Bunce, Valerie. "The Political Transition." In *Central and East European Politics: From Communism to Democracy,* ed. Sharon Wolchik and Jane Curry. Lanham, Md.: Rowman & Littlefield (2007): 33–54.

Bútorová, Zora., et al. *She and He in Slovakia: Gender Issues in Public Perception.* Bratislava: Focus, 1996.

Carroll, Susan, ed. *The Impact of Women in Public Office.* Bloomington: Indiana University Press, 2001.

Childs, Sarah. "Should Feminists Give Up on Critical Mass? A Contingent Yes." *Politics & Gender* 2, no. 4 (2006): 522–30.

Colton, Timothy J., and Stephen Holmes, eds. *The State after Communism: Governance in the New Russia.* Lanham, Md.: Roman & Littlefield, 2006.

Colton, Timothy J., and Michael McFaul. *Popular Choice and Managed Democracy: The Russian Elections of 1999 and 2000.* Washington, D.C.: Brookings Institution Press, 2003.

Cook, Linda J. *Post-Communist Welfare States: Reform Politics in Russia and Eastern Europe.* Ithaca, N.Y.: Cornell University Press, 2007.

Dahlerup, Drude. "The Story of the Theory of Critical Mass." *Politics & Gender* 2, no. 4 (2006): 511–22.

Daly, Mary E. "Gender Mainstreaming in Theory and Practice." *Social Politics: International Studies in Gender, State and Society* 12, no. 3 (Fall 2005): 433–50.

Dauderstadt, Michael, Andre Gerrits, and Gyorgy G. Markus. *Troubled Transition: Social Democracy in East Central Europe.* Bonn: Friedrich Ebert Stiftung, Wiardi Beckman Stichting, and Alfred Mozer Stichting, 1999.

Davis, Rebecca Howard. *Women and Power in Parliamentary Democracies: Cabinet Appointments in Western Europe, 1968–1992.* Lincoln: University of Nebraska Press, 1997.

Davidson-Schmich, Louise K. *Becoming Party Politicians: Eastern German State Legislators in the Decade Following Democratization.* Notre Dame, Ind.: University of Notre Dame Press, 2006.

Diamond, Irene. *Sex Roles in the State House.* New Haven, Conn.: Yale University Press, 1977.

Dyson, Kenneth, and Stephen Padgett, eds. *German Politics* (Special Issue on the Politics of Economic Reform in Germany: Global, Rhineland or Hybrid Capitalism?) 14, no. 2 (June 2005).

Einhorn, Barbara. *Cinderella Goes to the Market: Citizenship, Gender, and Women's Movements in East Central Europe.* London: Verso Books, 1993.

———. *Citizenship in an Enlarging Europe: From Dream to Awakening.* London: Palgrave Macmillan, 2006.

———. "Gender(ed) Politics in Central and Eastern Europe." *Journal of Global Ethics* 2 (2006): 139–62.

Fink-Hafner, Danica, and Milica G. Antić. "The 2002 Presidential Elections in Slovenia." *Electoral Studies,* no. 23 (2004): 143–82.

Forest, Maxine. "Emerging Gender Interest Groups in the New Member States: The Case of the Czech Republic." *Perspectives on European Politics and Society* 7, no. 2 (2006): 170–84.

Fultz, Elaine, Markus Ruck, and Silke Steinhilber, eds. *The Gender Dimensions of Social Security Reform in Central and Eastern Europe: Case Studies of the Czech Republic, Hungary and Poland.* Budapest: International Labor Office, 2003.

Funk, Nanette, and Magda Mueller, eds. *Gender Politics and Post-Communism: Reflections from Eastern Europe and the Former Soviet Union.* London: Routledge, 1993.

Fuszara, Malgorzata. "New Gender Relations in Poland in the 1990s." In *The Politics of Gender after Socialism,* ed. Susan Gal and Gail Kligman. Princeton, N.J.: Princeton University Press (2000): 259–85.

Gal, Susan, and Gail Kligman. *The Politics of Gender after Socialism.* Princeton, N.J.: Princeton University Press, 2000.

————, eds. *Reproducing Gender: Politics, Publics, and Everyday Life after Socialism.* Princeton, N.J.: Princeton University Press, 2000.

Grabbe, Heather. *The EU's Transformative Power: Europeanisation through Conditionality in Central and Eastern Europe.* Basingstoke, U.K.: Palgrave, 2006.

Graham, Ann, and Joanna Regulska. "The Parameters of the Political: Does Meaning Matter for Participation in Public Life for Women in Poland and Ukraine?" In *Women and Citizenship in Central and Eastern Europe,* ed. Jasmina Lukic, Joanna Regulska, and Darja Zavirsek. Burlington, Vt.: Ashgate (2006): 121–46.

Grey, Sandra. "Does Size Matter? Critical Mass and Women MPs in the New Zealand House of Representatives." Paper for the Fifty-First Political Studies Association Conference, Manchester, April 10–12, 2001.

————. "The New World? Women and Political Representation in New Zealand." In *Representing Women in Parliament: A Comparative Study,* ed. Marian Sawer, Linda Trimble, and Manon Tremblay. London: Routledge (2006): 134–87.

————. "Numbers and Beyond: The Relevance of Critical Mass in Gender Research." *Politics & Gender* 2, no. 4 (2006): 492–502.

Grey, Sandra J., and Marin Sawer. "Australia and New Zealand." In *Sharing Power: Women in Parliament in Consolidated and Emerging Democracies,* ed. Yvonne Galligan and Manon Tremblay. Aldershot, U.K.: Ashgate (2005): 171–87.

Guenther, Katya M. "Understanding Policy Diffusion across Feminist Movements: The Case of Gender Mainstreaming in Eastern Germany." *Politics & Gender* 4, no. 4 (2008): 587–613.

Grzymala-Busse, Anna. *Redeeming the Communist Past: The Regeneration of Communist Parties in East Central Europe.* Cambridge: Cambridge University Press, 2002.

Hale, Henry E. *Why Not Parties in Russia? Democracy, Federalism and the State.* New York: Cambridge University Press, 2006.

Hancock, Donald M., and Henry Krisch. *Politics in Germany.* Washington, D.C.: CQ Press, 2009.

Havelkova, Haná. "Abstract Citizenship? Women and Power in the Czech Republic." In *Gender and Citizenship in Transition,* ed. Barbara Hobson. New York: Routledge (2000): 118–38.

Hedin, Astrid. *The Politics of Social Networks.* Lund Political Studies 118. Lund: Department of Political Science, Lund University, 2001.

Heinen, Jacqueline, and Stephane Portet. "Political and Social Citizenship: An Examination of the Case of Poland." In *Gender Justice, Development, and Rights,* ed. Maxine Molyneux and Shahra Razavi. Oxford: Oxford University Press (2002): 141–69.

Heitlinger, Alena, ed. *Émigré Feminism: Transnational Perspectives.* Toronto: University of Toronto Press, 1999.

Heitlinger, Alena. "Women in Eastern Europe: Survey of Literature." *Women's Studies International Forum* 8, no. 2 (1985): 147–52.

————. *Women and State Socialism: Sex Inequality in the Soviet Union and Czechoslovakia.* London and Montreal: Macmillan and McGill–Queen's University Press, 1979.

Holmes, Leslie. *Rotten States? Corruption, Post-Communism, and Neoliberalism.* Durham, N.C.: Duke University Press, 2006.

Jahnert, Gabriele, Jana Gohrisch, Daphne Hahn, Hildegard Maria Nickel, Iris Peinl, and Katrin Schaefgen, eds. *Gender in Transition in Eastern and Central Europe.* Proceedings im Auftrag des Zentrums für Interdisziplinäre Frauenforschung an der Humboldt Universitat zu Berlin. Berlin: Trafo Verlag, 2001.

Jalušić, Vlasta, and Milica Antić. *Prospects for Gender Equality Policies in Central and Eastern Europe.* Social Consequences of Economic Transformation in East Central Europe, Project Paper 79. Vienna: Institute for Human Sciences, 2000. http://www.iwm.at/publ-spp/soco79pp.pdf.

Jancar, Barbara Wolfe. *Women under Communism.* Baltimore: Johns Hopkins University Press, 1978.

Jaquette, Jane S., ed. *The Women's Movement in Latin America: Feminism and the Transition to Democracy.* Boulder, Colo.: Westview Press, 1989.

———, ed. *The Women's Movement in Latin America: Participation and Democracy.* Boulder, Colo.: Westview Press, 1994.

Jaquette, Jane S., and Sharon L. Wolchik, eds. *Women and Democracy: Latin America and Central and Eastern Europe.* Baltimore: Johns Hopkins University Press, 1998.

Jasiewicz, Krsysztof. "Citizenship and Politics." In *Developments in Central and East European Politics 4,* ed. Stephen White, Judy Batt, and Paul G. Lewis. Durham, N.C.: Duke University Press (2007): 193–212.

Kamenitsa, Lynn, and Brigitte Geissel. "WPAs and Political Representation in Germany." In *State Feminism and Political Representation,* ed. Joni Lovenduski. Cambridge: Cambridge University Press (2005): 106–29.

Kathlene, Lyn. "In a Different Voice: Women and the Policy Process." In *Women and Elective Office: Past Present and Future,* ed. Sue Thomas and Clyde Wilcox. New York: Oxford University Press (1998): 188–202.

Kittilson, Miki Caul. *Challenging Parties, Changing Parliaments: Women and Elected Office in Contemporary Western Europe.* Columbus: Ohio State University Press, 2006.

Herbert Kitschelt, Zdenka Mansfeldova, Radoslaw Markowski, and Gabor Toka. *Post-Communist Party Systems: Competition, Representation, and Inter-Party Cooperation.* Cambridge Studies in Comparative Politics. Cambridge: Cambridge University Press, 1999.

Kligman, Gail. *The Politics of Duplicity: Controlling Reproduction in Ceausescu's Romania.* Berkeley: University of California Press, 1998.

Knox, Zoe, et al. "Parties of Power and Russian Politics: A Victory of the State over Civil Society?" *Problems of Post-Communism,* January–February 2006, 3–14.

Kochkina, Elena V. "Women in Russian Government Bodies." *Russian Social Science Review: A Journal of Translations* 42, no. 2 (2001): 44–59.

Kolinsky, Eva, and Hildegard Maria Nickel, eds. *Reinventing Gender: Women in Eastern Germany since Unification.* London: Frank Cass, 2003.

Kornai, Janos, Stephan Haggard, and Robert R .Kaufman, eds. *Reforming the State: Fiscal and Welfare Reform in Post-Socialist Countries.* Cambridge: Cambridge University Press, 2001.

Kostelecký, Tomáš. *Political Parties after Communism: Developments in East-Central Europe.* Washington, D.C., and Baltimore: Woodrow Wilson Center Press and Johns Hopkins University Press, 2002.

Kostova, Dobrinka. "Similar or Different? Women in Post-Communist Bulgaria." In *Women in the Politics of Post-Communist Eastern Europe,* ed. Marilyn Rueschemeyer. Armonk, N.Y.: M. E. Sharpe (1998): 249–66.

Kuehnast, Kathleen, and Carol Nechemias, eds. *Post-Soviet Women Encountering Transition: Nation Building, Economic Survival, and Civic Activism.* Washington, D.C., and Baltimore: Woodrow Wilson Center Press and Johns Hopkins University Press, 2004.

Kunovich, Sheri, and Pamela Paxton. "Pathways to Power: The Role of Political Parties in Women's National Political Representation." *American Journal of Sociology* 111, no. 2 (September 2005): 505–52.

Lagerspetz, Mikko, and Marek Skovajsa. "Non-Profit Foundations in Four Countries of Central and Eastern Europe." *Polish Sociological Review* 2, no. 154 (2006): 187–208.

Lapidus, Gail Warshofsky. *Women in Soviet Society: Equality, Development, and Social Change.* Berkeley: University of California Press, 1978.

Lewis, Paul G. *Political Parties in Post-Communist Eastern Europe.* London: Routledge, 2000.

Lewis, Paul G., and Zdenka Mansfeldová, eds. *The European Union and Party Politics in Central and Eastern Europe.* Houndmills, Basingstoke Hampshire: London: Palgrave Macmillan, 2006.

Linden, Ronald. *Norms and Nannies: The Impact of International Organizations on the Central and East European States.* Lanham, Md.: Rowman & Littlefield, 2003.

Lovenduski, Joni. *Women and European Politics: Contemporary Feminism and Public Policy.* Amherst: University of Massachusetts Press, 1986.

Lovenduski, Joni, ed., with Diane Sainsbury, Marila Guadagnini, Petra Meier and Claudie Baudino. *State Feminism and Political Representation.* Cambridge: Cambridge University Press, 2005.

Lubrani, Osnat, and Elizabeth Villagomez. "The Impact of Globalization on Women's Market Situation." In *Women's Social Rights and Entitlements,* ed. Audrey Guichon, Christien L. Van Den Anker, and Irina Novikova. London: Palgrave Macmillan (2006): 203–23.

Maniatopoulou, Theodora Hiou, and Maria Katsiyianni. "Current Approaches to Gender Equality in European Social Policies." In *Women's Social Rights and Entitlements,* ed. Audrey Guichon, Christien L. Van Den Anker, and Irina Novikova. London: Palgrave Macmillan (2006): 224–44.

Mansfeldová, Zděnka, et al. "Committees of the Chamber of Deputies of the Czech Republic." In *Committees in Post-Communist Democratic Parliaments: Comparative Institutionalization,* ed. David M. Olson and William E. Crowther. Columbus: Ohio State University Press, 2002.

Matland, Richard E., and Kathleen A. Montgomery, eds. *Women's Access to Political Power in Post-Communist Europe.* Oxford: Oxford University Press, 2003.

Moghadam, Valentine M., ed. *Democratic Reform and the Position of Women in Transitional Economies.* Oxford: Clarendon Press, 1994.

Moser, Robert G., "Electoral Systems and Women's Representation: The Strange System of Russia." In *Women's Access to Political Power in Post-Communist Europe,* ed. Richard E. Matland and Kathleen A. Montgomery. Oxford: Oxford University Press (2003): 153–72.

———. *Unexpected Outcomes: Electoral Systems, Political Parties, and Representation in Russia.* Pittsburgh: Pittsburgh University Press, 2001.

Mushaben, Joyce. "Girl Power, Mainstreaming and Critical Mass: Women's Leadership and Policy Shift in Germany's Red-Green Coalition, 1998–2002." *Journal of Women, Politics, and Policy* 27, no. $^{1}/_{2}$ (2005): 135–61.

Nelson, Barbara J., and Najma Chowdhury, eds. *Women and Politics Worldwide.* New Haven, Conn.: Yale University Press, 1994.

Nickel, Hildegard M. "Employment, Gender and the Dual Transformation in Germany." In *The New Germany in the East,* ed. Chris Flockton, Eva Kolinsky, and Rosalind Pritchard. London: Frank Cass (2001): 106–22.

Orenstein, Mitchell A., Stephen Bloom, and Nicole Lindstrom, eds. *Transnational Actors in Central and Eastern European Transitions.* Pittsburgh: University of Pittsburgh Press, 2008.

Outshoorn, Joyce, and Johanna Kantola, eds. *Changing State Feminism: Women's Policy Agencies Confront Shifting Institutional Terrain.* London: Palgrave Macmillan, 2007.

Posadskaya, Anastasia, ed. *Women in Russia: A New Era in Russian Feminism.* London: Verso, 1994.

Ramet, Sabrina, ed. *Gender Politics in the Western Balkans: Women and Society in Yugoslavia and the Yugoslav Successor States.* University Park: Pennsylvania State University Press, 1999.

Regulska, Joanna, and Magda Grabowska. "Will It Make a Difference? EU Enlargement and Women's Public Discourse in Poland." In *Gender Politics in the Expanding European Union,* ed. Silke Roth. Oxford: Berghahn Books (2008): 137–54.

Remington, Thomas F., and Steven S. Smith. *The Politics of Institutional Choice: The Formation of the Russian State Duma.* Princeton, N.J.: Princeton University Press, 2001.

Renne, Tanya. *Ana's Land: Sisterhood in Eastern Europe.* Boulder, Colo.: Westview Press, 1997.

Robinson, Jean. "Women, the State, and the Need for Civil Society: The Liga Kobiet in Poland." In *Comparative State Feminism,* ed. Dorothy McBride Stetson and Amy Mazur. Thousand Oaks, Calif.: Sage (1995): 203–20.

Rose-Ackerman, Susan. *From Elections to Democracy: Building Accountable Government in Hungary and Poland.* Cambridge: Cambridge University Press, 2005.

Rueschemeyer, Marilyn. *Professional Work and Marriage: An East-West Comparison.* London and New York: Macmillan for St. Antony's College, Oxford, and St. Martin's Press, 1981.

———, ed. *Women in the Politics of Post-Communist Eastern Europe.* Armonk, N.Y.: M. E. Sharpe, 1998.

Rueschemeyer, Marilyn, and Christiane Lemke, eds. *The Quality of Life in the German Democratic Republic: Changes and Developments in a State Socialist Society.* Armonk, N.Y.: M. E. Sharpe, 1989.

Rueschemeyer, Marilyn, and Szonja Szelenyi, "Socialist Transformation and Gender Inequality: Women in the GDR and Hungary." In *East Germany in Comparative Perspective,* ed. David Childs, Thomas A. Baylis, and Marilyn Rueschemeyer. London: Routledge (1989): 81–109.

Rusinow, Dennison. *The Yugoslav Experiment 1948–1974.* Berkeley: University of California Press, 1977.

Saxonberg, Steven. "Women in East European Parliaments." *Journal of Democracy* 11, no. 2 (April 2000): 145–58.

Schimmelfennig, Frank, and Ulrich Sedelmeier, eds. *The Europeanization of Central and Eastern Europe.* Ithaca, N.Y.: Cornell University Press, 2005.

Scott, Hilda. *Does Socialism Liberate Women? Experiences from Eastern Europe.* Boston: Beacon Press, 1974.

Siemieńska, Renata. "Elites and Women in Democratising Post-Communist Societies." *International Review of Sociology* 9, no. 2 (1999): 197–220.

———. *Women in the Polish Sejm: Political Culture and Party Politics versus Electoral Rule.* Oxford: Oxford Scholarship Online Monographs, 2003.

Šiklova, Jiřina. "Feminism and the Roots of Apathy in the Czech Republic." *Social Research* 64, no. 2 (Summer 1997): 258–80.

Sissenich, Beate. *Building States without Society: European Union Enlargement and the Transfer of EU Social Policy to Poland and Hungary.* Lanham, Md.: Rowman & Littlefield, 2007.

Slomczynski, Kazimierz M., and Goldie Shabad. "Structural Determinants of Political Experience: A Refutation of the 'Death of Class' Thesis." In *Social Patterns of Being Political,* ed. Kazimierz M. Slomczynski. Warsaw: IFIS (2000): 187–209.

Smyth, Regina. *Candidate Strategies and Electoral Competition in the Russian Federation: Democracy without Foundation.* New York: Cambridge University Press, 2006.

Sociologický časopis / Czech Sociological Review (Special Issue on Gendering Democracy in an Enlarged Europe; articles in English), no. 6, 2005.

Sperling, Valerie. *Organizing Women in Contemporary Russia: Engendering Transition.* Cambridge: Cambridge University Press, 1999.

Steinhilber, Silke. "Gender Relations and Labour Market Transformation: Status Quo and Policy Responses in Central and Eastern Europe." In *Gender in Transition in Eastern and Central Europe,* ed. Gabriele Jahnert, Jana Gohrisch, Daphne Hahn, Hildegard Maria Nickel, Iris Peinl, and Katrin Schaefgen. Proceedings im Auftrag des Zentrums für Interdisziplinare Frauenforschung an der Humboldt Universitat zu Berlin. Berlin: Trafo Verlag (2001): 201–14.

Stetson, Dorothy McBride, and Amy Mazur, eds. *Comparative State Feminism.* Thousand Oaks, Calif.: Sage, 1995.

Studlar, Donley T., and Ian McAllister. "Does a Critical Mass Exist? A Comparative Analysis of Women's Legislative Representation since 1950." *European Journal of Political Research* 41, no. 2 (March 2002): 233–53.

Swers, Michele L. *The Difference Women Make: The Policy Impact of Women in Congress.* Chicago: University of Chicago Press, 2002.

Thomas, Sue. "The Impact of Women on State Legislative Policies." *Journal of Politics* 53, no. 4 (November 1991): 958–76.

———. "Voting Patterns in the California Assembly: The Role of Gender." *Women and Politics* 9, no. 4 (1989): 43–53.

Thomas, Sue, and Susan Welch. "The Impact of Gender on Activities and Priorities of State Legislators." *Western Political Quarterly* 44, no. 1 (March 1991): 445–56.

Tinker, Irene. "Quotas for Women in Elected Legislatures: Do They Really Empower?" *Women's Studies International Forum* 27, nos. 5–6 (2004): 531–46.

Tremblay, Manon. "The Substantive Representation of Women and PR: Some Reflections on the Role of Surrogate Representation and Critical Mass." *Politics & Gender* 2, no. 4 (2006): 502–11.

Tuominen, Eila, and Sini-Laitinen-Kuikka. "Pension Policy in the European Union: Responses to the Changing Division of Labor in Family Life." *Gender Issues* 22, no. 3 (Summer 2005): 46–78.

Vachudova, Milada Anna. *Europe Undivided: Democracy, Leverage, and Integration after Communism.* Oxford: Oxford University Press, 2005.

van Hoven-Iganski, Bettina. "Rural Women's Perception and Experience of Local Democracy." In *Made in the GDR: The Changing Geographies of Women in the Post-Socialist Rural Society in Mecklenburg-Westpommerania.* Netherlands Geographical Studies 267 Utrecht: Koninklijk Nederlands Aardrijkskundig Genootschap (2000): 169–95.

Vardanian, R. A., and E. V. Kochkina. "Elections: The Gender Gap." *Russian Social Science Review* 49, no. 3 (May–June 2008): 64–65.

Wejnert, Barbara, Metta Spencer, and Slobodan Drakulic, eds. *Women in Post-Communism.* London: JAI Press, 1996.

White, Stephen, Judy Batt, and Paul G. Lewis, eds. *Developments in Central and East European Politics 4,* Durham, N.C.: Duke University Press, 2007.

Wolchik, Sharon L. "Elite Strategy toward Women in Czechoslovakia: Liberation or Mobilization?" *Studies in Comparative Communism* 14, nos. 2–3 (Summer–Autumn 1981): 123–43.

———. "Ideology and Equality: The Status of Women in Eastern and Western Europe." *Comparative Political Studies* 13, no. 4 (January 1981): 445–76.

———. "The Status of Women in a Socialist Order: Czechoslovakia, 1948–1978." *Slavic Review* 38, no. 4 (December 1979): 583–602.

Wolchik, Sharon L., and Jane L. Curry. *Central and East European Politics: From Communism to Democracy.* Lanham, Md.: Rowman & Littlefield, 2007.

Wolchik, Sharon L., and Alfred G. Meyer, eds. *Women, State, and Party in Eastern Europe.* Durham, N.C.: Duke University Press, 1985.

Ziblatt, Daniel F., and Nick Biziouras. "Doomed to Be Radicals: Organization, Ideology, and the Communist Successor Parties in East Central Europe." In *The Communist Successor Parties of Central and Eastern Europe,* ed. Andras Bozoki and John T. Ishiyama. Armonk, N.Y.: M. E. Sharpe (2002): 287–302.

Zielonka, Jan, ed. *Democratic Consolidation in Eastern Europe, Volume 1: Institutional Engineering.* Oxford: Oxford University Press, 2001.

———. "The Quality of Democracy after Joining the European Union." *East European Politics and Societies* 1, no.1 (2007): 162–80.

Contributors

Milica G. Antić is an associate professor of sociology and the sociology of gender at the University of Ljubljana, where she is also head of the Sociology Department. Her publications have appeared in academic journals in Slovenia and elsewhere, including *Delta, Družboslovne razprave, Feminist Review,* and the *Journal of Communist Studies and Transitional Politics.* She is the author or coauthor of several books, including *Women—Politics—Equal Opportunities: Prospects for Gender Equality Politics in Central and Eastern Europe* (with Vlasta Jalušić; Peace Institute of Ljubljana, 2001); and *Women in Parliamentary Politics: Hungarian and Slovene Cases Compared* (with Gabriella Ilonski; Peace Institute of Ljubljana, 2003).

Linda J. Cook is a professor of political science at Brown University and an associate at the Davis Center for Russian and Eurasian Studies at Harvard University as well as at the Watson Center for International Studies at Brown. She is the author of *The Soviet Social Contract and Why It Failed* (Harvard University Press, 1993) and *Postcommunist Welfare States: Re-*

form Politics in Russia and Eastern Europe (Cornell University Press, 2007) and the coeditor of *Left Parties and Social Policy in Post-Communist Europe* (with Mitchell A. Orenstein and Marilyn Rueschemeyer; Westview Press, 1999).

Kristen Ghodsee is an associate professor of gender and women's studies at Bowdoin College. She is the author of *The Red Riviera: Gender, Tourism, and Postsocialism on the Black Sea* (Duke University Press, 2005) and *Muslim Lives in Eastern Europe: Gender, Ethnicity, and the Transformation of Islam in Postsocialist Bulgaria* (Princeton University Press, 2009). Her articles on economic transformation, development, and women have been published in journals such as *Signs: Journal of Women in Culture and Society; Women's Studies Quarterly; International Journal of Politics, Culture, and Society;* and *L'Homme: Zeitschrift für Feministische Geschichtswissenschaft.* She has won numerous fellowships to support her ongoing fieldwork in Bulgaria and has been the recipient of residential fellowships at the Woodrow Wilson International Center for Scholars and the Institute for Advanced Study.

Carol Nechemias is an associate professor of public policy at Pennsylvania State University, Harrisburg, where she also serves as coordinator of the Public Policy Program and Political Science Program. Her work on Russian living standards has appeared in *Slavic Review, Soviet Studies, Urban Studies, Studies in Comparative Communism,* and *Social Science Quarterly.* Her essays on women's status in post-Soviet Russia have been published in the journals *Women and Politics* and *Demokratizatsiya,* and she is the coeditor of two books, *The Encyclopedia of Russia Women's Movements* (with Norma Corigliano Noonan; Greenwood Press, 2001); and *Post-Soviet Women Encountering Transition: Nation Building, Economic Survival, and Civic Activism* (with Kathleen Kuehnast; Woodrow Wilson Center Press and Johns Hopkins University Press, 2004).

Marilyn Rueschemeyer is a professor of sociology emerita at the Rhode Island School of Design, chairs the European Politics Seminar Series at the Watson Institute of International Studies at Brown University, and is an associate of Harvard University's Davis Center for Russian and Eurasian Studies. She is the author, most recently, of *Art and the State: The Visual Arts in Comparative Perspective* (with Victoria Alexander; Palgrave Macmillan for St. Antony's College, Oxford, 2005). Her earlier books include *Profes-*

sional Work and Marriage: An East-West Comparison (Macmillan for St. Antony's College, Oxford, and St. Martin's Press, 1981); *Soviet Émigré Artists* (with Igor Golomshtok and Janet Kennedy; M. E. Sharpe, 1985); and *Women in the Politics of Post-Communist Eastern Europe* (M. E. Sharpe, 1998). She has also published extensively on the German Democratic Republic. Rueschemeyer has been a guest at the Wissenschaftszentrum Berlin für Sozialforschung (Social Science Center) and a fellow at the Swedish Collegium for Advanced Study in the Social Sciences, the Stockholm Institute of Soviet and East European Economics, and the Department of Sociology at Hebrew University of Jerusalem.

Renata Siemieńska is a professor and chair of the department of sociology of education at the Institute of Sociology at Warsaw University, as well as head of the Center of Interdisciplinary Gender Studies at the Institute for Social Studies. She was a participant in the international mission of the United Nations analyzing women's status and their role in the process of democratization by governments and nongovernmental organizations in Kazakhstan, Kyrgyzstan, Tajikistan, and Uzbekistan for the 1995 World Women's Conference in Beijing. She has published several books on comparative cross-national value systems, ethnic relations, women's public participation, the reconciliation of work and family, and the family and socialization.

Sharon L. Wolchik is a professor of political science and international affairs at George Washington University. She is the author of *Czechoslovakia in Transition: Politics, Economics, and Society* (Pinter, 1991). She is the coeditor of *Central and East European Politics: From Communism to Democracy* (with Jane Curry; Rowman & Littlefield, 2007); *Women and Democracy: Latin America and Central and Eastern Europe* (with Jane S. Jaquette; Johns Hopkins University Press, 1998); *Ukraine: The Search for a National Identity* (with Volodymyr Zviglyanich; Rowman & Littlefield, 2000); *The Social Legacy of Communism* (with James R. Millar; Cambridge University Press, 1994); and *Women, State, and Party in Eastern Europe* (with Alfred G. Meyer; Duke University Press, 1985). She is currently conducting research on the electoral revolutions in post-Communist Europe and Eurasia, with Valerie Bunch, and on women's political roles in post-Communist states.

Index

Figures, notes, and tables are denoted by f, n, and t following the page number.

abortion rights: in Bulgaria, 177; in Germany, 138, 146, 155; in Poland, 74, 87, 90, 259; in Slovenia, 227
Act on Equal Opportunities of Women and Men (Slovenia), 100
administration as occupational background, 75
adoption process, 80
Againe, Ralitza, 171
age differences in parliamentarians, 74, 115
aging population, 177, 198. *See also* birthrate issues
Alliance 90 / Greens (Germany), 136, 137*t*, 138, 142, 255

Alternative Social Movement (Poland), 74
Andreeva, Kina, 181, 243
Antić, Milica G., 93, 162, 256, 260, 261
Anti-Fascist Movement, 93
Anti-Fascist Women's Front, 94
Aparina, Alevtina, 28, 29
apprenticeships, 133
Artificial Insemination Act (Slovenia), 228
associations, professional, 142
Attack (political party, Bulgaria), 184, 185, 186–87*t*
Attwood, Lynne, 33–34

Baburin, Sergei, 194
Beck, Kurt, 160*n*35
Behm, Cornelia, 153
Bielecki, Jan Krzysztof, 209
Bill on Equal Opportunities for Men and Women (Bulgaria), 246, 249
birth control, 177
birthrate issues: in Bulgaria, 176–77; in Germany, 152; in Russia, 198, 261
Boris III, 167, 189*n*12
Borrisov, Boiko, 187
Brancheva, Adrianna, 171
Brandt, Willy, 235
Brzinski, Joanne B., 139
BSP. *See* Bulgarian Socialist Party
Buckley, Mary, 34
Budget and Finance Committee (Bulgaria), 175, 175*t*
budgetary impact of policy, 180, 260
Budget Committee (Czech Republic), 117
Bulgaria Gender Research Foundation, 163, 180
Bulgarian Communist Party, 164
Bulgarian Parliament, 161–90, 243–49; constituencies for women in, 172–74; future trends in, 183–88; historical background, 3, 7, 163–66; and NMSS, 167–70; and Saxecoburgotski, 167–70; social backgrounds of women in, 170–72; women in, 164*t*, 166*t*, 174–83, 186*t*; and women's issues, 174–83
Bulgarian People's Union, 184, 186–87*t*
Bulgarian Socialist Party (BSP): electoral results of, 164, 166*t*, 184–85; on NMSS, 172; and quotas, 173, 255; women in, 171, 184–85, 186–87*t*; on women's issues, 177, 178
Bulgarian Women's Party, 167
Bundesrat (Germany), 157*n*2, 158*n*14
Bundestag. *See* German Bundestag
Buzkova, Petra, 117

cabinet positions, 116–18
career path. *See* occupational background of parliamentarians
Catholic Church in Poland, 3, 70, 80, 86, 90, 259
CDP. *See* Civic Democratic Party
CDU. *See* Christian Democratic Party
CDU-PP. *See* Christian Democratic Union–Peoples' Party
CEDB (Citizens for European Development of Bulgaria), 187–88
Charter of the Rights of the Family (Catholic Church), 86
child care: in Bulgaria, 178, 179; under Communism, 253; in East Germany, 134; in Germany, 152–53; in Poland, 82; in Russia, 198
Children, Youth, and Sports Affairs Committee (Bulgaria), 175, 175*t*
Childs, Sarah, 16
Chilova, Nina, 171
Christian Democratic Party (CDU, Germany): and elections of 2005, 148–51; electoral results of, 135, 137*t*; Green Party coalition with, 160*n*33; and quotas, 158*n*13, 255; religious affiliations of, 142; and social policies, 261; women in, 139, 141
Christian Democratic–Social Democratic coalition government (Germany), 133, 148–51
Christian Democratic Union–Peoples' Party (CDU-PP, Czech Republic), 113, 115, 116*t*
churches. *See* Catholic Church in Poland; religion and politics
Cimoszewicz, Włodzimierz, 206
Citizens for a Green Sofia, 246
Citizens for European Development of Bulgaria (CEDB), 187–88
Civic Democratic Party (CDP, Czech Republic), 114, 115, 116*t*

Civic Platform (CP, Poland): and election of 2005, 71, 72; women in, 64–66*t*, 71*t*, 73*t*; and women's issues, 74

civil society groups, 256

Clinton, Hillary, 1

closed-list system, 165

Coalition for Equal Opportunities (Slovenia), 227

Coalition for Equal Representation of Women in Public Life (Slovenia), 105

Coalition for Parity (Slovenia), 97–98

collective bargaining, 150, 159*n*20

commissions and committees: in Bulgaria, 174–75, 175*t*, 190*n*40; in Czech Republic, 116–18; in German Bundestag, 145–46, 159*n*15; in Polish Parliament, 76–89, 78–80*t*, 262; in Slovene Parliament, 102–3, 108, 228–29. *See also specific commissions and committees*

common-law marriages, 227

Communist Party: in Bulgaria, 244–45; in Czech Republic, 114; political power of, 7–8, 255; in Slovenia and Yugoslavia, 8, 93–94; women's participation in, 2, 9, 94, 113

Communist Party of the Russian Federation (CPRF), 27, 28, 29, 32, 257

Communist vs. post-Communist politics, 7–12, 19*nn*12–13; and education of women, 133; and gender quotas, 173; role of women in, 253. *See also specific Central and East European parliaments*

company-based collective bargaining, 150, 159*n*20

Congress of People's Deputies (Russia), 193

constituencies for women in Bulgarian Parliament, 172–74

Constitution, Russian Federation, 34

Constitutional and Legal Committee (Czech Republic), 116

Cook, Linda J., 25, 256, 258

cooperation among parliamentary women, 15, 89. *See also* cross-party connections

Copenhagen Summit (EU), 16

Cox, Pat, 240–41

CP. *See* Civic Platform

CPRF. *See* Communist Party of the Russian Federation

critical mass of women in parliaments, 62, 91, 124

cross-party connections: in Germany, 144–45, 154–55; in Polish Parliament, 89, 90, 265; as research issue, 15; in Russia, 201; in Slovenia, 105, 107

Culture, Education, Youth, Science, and Sports, Committee for (Slovenia), 102

Culture and Media, Commission of (Poland), 206

Čurdová, Anna, 231–34

Cyprus and European Parliament, 240

Czech Academy of Science, 112

Czech Parliament, 111–30; committees and cabinet positions, 116–18; Čurdová interview on, 231–34; and European Parliament, 240; future trends, 127–28; group identification and representation of interests in, 120–21; historical background, 3; and party programs, 120–21; and party system, 115–16, 116*t*; perceptions of women's roles in, 119–20; political ambition of women in, 118–19; representation of women's interests in, 123–27; social backgrounds of women in, 113–15; women in, 112–13, 113*t*, 116*t*; and women's interests, 121–33

day care. *See* child care

debate: in Bulgarian Parliament, 178;

East vs. West Germany differences in, 145

decommunization, 69

Democratic Left Alliance (DLA, Poland): and abortion rights, 80, 259; and election of 2005, 72; and gender quotas, 70; and Kempka, 206, 211, 214; political alignment of, 218; women in, 64–66*t*, 71*t*, 73*t*, 215–16; and women's issues, 73–74; and WPG, 77–78, 81

Democratic Party of Pensioners (Slovenia), 226

Democratic Union (UD, Poland), 64–66*t*, 77

Democrats for a Strong Bulgaria, 168, 184, 186–87*t*, 247

demographic issues, 177, 198. *See also* birthrate issues

de-Stalinization period, 8

d'Hondt formula, 99

Dimovska, Siyka, 171

discrimination: Bulgarian legislation on, 179–80, 181, 260; Czech Republic legislation on, 121; Polish legislation on, 74, 219; Russian legislation on, 198; under socialism, 94. *See also* equal rights

division of parliamentary work, 84. *See also* commissions and committees

divorce process, 80

DLA. *See* Democratic Left Alliance

domestic violence as advocacy issue: in Bulgaria, 162, 177, 180, 183, 190*n*47, 257; in Czech Republic, 127

Doncheva, Julianna, 171

Doncheva, Tantanya, 187

East German Social Democratic Party, 236

East Germany: political preferences of, 149, 150*t;* population of, 159*n*16;

transition to unified Germany, 131–32; women in, 133–35. *See also* German Bundestag

Economic Policy Committee (Bulgaria), 175, 175*t*

economics as occupational background, 75, 101

economic trends, 10–11

Economy, Committee of the (Czech Republic), 117

education: of Bulgarian electorate, 173; of Bulgarian parliamentarians, 170–72, 171*t;* of Czech parliamentarians, 113–14, 127–28; in East Germany, 133; of Polish parliamentarians, 75, 76; in Slovenia, 94, 107

Education and Science Committee (Bulgaria), 175, 175*t*

Election Action Solidarity (Poland), 71*t*

election committees, 70–71, 71*t*

electoral system: in Bulgaria, 165; of European Parliament, 226; in Germany, 139–40, 158*n*11; in Poland, 63–67; in Russia, 39–41; in Slovenia, 98, 99–100, 110*n*15

elites, political, 67, 126

employment. *See* labor force participation

Employment Act (Slovenia), 108, 262

entrepreneurial background for parliamentarians, 195

environmental issues, 132, 141, 142

Equal Opportunities Act (Slovenia), 108, 227, 262

equal rights: in Bulgaria, 181, 246, 249; in Czech Republic, 117, 125; and European Union, 87; in Poland, 80–81, 215; in Slovenia, 100, 102–3, 105, 227, 262

Estonia and European Parliament, 240

ethnic minorities: in Bulgaria, 184; in Slovenia, 99, 103, 228

European Affairs, Committee on (Czech Parliament), 232
European Parliament: and Bulgaria, 187–88; electoral system for, 226; gender quotas for, 98, 107, 108–9, 241–42; Krehl at, 236; women in, 228, 237, 239–40, 239–40*f*
European Union: and antidiscrimination legislation, 16–17; Bulgaria's accession to, 182, 184, 185, 188; and Czech Republic, 127, 128, 234; Elections Act, 226; and gender mainstreaming, 67, 87, 151–52, 159*n*24, 220, 259; influence of, 3, 12, 16, 18, 108; pension policy of, 151; Poland's accession to, 72, 80, 87, 90, 91, 220; and quotas, 255; Slovenia's accession to, 228, 256; Social Charter of, 201
executive positions held by women, 134

Family Affairs, Senior Citizens, Women, and Youth, Committee for (Germany), 146
Family Affairs and Equal Opportunities, Committee on (Czech Parliament), 232
Family and Guardians' Code (Poland), 80
family roles, 122–23, 263–64. *See also* perceptions of women's roles
FDP. *See* Free Democratic Party
Federal Job Agency (Germany), 147
Federal Republic of Germany, 131. *See also* German Bundestag
Fedulova, Alevtina, 28
feminism: attitudes toward, 16; in Bulgaria, 183; in German Democratic Republic, 237; organizations and activists for, 16–17; state feminism, 94; Western, 176, 180, 184, 257
Ferdinand Saxe Coburg von Gotha, 167
Filipová, Daniela, 118

Filipova, Pavlina, 176, 181
Foreign Affairs Committee (Czech Republic), 117
Foreign Policy, Defense, and Security Committee (Bulgaria), 175, 175*t*
Forest, Maxine, 259
Free Democratic Party (FDP, Germany): constituencies of, 142; electoral results of, 135, 137*t;* and quotas, 255; women in, 139, 154
Freedom Party–Democratic Union (FP-DU, Czech Republic), 115
Freedom Union (Poland): and gender quotas, 70; women in, 64–66*t,* 71*t;* and women's issues, 73–74

Gal, Susan, 162
gay rights, 87
GDR (German Democratic Republic). *See* East Germany
gender differences: in family roles, 122–23; in Polish Parliament, 74–76
gender empowerment, 183
gender equality. *See* equal rights
Gender Equality, Commission for (Slovenia), 102
gender mainstreaming, 67, 87, 151–52, 159*n*24, 217, 220, 241, 259
Gender Project, 246
German Bundestag, 131–60, 235–42; and early unification years, 3, 12, 135–39; and election of 2005, 148–51; and electoral system, 139–40; future trends in, 155–57; and NGOs, 258; party system of, 140–44, 150*t,* 238*f;* representation of women's interests in, 151–55; social reform issues in, 146–48; women in, 140*t,* 144–46, 149*t,* 238*f*
German Democratic Republic (GDR). *See* East Germany
German Minority Party (Poland), 73

Ghodsee, Kristen, 161, 257, 258, 260
Gierek, Edward, 208
Golikova, Tatyana, 29
Goryacheva, Svetlana, 28, 200
Governmental Office for Women's
  Politics (Slovenia), 96
Green Party (Czech Republic), 116
Green Party (Germany), 138, 139,
  145–47, 160n30, 160n33, 255
group identification: in Czech
  Parliament, 120–21; in Polish
  Parliament, 88–89

Hartz IV reforms, 148, 160n35
Havelková, Hana, 126
Health, Labor, Family, Social Policy,
  and the Disabled, Committee for
  (Slovenia), 102
health care: in Bulgaria, 188; contributions for, 150; in Germany, 147, 148,
  159n21
Health Care, Committee on (Poland), 77
Health Care and Health Insurance Act
  (Slovenia), 108
Health Care Committee (Bulgaria), 175,
  175t
High-Level Group on Gender Equality,
  241
Hildebrandt, Regine, 235, 236
Home Affairs, Committee for (Slovenia),
  100, 102
homosexual rights, 87
humanities as educational background,
  75, 101
human rights, 228
human trafficking, 181, 242
Hungarian minority in Slovenia, 99, 103
Hungary and European Parliament, 240

Indjova, Reneta, 165
Institute for Social Studies at Warsaw
  University, 205

Institute of Sociology of the Czech
  Academy of Science, 112
International Monetary Fund, influence
  of, 16, 166, 184–85
international organizations, 201. *See also*
  specific organizations
International Women's Movement,
  266n2
interparty women's initiatives, 154–55.
  See also cross-party connections
intraparliamentary conflicts, 178
Italian minority in Slovenia, 99, 103

Jalušić, Vlasta, 162
Just Russia, 29

Kaczyński, Jarosław, 71
Kaczyński, Lech, 71
Kempka, Dorota, 205, 258
Khakamada, Irina, 29
Kligman, Gail, 162
Konstantinovna, Liubov, 201
Kostov, Ivan, 166, 167, 184, 247
Krehl, Constanze, 151–52, 235, 259
Kresal, Katarina, 108
Krook, Mona Lena, 16
Kučan, Milan, 96
Kunovich, Sheri, 266n2
Kwasnieski, Aleksander, 206
Labor and Social Policy Committee
  (Bulgaria), 175, 175t
Labor Code and Act on Employment
  (Czech Republic), 127
labor force participation: in Czech
  Republic, 114; in East Germany,
  133, 134–35, 151, 236; in Germany,
  136–38, 142; in Russia, 32; in
  Slovenia, 94, 107; in West Germany,
  134
labor issues: in Germany, 148, 150,
  159n20; in Slovenia, 103. *See also*
  unions

Labor Office (Germany), 147

Labor Union (LU, Poland): and abortion rights, 80, 259; and gender quotas, 70; women in, 64–66*t*; and women's issues, 73–74; and WPG, 81

Labuda, Barbara, 209

Lafontaine, Oskar, 148

Lagerspetz, Mikko, 266*n*3

Lakhova, Ekaterina, 200, 201

Latvia and European Parliament, 240

Law and Justice (L&J, Poland): and election of 2005, 71, 72; women in, 66*t*, 71*t*, 73, 73*t*; and women's issues, 82

law as occupational background, 75

Law on Equal Opportunities (Bulgaria), 181

Law on Political Parties (Russia), 256

Law on the Protection of the Child (Bulgaria), 180, 260

Law on the Rights of the Children (Russia), 201

LDP. *See* Liberal Democratic Party

LDS. *See* Liberal Democracy of Slovenia

League of Communists, 95

League of Polish Families (LPF): and election of 2005, 71, 72; and quotas, 70, 255–56; women in, 66*t*, 71*t*, 218; and women's issues, 82

League of Polish Women, 218

Left Party (Germany), 148–51, 155, 160*nn*34–35

Legal Affairs Committee (Bulgaria), 175, 175*t*

Liberal Democracy of Slovenia (LDS), 96, 105, 108, 223

Liberal Democratic Party (LDP, Russia), 27, 29–30

Lithuania and European Parliament, 240

Local Elections Act (Slovenia), 226

Local Government Initiative (Bulgaria), 163

local politics, 119, 162

Local Self-Government and State Administration, Commission for (Poland), 206

LPF. *See* League of Polish Families

LU. *See* Labor Union

Lybacka, Krystyna, 216

Majcher, Agnieszka, 205

Malta and European Parliament, 240

Mandates and Immunity Committee (Czech Republic), 116, 117

mandatory retirement age, 74

Marriage and Family Relations Act (Slovenia), 108, 262

marriages: common-law, 227; and divorce process, 80; of parliamentarians, 263–64

Marxist-Leninist ideology, 7, 9

Maslarova, Emilia, 187

maternity leave: in Bulgaria, 176–77; in East Germany, 135; in Germany, 152; in Poland, 82

Matvienko, Valentina, 204

Maximum magazine on Doncheva, 171–72

media coverage of women's issues, 225, 248

medicine as occupational background, 75

Medvedev, Dmitri, 10

Merkel, Angela, 148–49, 150, 262, 264

middle management positions held by women, 134

Milailova, Nadezhda, 166

ministerial positions held by women: in Bulgaria, 165, 166, 169; in Czech Republic, 117–18; in Germany, 139, 149, 151; in Poland, 67, 262; in Slovenia, 229, 262

minorities: in Bulgaria, 184; in Slovenia, 99, 103, 228

motivations for political participation, 118–19

municipal politics, 119, 162

Nabiullina, Elvira, 29
National and Ethnic Minorities, Committee for (Poland), 77
National Assembly Elections Act (Slovenia), 226
National Association of Municipalities in the Republic of Bulgaria, 163
National Council for Culture (Poland), 208
National Equality Law (Slovenia), 107
nationalism, 132, 184
National Movement of Simeon the Second (NMSS): creation of, 167–68; educational backgrounds of candidates of, 170–72, 171*t;* and elections of 2001, 168; and elections of 2005, 184–86; electoral results of, 161–62, 163; occupational backgrounds of candidates of, 170–72, 171*t;* parliamentary delegates from, 169; social legislation proposed by, 260; women as candidates for, 166*t,* 168–70, 182, 186, 261
National Plan of Action for Women (Russia), 201
Nechemias, Carol, 25, 193, 256, 258, 263
negotiated transition process, 95
Neicheva, Silvia, 171
newborn allowances, 82
New Economic Policy (NEP, Russia), 194
New Slovenia, 226
New Time (Bulgaria), 174, 185
NGOs. *See* nongovernmental organizations
NMSS. *See* National Movement of Simeon the Second
nomenklatura, 164
nongovernmental organizations (NGOs): in Bulgaria, 246; in Czech Republic, 126, 128; feminist organizations and

activists, 16–17; links to, 258; lobbying by, 259; role of, 256; in Russia, 199–200

Oborishte National Revival Party, 167
occupational background of parliamentarians: in Bulgaria, 170–72, 171*t;* and commitment to professions, 103; under Communism, 253; in Czech Republic, 114, 118–19, 127–28; in Germany, 142–44, 143*t,* 155; in Poland, 75, 85, 88; in Russia, 36–37, 37*t,* 195; in Slovenia, 101, 101*t*
Ostrowska, Małgorzata, 216
Our Home Is Russia, 28
outside actors, influence of, 16. *See also specific organizations*

parental leave: in East Germany, 134–35; in Europe, 242, 259; in Germany, 152; in Slovenia, 107
Parenthood and Family Earnings Act (Slovenia), 108, 262
Parliamentary Association of Women (Poland), 206, 209
Parliamentary Commission for Women's Politics (Slovenia), 96
parliamentary committees. *See* commissions and committees
part-time employment, 153, 154
party caucuses in German Bundestag, 158*n*15
party list voting, 165, 168
party loyalty: in Czech Republic, 120–21, 125; in German Bundestag, 146; in Poland, 89, 90; in Slovenia, 105–6, 107
Party of Democratic Socialism (PDS, Germany), 136, 137*t,* 139, 140, 142
party programs: and Czech Parliament, 120–21; and Polish Parliament, 73–74; and Russian State Duma, 46–47

party recruitment system, 125, 128

party system: and Bulgarian Parliament, 163–66, 166*t;* and Czech Parliament, 115–16; and German Bundestag, 132, 140–44, 145; in post-Communist era, 10; in Slovenia, 96–97; and women as leaders, 14

Pau, Petra, 149

Pavlov, Nikolai, 194

Paxton, Pamela, 266*n*2

PDS. *See* Party of Democratic Socialism

peace activist groups, 132, 141

pension costs: in Bulgaria, 177; and European Union policy, 151; in Germany, 147

perceptions of women's roles: in Communist vs. post-Communist period, 9–10; in Czech Parliament, 119–20; in Polish Parliament, 67–69, 68*f,* 69*f,* 79*t,* 82–86; in post-Soviet Russia, 34–35; as research issue, 14

personal life of parliamentarians, 263–64

Petitions, Human Rights, and Equal Opportunities, Committee for (Slovenia), 100, 102–3

Polish Parliament, 61–92, 205–21; and European Parliament, 240; future trends in, 89–91; gender differences in, 74–76; group identification and representation of interests in, 88–89; historical background, 3; increase of women's presence in (1997 and 2001 elections), 63–73; lack of cooperation among women in, 89; parliamentary committees, women's participation in, 76–89; and party programs, 73–74; perceptions of women's roles in, 82–86; women in, 62–76, 64–66*t;* and women's interests, 62, 86–88

Polish Peasant Party (PSL): and election of 2005, 71, 72; women in, 64–66*t,* 71*t,* 73, 73*t*

Polish Scouting and Guiding Association (ZHP), 205, 206–7, 220

Polish United Workers' Party, 206, 208, 209

political career development, 106

political participation of women: in Czech Republic, 112–13, 113*t,* 118–19; in Germany, 135–36; in Poland, 216; and proportional representation systems, 14; in Russia, 35–36; in Slovenia, 96–99, 97*t,* 98*t;* trends in, 1–3, 4–6*t. See also specific Eastern European parliaments*

positive discrimination, 121

Pre-Electoral Coalition of Women (Poland), 69, 256

preschools in Germany, 152

Presidium (Russia), 29

privatization, 69

professional associations, 142

proportional representation, 14, 110*n*15, 158*n*11, 165

Provincial Electoral Board (Poland), 206

PSL. *See* Polish Peasant Party

public health insurance, 147. *See also* health care

public opinion of women in politics. *See* perceptions of women's roles

Pučnik, Jože, 96

Putin, Vladimir, 10, 198, 261

quotas: adoption of, 255; in Bulgaria, 165, 173; in Czech Republic, 112, 124; in East Germany, 133, 237; effectiveness of, 264; in European Parliament, 98, 107, 108–9; in Germany, 138, 139–40, 154, 237, 239*f;* in Poland, 70; in Russian State Duma, 52–53; in Slovene Parliament, 97, 104

Rakusanova, Petra, 112

recruitment pools: for Czech Republic, 125; for Russian State Duma, 36–39

Reformed Communist Party (Germany), 136, 159*n*15

Regulations and Senat Affairs, Commission for (Poland), 206

religion and politics: in Bulgaria, 3, 7; and Communist Party, 7; in Czech Republic, 3; in Germany, 142; in Poland, 3, 70, 80, 86, 90, 259

reproductive rights, 177, 228

research methodology, 12–18

retirement age, 74

right-to-die, 87

Rodina (Motherland, Russia), 27

Rueschemeyer, Marilyn, 1, 131, 251, 255

Rural Association of Housewives (Poland), 218

Russia: Constitution of, 34; de-democratization in, 10, 27; economy in, 11; feminist influences on, 12. *See also* Russian State Duma

Russian State Duma, 25–59, 193–204; electoral system and parties as gatekeepers for, 27, 39–41; future trends in, 53–55; and gender consciousness in post-Soviet Russia, 34–35; gender issues in running for, 41–46; historical background, 7; and NGOs, 258; obstacles and challenges for women, 32–41, 195–96; and party programs and societal ties, 46–47; and political ambition of women, 35–36; quotas in, 52–53; recruitment pools for, 36–39; representational structure of, 14; and Soviet Communist legacy, 32–34; women in, 27–32, 30–31*t*, 254; and women's interests, 46–53, 49*t*

Safe Children, 246

Saxecoburgotski, Simeon, 163, 167–70, 187. *See also* National Movement of Simeon the Second (NMSS)

Schröder, Gerhard, 133, 148

Science and Education, Committee for (Czech Republic), 117

Science, Education, Culture, Youth, and Sport, Committee on (Czech Republic), 116–17

SDP. *See* Social Democratic Party (Czech Republic)

Secret Services, Committee for the (Poland), 77

Sega (newspaper) on women in Bulgarian politics, 169

Self-Defense of the Polish Republic (SD), 66*t*, 71–72, 71*t*, 73*t*

Senat Club of the Democratic Left Alliance (Poland), 206

sexual harassment, 162, 177, 190*n*47, 257

Shuleva, Lydia, 169

Siemieńska, Renata, 61, 255, 256, 260

Simeon II. *See* Saxecoburgotski, Simeon

Širca, Majda, 223

Skovajsa, Marek, 266*n*3

Sliska, Lyubov, 29, 201

Slovakia and European Parliament, 240

Slovene Democratic Party, 226

Slovene Parliament, 93–110, 223–29; and Communism, 8; electoral system of, 99–100; and European Parliament, 240; future trends, 107–9; historical background, 3; interviews, 103–7; women in, 95, 96–99, 100–103, 104*t*, 261

Slovene People's Party, 97, 226

Slovenian Democratic Party, 97

Social Affairs, Committee on (Czech Parliament), 232

social backgrounds of women: in Bulgarian Parliament, 170–72; in Czech Parliament, 113–15; as research issue, 14

Social Democratic Party (SDP, Czech Republic): and Čurdová, 231, 233;

educational levels of deputies from, 114; and party loyalty, 120; and quotas, 255; women in, 115–16, 116*t*

Social Democratic Party (SPD, Germany): east-west differences in, 145; and elections of 2005, 148–51; electoral results of, 135–36, 137*t;* formation of, 255; and quotas, 138; religious affiliations of, 141; and Socialist Unity Party, 143; women in, 139; and women's issues, 147, 154

socialism, transition from, 95

social issues vs. women's issues, 94, 162, 174–75

Socialist Unity Party (Germany), 135, 143

Social Policy and Family Affairs, Committee for (Poland), 77

social reform issues: in German Bundestag, 146–48; as research issue, 15

social sciences as occupational background, 101

social security system in Germany, 147

socioeconomic issues, 47–48, 107, 197, 201, 257

Sofianski, Stefan, 184

Solidarity in Poland, 255

Souckova, Marie, 117

Soviet Communist legacy, 32–34

SPD. *See* Social Democratic Party (Germany)

speeches in Parliament: in Czech Republic, 123; in Slovenia, 103

Standing Committee on the Family and Equal Opportunity (Czech Republic), 117, 125

Stanishev, Sergei, 184

state feminism, 94

state politics, 148, 158*n*14

stem cell research, 146

subcommissions in Polish Parliament, 86

Suchocka, Hanna, 91

Suessmuth, Rita, 138, 157*n*3

Sweden, women legislators in, 1

taxes: and child care cost deductions, 152–53; value-added tax, 150–51; and women's issues in Bulgaria, 179

technical studies as occupational background, 75. *See also* education

Temkina, A. A., 33

Thatcher, Margaret, 243–44

Tisheva, Genoveva, 180–81

Tito, Josip, 7–8

Tomšič, Vida, 109*n*3

trafficking in persons, 181, 242

Treaty of Amsterdam (1999), 159*n*24

Treuhand, 131

Türk, Danilo, 108

Turkish Movement for Rights and Freedoms (MRF, Bulgaria), 184, 185, 186

two-party system, 166, 168

UD. *See* Democratic Union

unemployment, 11, 253; in Germany, 136, 138, 147–48, 150, 151, 155, 158*n*9, 160*n*35, 258, 261; in Poland, 86, 90, 219; in Russia, 51; in Slovenia, 107. *See also* labor force participation

Union of Democratic Forces (UDF, Bulgaria): and Andreeva, 244–45; women in, 163, 165–66, 166*t*, 171–72, 185, 186–87*t;* on women's issues, 178

Union of Right Forces (Russia), 195

unions, 131–32, 142, 150, 159*n*20

United List of Social Democrats (Slovenia), 95, 96–97

United Nations, 67, 201

United Russia (UR): emerging dominance of, 27; and Putin, 10; women aligned with, 26–27, 29, 32; and women's issues, 257

Uprising of Wielkopolska, 206

value-added tax (VAT), 150–51
van Hoven-Iganski, Bettina, 160n33
vocational training, 133
Volkskammer (GDR), 133–35
von der Leyen, Ursula, 151, 152
voting records, 123

wage equality, 90
Warsaw University, 205
welfare state crisis, 147
West Germany, 131, 136–37, 149, 150t.
  See also German Bundestag
Wielkopolska, Uprising of, 206
Wolchik, Sharon L., 1, 111, 251, 257, 258
Women, Family, and Children, Committee on (Russia), 200
Women of Russia (WR), 26, 28, 32, 254, 257
"Women Run, Women Vote" campaign, 70
Women's Alliance for Development, 163, 181
women's interests: in Bulgarian Parliament, 174–83; in Czech Parliament, 121–33, 232–33; in German Bundestag, 151–55; in Polish Parliament, 62, 86–88; as research issue, 14, 15–16; in Russian State Duma, 41–53, 49t, 198; in Soviet

Communist system, 32–34. *See also* feminism
women's lobby, 69. *See also* non-governmental organizations (NGOs)
women's movement in German unification, 135
Women's Parliamentary Group (WPG, Poland), 77–82; and abortion rights, 259; and Kempka, 212–13, 215; political alignment of, 260; and Pre-Electoral Coalition of Women, 70, 256; training by, 217
Women's Party (Poland), 72
Women's Rights and Gender Equality Committee (EU), 241
Work, Family, Social Affairs, and the Disabled, Committee for (Slovenia), 102–3
WR. *See* Women of Russia

Yabloko (Russia), 28, 29, 194–95, 258
Yavlinskii, Grigorii, 195
Yeltsin, Boris, 194
youth issues, 183
Yugoslavia, Communism in, 8

Zhivkov, Todor, 164
Zhivkova, Jenny, 182–83
Zhivkova, Lyudmila, 164
ZHP. *See* Polish Scouting and Guiding Association